INDEX
ON CENSORSHIP

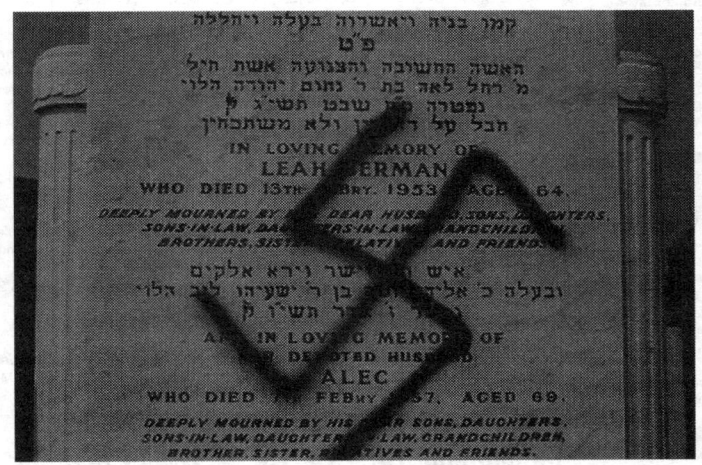

INDEX ON CENSORSHIP 1 1998

INDEX

Volume 27 No 1 January/February 1998 Issue 180

WEBSITE NEWS UPDATED EVERY TWO WEEKS
www.oneworld.org/index_oc/
indexoncenso@gn.apc.org
tel: 0171-278 2313
fax: 0171-278 1878

Editor & Chief Executive
Ursula Owen

Deputy Editor
Judith Vidal-Hall

News Editor
Michael Griffin

Production Editor
Frank Fisher

Eastern Europe Editor
Irena Maryniak

Editorial Co-ordinator
Nevine Mabro

Fundraising Manager
Elizabeth Twining

Fundraising Executive
Joe Hipgrave

Circulation & Marketing Director
Louise Tyson

Promotions Manager
Ann McCarthy

Subscriptions Manager
Syra Morley

Office Manager
Gary Netherton

Contributing Editor
Maria Margaronis

Africa Researcher
Penny Dale

Volunteer Assistants
Andrew Blick
Rupert Clayton
Eli Fenés
Hugo Grieve
Lucy Hillier
Andrew Kendle
Simon Martin
Randip Panesar
M. Siraj Sait
Nicky Winstanley-Torode

Cover design: Furry Dice, 01606 41314
Printed by Unwin Brothers Ltd, UK
Photo previous page: Rex

Index on Censorship (ISSN 0306-4220) is published bi-monthly by a non-profit-making company: Writers & Scholars International Ltd, Lancaster House, 33 Islington High Street, London N1 9LH. *Index on Censorship* is associated with Writers & Scholars Educational Trust, registered charity number 325003
Periodicals postage: (US subscribers only) paid at Newark, New Jersey. Postmaster: send US address changes to *Index on Censorship* c/o Mercury Airfreight Int/ Ltd Inc, 2323 Randolph Avenue, Avenel, NJ 07001, USA
© This selection Writers & Scholars International Ltd, London 1997
© Contributors to this issue, except where otherwise indicated

Directors Louis Blom-Cooper, Ajay Chowdhury, Caroline Moorehead, Ursula Owen, Peter Palumbo, Martin Neild, Helen Alexander, Anthony Smith, Judith Vidal-Hall, Sue Woodford (Chair)

Council Ronald Dworkin, Amanda Foreman, Thomas Hammarberg, Clive Hollick, Geoffrey Hosking, Michael Ignatieff, Mark Littman, Pavel Litvinov, Robert McCrum, Uta Ruge, William Shawcross, Suriya Wickremasinghe

Patrons Chinua Achebe, David Astor, Robert L Bernstein, Harold Evans, Richard Hamilton, Stuart Hampshire, Yehudi Menuhin, Iris Murdoch, Philip Roth, Tom Stoppard, Michael Tippett, Morris West

Australian committee Phillip Adams, Blanche d'Alpuget, Bruce Dawe, Adele Horin, Angelo Loukakis, Ken Methold, Laurie Muller, Robert Pullan and David Williamson, c/o Ken Methold, PO Box 825, Glebe NSW 2037, Australia
Danish committee Paul Grosen, Niels Barfoed, Marie-Louise Lycke, Claus Sønderkøge, Herbert Pundik, Toni Liversage and Björn Elmquist, c/o Claus Sønderkøge, Utkaervej 7, Ejerslev, DK-7900 Nykobing Mors, Denmark
Dutch committee Maarten Asscher, Gerlien van Dalen, Christel Jansen, Chris Keulemans, Wieke Rombach, Mineke Schipper and Steven de Winter, c/o Gerlien van Dalen and Chris Keulemans, De Balie, Kleine-Gartmanplantsoen 10, 1017 RR Amsterdam
Norwegian committee Trond Andreassen, Diis Bøhn, Helge Rønning and Sigmund Strømme, c/o Trond Andreassen, Tyrihansveren 8, N-0851 Oslo, Norway
Swedish committee Gunilla Abrandt and Ana L Valdés, c/o Dagens Nyheter, Kulturredaktionen, S-105 15 Stockholm, Sweden
USA committee Ariel Dorfman, Rea Hederman, Peter Jennings, Harvey J Kaye, Susan Kenny, Jane Kramer, Jeri Laber, Gara LaMarche, Anne Nelson, Faith Sale, Gay Salisbury, Michael Scammell, Vivienne Walt

Subscriptions (6 issues per annum)
Individuals: UK £39, US $52, rest of world £45
Institutions: UK £44, US $80, rest of world £50
Speak to Syra on 0171 278 2313

Index on Censorship and Writers & Scholars Educational Trust depend on donations to guarantee their independence and to fund research. The Trustees and Directors would like to thank all those whose donations support Index and WSET, including
The Bromley Trust
Demokratifonden, Denmark
European Commission
Institusjonen Fritt Ord
The Onaway Trust

Former Editors: Michael Scammell (1972-81); Hugh Lunghi (1981-83); George Theiner (1983-88); Sally Laird (1988-89); Andrew Graham-Yooll (1989-93)

EDITORIAL

A suitable case for censorship?

At the end of the Maastricht summit, the Council of Ministers reported on what they saw as a paradox of history: that racism had increased as democracy spread through the post-Communist world. Not such a paradox really: as Hans Magnus Enzensburger once said, 'With democracy, all the dirt comes out.'

'Hate speech', as Americans call it – abusive and dehumanising, inciting to discrimination and violence – is an integral part of this dirt, usually directed at ethnic minorities, gays or women. And it is, say the free speech absolutists, the painful price we must pay for safeguarding free expression above all other rights.

But how high is this price, and who exactly is paying it? *Index* looks at old style hate radio in Rwanda and the new language of hate in the USA, at media hate speech in former Yugoslavia and the banning of revisionist Holocaust history in Germany; and asks whether there are circumstances in which speech must be censored or even criminalised, to protect the vulnerable.

Such a group are the Gypsies, or Roma, now the most persecuted group in Europe. Eight hundred of them arrived in Britain last month (described by the British press as a 'flood of immigrants looking for handouts') from Slovakia and the Czech Republic where they were routinely subjected to 'Black swine, we'll kill you' and 'Gypsies to the gas chambers'. It's not easy to define what hate speech is, nor for a free expression magazine to suggest the need for censorship. But we believe it is a debate we must have in our pages, one of the most important of our time.

The issues were clearer when *Index* was founded in 1972 in response to pleas from Russian dissidents. Last year there was a sense of things coming full circle when we launched a quarterly Russian-language sister journal, *Dos'e na tsenzuru*, with the Glasnost Defence Foundation in Moscow. Here, from its second issue, we publish Alexei Simonov on the state they're in – attacks on the mass media and a woefully inadequate press corps – a poignant account by our own correspondent, Irena Maryniak, of Russians facing winter on the streets in sub-zero temperatures and Mikhail Gorbachev, who despite everything, is not pessimistic and believes that 'the last dictators are leaving the political scene'. ❑

contents

America's militias are preparing for war. Oklahoma City was just the beginning. Ed Vulliamy reports

Page 61

Irena Maryniak – zero tolerance in sub-zero Moscow

Page 108

Adam Michnik's visit to Burma reminds him of Poland's own confrontation with military dictators

Page 17

CONTENTS

5	**EDITORIAL** URSULA OWEN A suitable case for censorship?
8	**IN THE NEWS**
17	**OPINION** ADAM MICHNIK An anatomy of dictatorship
25	**NEWS ANALYSIS** FRANCOIS MISSER Rough diamonds
30	**COVER STORY: HATE SPEECH**
32	URSULA OWEN The speech that kills
40	CLAUDE CAHN, MICHAEL FOLEY, JEREMY HARDY No port in a storm
52	PAUL OPPENHEIMER In the name of democracy
57	ARYEH NEIER Clear and present danger
61	ED VULLIAMY The tapes of wrath
72	**REVIEW** JULIAN PETLEY Another year over
	INDEX INDEX
76	MICHAEL GRIFFIN Paper Tigers
106	**COUNTRY FILE OUR HOME IS RUSSIA**
108	IRENA MARYNIAK Sub-zero tolerance
115	MIKHAIL GORBACHEV Look to the people
120	SVETLANA ALEKSIYEVICH A prayer for Chernobyl
130	OLGA BAGAUTDINOVA Diary of a hostage
138	ALEXEI SIMANOV A matter of honour
142	ANATOL LIEVEN New Russia: what the people think
148	**PHOTO FEATURE** OLGA KHABAROVA Out of the depths
156	**BABEL** Roma voices, skinhead voices
162	**NEW MEDIA** DAVID BANISAR & SIMON DAVIES The code war
170	**DIARY** ALEX REYNOLDS Asian values and all that
177	**SPECIAL REPORT** ADEWALE MAJA-PEARCE Disabled Africa

IN THE NEWS

- **Torn veil** An Italian-born designer of Iranian descent has won the fashion world's first unofficial *fatwa*, following a show in Rome which combined nudity with the Islamic *chador*. Three 'models' strode in from the street, covered from head to toe in *chador* which they then let fall to the ground. One turned out to be a man, naked but for a chastity belt. The two others were women; one wore only a live python, the other a skimpy dress opened to reveal a padlock at the crotch. A few days later, after a series of threatening phone calls, designer Farhad Rahbarzadeh was beaten up by unidentified assailants.

- **Copyright comes to cyberspace** A group of UK companies, including British Telecom, Marks and Spencer, Sainsbury and Virgin Enterprises, won a landmark ruling on 30 November 1997 which bans Internet domain name speculators from infringing the trademarks of registered companies. Richard Conway and Julian Nicholson were accused of registering domains such as ladbrokes.com, burgerking.co.uk and even spice-girls.net, without their 'owners'' consent, and offering them for sale to the companies concerned. They were ordered to pay costs of £65,000 (US$102,000) and to assign the disputed names to the plaintiffs. 'Surveys have shown,' said Nicholson after the verdict, 'that 41 per cent of domain names include parts of other people's trademarks. The judgment doesn't address that.'

- **Language barrier** A test case in Texas will establish whether English is still the official US language at work after two women, Rosa

IN THE NEWS

Gonzales and Ester Hernandez, who speak both English and Spanish fluently, were sacked by Allied Insurance Agency (AIA) in Amarillo for speaking Spanish in the office. AIA operates an English-only policy. In 1996, a Texan judge ruled that a Mexican-American woman involved in a custody battle should only speak English to her five-year-old child to avoid being found guilty of 'abusing' the child.

- **Loss therapy** 'Nobody believes in penis envy or castration anxiety anymore,' whined Edgar Levenson of the William Alanson White Institute in late October 1997. According to recent estimates, psychoanalysts in New York suffered an 11,000-hour drop in patient therapy hours over the year as the city basked in a rare and extended feel-good mood. One reason may the increased use of such anti-depressants as Prozac or Zoloft. The Asian stock market crash, hopefully, will nip this disturbing trend before it becomes too deeply entrenched.

- **Poetry and libel** An 'exhortation of chastity' written in prison by Lord Alfred Douglas, the lover of Oscar Wilde, ignited a Home Office controversy in World War II because of a criminal libel case involving the then-Prime Minister Winston Churchill. Bosie, as Wilde called him, wrote *In Excelsis* while serving a six-month sentence for criminal libel against Churchill. He had accused the war leader of falsifying a communique about the Battle of Jutland to make money on the stock market. In 1942, according to documents recently released to the public, Bosie asked the Home Office to return the manuscripts. The poems had already been published, but the Home Office was worried that, if the public was reminded of the libel, the manuscript would become more valuable and so create 'a good deal of undesirable publicity'.

- **Penultimate high** A federal appeal court in November last year rejected freedom of speech arguments and ruled that a personal injury claim against murder-manual publisher, Paladin Press in Boulder, Colorado could go ahead. *Hit Man: A Technical Assault Manual For Independent Contractors*, published in the early 1980s, was used by a convicted assassin, James Perry. Perry read victims should be shot in the eye sockets and that he would feel 'superiority, a new independence and self-assurance after a murder'.

- **Americans prefer less liberty** A major study of public opinion, commissioned by the American Society of Newspaper Editors in 1990 to observe the 200th anniversary of the Bill of Rights, has found that most Americans reject the current concepts of free press and free speech. The study found that a majority of adults would prefer journalists to obtain a licence before practising and wanted more liberalised libel laws to make it easier for plaintiffs to win judgments against newspapers.

- **Cruel and unusual Manilow** A six-week police siege of Shirley Allen, beginning late September last year, cost more than US$500,000 and alienated all 100 residents of the Illinois village where she owns a homestead. Allen had refused to comply with a judge's order to undergo psychiatric examination. Allen's trials during the stake-out were legion; telephone, water and electricity were cut off; tear-gas was fired into her home; and she was psyched out by the amplified music of Barry Manilow. Neighbours rallied to Allen, whom they say was being victimised by greedy relatives, although police argued she had links with anti-government militia groups.

- **Privatised intelligence** Hot from its legal battles over the export of encryption technology, the US faces what may prove a more immediate threat to domestic security in the EarlyBird satellite, launched from the Svobodny Cosmodrome in Russia in mid-December. EarlyBird provides paying customers with three-metre resolution images of any co-ordinates in the world. Likely customers include relief and environmental agencies, estate agents, map-makers and foreign intelligence departments with no spy satellite to call their own. EarthWatch, the company handling EarlyBird contracts in the US, may find itself forced to include a 'shutter control' to prevent clients inspecting US defence sites.

- **Privy chambers** Foreign Minister Bronislaw Geremek, has called for changes in journalists' rights of access within the two-floor Sejm, Poland's parliament. Reporters have become so intrusive that members can no longer confer privately without a microphone being thrust under their sensory organs. Geremek suggests three possible strategies: a) journalists are permitted on the ground floor, but only 'unarmed' (ie no microphones); b) journalists are permitted on both floors, but the toilets are off-limits; c) journalists are permitted to enter the toilets, but they must be strictly single-sex units. One cannot help but wonder what kind of 'leaks' the Sejm has been suffering.

• **Hungary for change** During last October's referendum on whether Hungary should cleave to NATO, Daniel McAdams of the British Helsinki Human Rights Group was refused admission and prevented from checking documents at seven of the nine voting stations he visited in Budapest. The National Election Commission explained that McAdams had deviated from a list of 'recommended' stations prepared for foreign observers. The authorities greatly favoured a 'yes' vote. The government ran TV spots and inserted a character in a children's television show to extol the virtues of the western defence umbrella. Public meetings in rural areas were discouraged because the issues 'were too complex [for country people] to understand'.

• **Tobacco road** As Tony Blair withstood a nicotine-stained image crisis, following accusations that he had reprieved Formula One racing from a ban on tobacco sponsorship in exchange for a £1 million donation to Labour Party funds, cigarette manufacturer L&M was going cold turkey in Massachussetts on the contents of its more infamous blends. The recipe includes high-fructose corn syrup, sugar, natural and artificial licorice flavour, menthol, artificial milk chocolate, natural chocolate flavour, valerian root extract, molasses, vanilla and less salubrious additives, such as glycerol, propylene glycol, isovaleric acid, hexanoic acid and 3-methylpentanoic acid. But what's this? Patchouli, the Indian perfume so beloved of hashish abusers that it launched a thousand 'stop and searches'. Is nothing sacred?

• **More Russian negligence** The case of Aleksandr Nikitin, the former Russian naval officer charged with espionage after leaking information on nuclear waste-dumping to the Norwegian environmental organisation Bellona, is now entering its third year – and continues to produce bizarre twists. In a rare press conference, Nikitin said the information he had transmitted could not affect defence capability, combat readiness or state security. However, he says, the federal security service fear that 'terrorists could get hold of that radioactive waste and start chucking it around.' Accordingly, the authorities are still trying to prevent this information reaching the Russsian public. A few months ago, the St Petersburg police seized 1,500 copies of the Bellona report and these have now been put in as further evidence against Nikitin. The authorities seem to have overlooked one fact. The Bellona report is already on the Internet.

- **Native correct** After five years of meetings between staff of Mesa Verde National Park, Colorado and the 24 tribes in the area, the park is correcting its publications to more accurately reflect ethnic sensibilities. The Navajo term *Anasazi* means 'ancestral enemies' but other tribes descended from those 'enemies' say it is offensive. *Anasazi* will now be replaced by 'ancestral Puebloans'. However, 'ancestral Puebloans' will no longer be referred to as an 'ancient' people. Tribal leaders correctly pointed out that, while their social structures may be ancient, the people were not. The term 'early' is preferred.

- **Déjà vu** *'He sways on his stool in the Station Bar and calls for a short white wine/ And knocks it back and sheds a tear and damns the party line.'* So begins the Kiplingesque 'Kobus Le Grange Marais', written exactly 25 years ago in a English-Afrikaans patois by South African poet Christopher Hope. It was promptly banned by the South African Broadcasting Corporation (SABC) for being 'calculated to give offence'. Kobus, the protagonist, peppers his complaint with a few choice expletives and the kind of racist *aperçus* not untypical of a drunken railway-worker brushed aside by modernisation. The ANC didn't care much for the poet's slant either: several years later, at Natal University, a member of the current government denounced the verses as 'not deserving to be heard'. Singer David Kramer disagreed and set them to music in 1996, including them on his new CD. Once again, SABC reached for the scissors. 'The official South African media,' recalls Hope, now living in France, 'were once memorably described as government glove puppets. But, back then, they had to be instructed what to ban. Now they do it without being told. Once a glove puppet, always a glove puppet.'

- **No sex please, we're Kosher** A phone-in sex advice programme on Jerusalem's Radio Yerushalayim has been taken off the air. Station owner Micha Levy said the show had been 'delayed' for 'evaluation' but a story in the *Jersualem Post* suggested a more intriguing explanation. Quoting a 'source close to the station', the paper claimed that the ultra-religious *haredim* had put pressure on Levy, who owns a banqueting hall in the district of Bayit Vagan. If the programme were not cancelled, the *haredim* threatened, they would see that the hall lost its *kashrut* certificate, which guarantees that all food served is prepared according to the rules of religious purity. The programme's resident 'sexpert', Dr Yaakov Meir-Weil said there had been no attempt to censor or change its contents or language. Fellow sexologist Dr Uri Wernik told the *Jerusalem Post* that he was surprised at the cancellation since 'Judaism has a very positive attitude towards sex; it's regarded as a *mitzvah*, a good deed commanded by the Almighty, not just for having children, but also for the couple to be together.'

- *Sic transit gloria* **Banda** The man in the shades, the three-piece suit and the Homburg hat has gone. Dr Hastings Kamuzu Banda, former president of Malawi, was one year short of a century, when he shuffled off in late November last year to discuss terms with his Maker. After 29 years of autocratic power, he was tipped to make a pretty good fist of it. When the first squeeze on his autocracy was signalled by a referendum in 1993, the doctor was renowned as a 'One Man Banda', because of all the portfolios he had seized. Nothing much changes in sleepy Malawi even under democratic rule. New ululations tear the air, but they have a familiar pitch. Banda's successor, President Bakili Muluzi, has not repealed Banda's notorious Censorship Act, which was used to send poet Jack Mapanje off to prison.

IN THE NEWS

- **The cracked rice-bowl** 'It's rather like the plot of *Rashomon*,' explained an official from the World Food Programme (WFP). 'You have seven different witnesses to the murder, but each is telling a different story.' Nick Kristof of the *International Herald Tribune*, pushed the imagery further. He called public perceptions of North Korea's on-again, off-again, flood-drought-famine a type of kaleidoscopic roulette. Twist the tube and you get an entirely different picture.

However fragmentary the detail, the statistics which emerge from North Korea, three years after flooding laid waste its rice fields, are consistently ominous. WFP estimates food production in 1998 will drop to 1.9 million tonnes, from a basic national requirement of 7.5 million tonnes. The state system of rationing, fixed at 100-150 grams – or half a bowl of rice – no longer reaches three-quarters of the North's 23 million people. One of the country's rare visitors reported railway carriages, freighted with the protein-hungry, heading to the coasts to gather the seaweed once exported to restaurants in Japan. By the time this is published, winter will have fallen, bringing more isolation and silence.

Last spring, cross-border traders returned to China with tales of cannibalism and cadavers. An estimated seven million peasants had reportedly been displaced into the mountains near the frontier when floods swept away their dykes and livelihoods. Despite fears of a disaster on an Ethiopian scale, however, the bodies have failed to materialise.

'There is malnutrition,' conceded Dr Eric Goemaere of *Médecins Sans Frontières* (MSF), 'the problem is to see it.' In the three provinces of South Pyongyang, North Hwangae and Kangwon, where MSF has been working, only 1,500 under-fives have been treated for severe malnutrition in two and a half months. MSF has unlimited access to village clinics, Dr Goemaere adds, but it cannot put a foot across a family's threshold.

With 17 personnel and unlimited use of helicopters, WFP has not pinpointed anything more grievous than 'attritional hunger' - poignant, wasting, but still a far cry from Ethiopia. Paranoid about its place in the scheme of things, Pyongyang allows air reconnaissance of all but two provinces located along the Chinese border in the northeast. Officially, the reason for their exclusion is that they are hard of access and already supplied from beyond the border. Unofficially, they may contain defence installations, gulags or nuclear bunkers. 'Perfect shelter for the dispossessed,' murmured the official.

Dr Goemaere has a different take. The real cause of the emergency, he says is the crash in the economy since the collapse of COMECON in 1989-90. 'There are doctors and buildings, but no aspirin, no anaesthetic, no basic medicines, no heating, no soap and no milk and, therefore, no patients.' After half a century of Kim Il Sung's national goal for self-sufficiency, North Koreans have been left with minimal 'coping mechanisms'. There are no markets, no money and they cannot move freely.

North Koreans are also hostage to regional and international politics. Washington wants to improve relations with East Asia's second nuclear power, but it does not want to rescue the shaky leadership of Kim Jong-Il. 'It wants to keep North Korea above the water line,' said Dr Goemaere, 'but it doesn't want it to stand up.' In early December, the USA, Japan and South Korea unsuccessfully tried to block a US$29 million programme by the UN's International Fund for Agricultural Development which would have given peasants credit for projects in poultry-rearing, pig-breeding and other key rural survival trades.

A drop in the ocean of North Korea's needs, perhaps, but the loan marks a significant transition in Pyongyang's identity from nuclear maverick to a self-recognition of its naked shambles. As a policy, the aid-for-sovereignty card augurs badly for the key players in North Korea's phantom famine.

Anticipate bones when the snow melts. And few witnesses.
Michael Griffin

• **No more dissent** On 14 November last year, three editors of a British newspaper were each imprisoned for three years. Nowhere did this make the headline news you would have expected. Nor did it attract the attention of pressure groups. During the trial the editors complained that they had been ignored by Liberty and others, from whom they had expected – and in some cases been promised – support. Liberty's director, John Wadham, issued an anodyne statement after the verdict. Yet this was one of the most serious attacks for many years on press freedom in Britain.

Of course, the paper wasn't one that many people had heard of. But even with a circulation of only 2,000 or so, the radical newspaper *Green Anarchist* is the only paper regularly and exhaustively reporting the many protests and actions that make up the direct-action movement in the 1990s. Its 'diary' columns typically fill three or four tabloid pages in every issue and list hundreds of actions worldwide, mostly without editorial comment.

It is these pages that appear to have led to the editors' prosecution; the prosecution successfully argued that by publishing such reports, the editors were 'conspiring to incite persons unknown to commit further acts of violence'.

In common with many contemporary protest groups and movements (such as Earth First!), *Green Anarchist* supports direct action that may lead to 'ecotage', that is, the disabling and damaging of machinery and property (such as earth-moving vehicles on the sites of new roads).

Yet support is not the same as incitement, nor need it entail conspiracy. As Nick Cohen of the *Observer* pointed out, to encourage readers by favourable reporting isn't even an issue when the tabloid press support 'victims of crime who fight back'. Encouraging vigilante neighbourhood watch schemes to shoot on sight is, it appears, neither here nor there.

No evidence was presented during the course of the trial that the accused as a group had ever conspired together. The prosecution was reduced to making much of the popular perception that sees anarchism and terrorism as synonymous. Summing up, the judge himself described the journalists as 'terrorists'.

Green Anarchist may be only the first to feel the force of the law: other direct-action publications were cited in court as further examples of 'conspiracy to incite', among them Earth First!'s annual journal *Do or Die*. None of these papers have circulations more than a few thousand, yet together they provide a remarkable communications network for the many and varied direct action groups working independently in loose alliance.

The verdict against *Green Anarchist* could spell the end of that network. More important, it threatens a long and honourable tradition of political dissent in Britain that includes names like John Milton, Tom Paine, William Blake and many others.

The imprisoned journalists, Noel Molland, Saxon Burchnall-Wood and Steve Booth, have appealed their sentences but no date has yet been set for the hearing.
Chris Atton

For updates on this and other cases, plus links to the offending *Green Anarchist* articles, see our news at www.oneworld.org/index_oc/news.html

ADAM MICHNIK

An anatomy of dictatorship

Independent Burma is 50 this year. For many there is little to celebrate after 35 years of military rule. Could this be the year of change, asks a Polish observer who finds much in Rangoon to remind him of Poland's own confrontation with dictatorship

The unreconciled will always resist where systematic lies and violence prevail. They know the taste of hypocrisy; the smell of fear; the touch of cruelty. And with unfailing instinct, too, they recognise their fellows: their heroism, determination and courage.

In Rangoon, I heard the arguments of the defenders of the military dictatorship. They spoke of 'reasons of state' and 'irresponsible, destabilising elements'.

And I saw people so paralysed by fear of the police that they would not speak to a foreigner.

Not least, I saw functionaries of the Burmese security services who would not allow anyone to enter the home of Nobel Prize winner and leader of the National league for Democracy (NLD) Aung San Suu Kyi.

Looking at Burma, I thought of Poland. Thinking of the Polish experience, I saw Burma. I belong to the 'unreconciled'. I remember well what dictatorship means. I am not in the least tempted to relativism about what I experienced then: the abject humiliation and the fear. Burma has its 'hope', its '*Solidarnosc*' in the NLD. It went through its August 1980 (the two-week strike in the Gdansk shipyard that led to the birth of Solidarity) in 1988. It has been through its martial law; it has its WRON (Jaruzelski's Military Council for the Salvation of the Nation) called the SLORC (State Law and Order Restoration Council, reborn in November 1997 as the State Law and Development Council.) It has its Lech Walesa in Daw Aung San Suu Kyi. It does not yet have its General Wojciech Jaruzelski mark 1989 (the year of the Polish Round Table at which all sectors of society met), although it does have its Jaruzelski mark 1981 (the declaration of martial law in Poland). Will a Burmese Jaruzelski willing to open a Round Table emerge?

> 'As a rule, dictatorships guarantee safe streets and terror of the doorbell'

The NLD won an overwhelming victory in the 1990 elections only to have victory snatched away by the military who remained in charge as they had done since 1962. NLD leaders were confined to prison. I visited NLD leaders at night and in secret. While Pawel, my colleague from *Gazeta Wyborcza* kept muttering, '*Junta* shit,' I remembered the police blockade of Lech Walesa's flat in Gdansk, the ubiquitous presence of the secret police, house searches, detentions and arrests, the anxiety of neighbours and later their discreetly expressed admiration. *Déjà-vu*, I thought. In Rangoon I felt 20 years younger.

Dictatorship emerges from the weaknesses of democracy and from a lack of consensus on the rules of the democratic game. Those who muddy the waters in the name of social justice, historical truth or the battle against corruption generally do so for serious reasons. The Bolsheviks sought to end World War I and promised radical agricultural reform; the Nazis intended to control inflation and overcome anarchy, unemployment and the stifling humiliation of the Treaty of Versailles. Jaruzelski aimed to stem the progressive disintegration of the Communist state and secure Poland from the threat of 'fraternal intervention'. The Burmese generals sought to guarantee the unity of a country torn by ethnic warfare and bring safety to city streets they claimed were ruled by gangs of thugs. For many people the distinction between order and chaos carries greater weight than the difference between democracy and dictatorship.

Dictatorship is security as well as fear. It is liberation from the need to make choices. Others decide: as for me, I am free of the threat of risk and the burden of responsibility; my obedience is the key to happiness and a career. But security also means danger. The institution which prompted the greatest fear in Communist Poland was the Ministry of

BURMA: A NEW PERSPECTIVE

Rangoon 1988: Burmese democracy campaign– Credit Miladinovic/Rex

Public Security. The security apparatus was a state within the state: its agents and informers became the bearers of an all-pervading fear. Laughter died, conversations slipped into silence. Safety became transfigured into danger: a security service colonel was more loathed than the leader of a band of criminals.

In a dictatorship, the security chief is as unassailable as the head of an underworld mafia in times of freedom. But who is more to be feared? Those aspiring to a role in public life are more likely to be fearful of the security colonel; those who want a quiet life will be more concerned about the mafia terrorising the city in a fragile, corrupt and helpless parliamentary democracy. As a rule, dictatorships guarantee safe streets and terror of the doorbell. In a democracy the streets may be unsafe after dark, but the most likely visitor in the early hours will be the milkman. Democracy is uncertainty, risk and responsibility, but it seldom enforces its policies through violence. Dictatorship means violence daily; it is fear, humiliation and silence. But it is the charm of dictatorship that it liberates people from responsibility: the state answers for everything. You cease to be a citizen and become state property.

Dictatorship will always have its acolytes: its aims are attractive to thousands. There may be a revolutionary transformation of ownership (agricultural reform or the expropriation of foreign capital); the defence of sovereignty and the integrity of the state; or a check on the growth of anarchy. Concrete aims such as these generally run hand in hand with broader ideas and more detailed action: the creation of a national state as a bulwark against ethnic minorities; a constitutional imperative to respect religious values against heretics, sectarians and the godless; the establishment of social justice in the face of the owners, exploiters and bloodsuckers of yesteryear, who must be punished by way of public example. Dictatorship exists for its enemies: members of the old order, anarchists, revolutionaries and subversives, agents of foreign services, individuals alienated from the national spirit. The accusations Burma's *junta* levels at its opposition are redolent of the language of Polish secretaries of state and generals speaking about the Workers' Defence Committee (KOR) or Solidarity. Dictatorships ever see themselves as saviours of the nation or guardians of the peace. Democracy is dismissed in favour of higher ideals (Communism, national socialism or the religious state), or because of the 'immaturity' of the population. And there will always be that sympathetic Anglo-Saxon ready to acknowledge that though democracy was an excellent discovery for the Anglo-Saxon world, it isn't culturally suitable for Poles, Russians or Burmese.

One wise Burmese interlocutor of ours spoke of the success of the Asian 'tigers': 'You Europeans are so obsessed by economic growth,' he said, 'that you have failed to see the increased democratic awareness in Asian countries. Democratic traditions are born of pain; they are vulnerable and constantly threatened by disaster, but in the late twentieth century, they are essential to everyone.' If there were no desire for freedom in Burma, why the tanks on the streets of Rangoon and the secret services outside the house of Aung San Suu Kyi?

Every dictatorship is controlled by economics. If the economy collapses, the desperate come out onto the streets demanding bread. When the police begin to shoot they demand bread and freedom. If the economy develops well, there will be a limited period of peace, but people whose elementary needs – and particularly their children's – are met will eventually seek civic freedoms. Such is the natural order of things. Economic collapse leads to revolt born of despair, economic growth to rebellion born of aspiration.

This rebellion also permeates the inner reaches of the dictatorship. Increasing numbers of people from the ruling apparatus find they no longer want to be sitting on a time-bomb. They are tempted to introduce a rationalised system of democratic reform. Reforms introduced from within the dictatorship are invariably intended to change everything so that nothing changes. The dialectic of change depends on that singular encounter between a reformer from within the dictatorship and a reformer from the opposition. In Burma I met both: people from the *junta* responsible for the crimes of martial law and long-term political prisoners from the opposition. And both asked me hopefully: what is this Jaruzelski of yours really like?

Jaruzelski is a kind of positive symbol. To some he is a progressive Pinochet who saved the country from collapse. For others he is the head of the *junta* who proved himself capable of critical self-reflection leading to the Round Table with the opposition and a bloodless dismantling of Poland's old regime. This is what Aung San Suu Kyi and members of the NLD are considering. But the SLORC has not yet produced its Jaruzelski.

Before the Round Table, Jaruzleski sought merely to achieve an impression of a consensus. That was the intention behind the Consultative Council. It was a purely decorative body to which selected opposition politicians were invited. The council had no powers. It was a kind of valve for opposition views: a few people talked to their hearts' content and the system continued to function as before. Which was why the leadership of the Solidarity underground called for the council to be boycotted.

But this fictional creation also had a symbolic significance: the opposition – though moderate and controlled – had appeared in the official arena. Evidently there was room for them outside prisons after all.

The Consultative Council was a trick, but it gave symbolic recognition to the opposition's existence. The same is true of Burma which has its SLORC-convened Ntional Convention. Any Consultative Council is a grotesque creature, created by the dictatorship of the generals, and although the NLD has withdrawn its representatives, a wide range of people are taking part in it. Which is why it may become a useful instrument for dialogue on democratisation.

Dictatorship hates reform and loves 'development and improvement'. But, despite everything, reform keeps knocking at the gate. Because, at some quite arbitrary moment, people rebel. Police squadrons disperse the crowd. There are victims: the wounded, the arrested and the dead. The people have their martyrs. Police batons and arrests act as agents of integration and new leaders are its hallmark. And though later they may be arrested, smeared and abused, they remain a sign of hope in the collective memory. Solzhenitsyn and Sakharov, Walesa and Havel – and Aung San Sui Kyi. Social resistance is no longer a shapeless river of stones spewed up from riot-riven streets onto government buildings; there are leaders now to articulate political proposals with whom the authorities can negotiate. If – and this is the crux – the will is there on both sides.

And so the arguments begin, in the corridors of power and among the opposition as well as in the democratic world without. Inside the establishment 'men of concrete' talk of closing ranks in the face of an outside threat. Any change will be read as a sign of weakness, they argue. The opposition want only to destroy us. Its success will lead to chaos and collapse, and take us to prison or the hangman's noose. It will be a gift for foreign enemies, whom the opposition in this country represent. And government reformers are unconscious tools of the destruction the opposition seek to wreak. How can reformers now persuade their comrades in the dictatorial camp that the more inflexible they remain, the harder they are working to self-destruct? Blind faith in the principles of traditional doctrine has to lead to rebellion, bloodshed, chaos and the collapse of the state.

The result of the debate between 'men of concrete' and the reformers is also determined by signals from the democratic opposition and from abroad. The opposition – previously held together by the firmness of its resistance to the dictatorship – begins to break up. Should it focus on public protest or seek routes to negotiation? Should it demand punishment for the dictators or agree to compromise, reconciliation and reform?

At the critical moment, that is the dilemma. The 'revolutionaries'

> ...negotiations with yesterday's enemy must be undertaken, to find ways to a peaceful dismantling of the dictatorship...'

continue to repeat their arguments: the dictatorship has innocent blood on its hands, it is an absolute evil and its people are the carriers of that evil. The evil must be exposed and destroyed and its carriers appropriately punished. That is what justice demands; that is our duty to the victims of the dictatorship. Any attempt at compromise with evil is a gesture of support for it, the destruction of the purity of the 'Idea', moral fraud and political folly. The thing to do is to wait for the Great Explosion when people take to the streets. That is the time to stand up and lead, and overturn the dictatorship. Only then will truth and liberty triumph, justice be victorious, virtue rewarded, treachery and transgression punished. 'Reformers' see things differently. We could be waiting for the Great Explosion for a long time, they say. It holds immense risk: social suicide, civil war, new wrongs and new victims. Life is short, the country is going to waste and the people have not yet recovered from earlier revolutions. That is why negotiations with yesterday's enemy must be undertaken, to find ways to a peaceful dismantling of the dictatorship, and to compromise.

To the revolutionary, compromise is opportunism and lack of principle. To the reformer it is essential. The reformer abandons the logic of revolution for the logic of negotiation. Earlier, he had sought out everything that divided him from the dictatorship; now he must search for whatever they have in common. He is exposed to allegations of betrayal. For it is in the nature of compromise that some principles are abandoned; that victory isn't absolute; that yesterday's enemy must be allowed full citizen's rights and a place under the sun. If, in the dictatorial establishment, the 'men of concrete' prevail, there can be no hope of compromise; nor if the revolutionaries do so in society. But if reformers from both sides emerge victorious, the country has won its prize on the lottery.

The Poles won their lottery in Spring 1989. And what of Burma?

In foreign capitals, the transformations of a creaking dictatorship are carefully watched. Tactics are considered: political boycott and economic sanction, or flexibility and 'politically realistic' silence on human rights. Or perhaps the carrot and stick, pressuring the dictatorship to tolerate the expansion of civil society.

ADAM MICHNIK

If pressure from abroad – economic, political and diplomatic – is in the interest of the reformers from the power camp and reformers from the democratic position, the chances for a peaceful transformation are very real. That was the formula in the Polish Velvet Revolution. No-one gives up power faced with the spectre of a guillotine. People from the regime must have some guarantees of safety. Otherwise they will defend their power to the end, drowning the country in blood. Only after their total defeat will real justice triumph – amid burned-out cities, orphaned families, thousands of newly dug graves. Negotiation brings disappointment, bitterness, a sense of injustice and unpaid debts. But it spares the victims: those who are disappointed are at least still living. Negotiations are possible when democratic resistance is strong enough for the dictatorship not to destroy it, and while the dictatorship itself is strong enough for the democratic opposition not to overthrow it overnight.

The country has its chance in the weakness of both sides. ❏

Adam Michnik *is editor in chief of* Gazeta Wyborcza, *the leading Polish daily.*
Translated by Irena Maryniak

FRANÇOIS MISSER

The diamond wars

A power shift in the diamond industry is the key to the recent series of conflicts that are changing governments in West and Central Africa.

Times have changed since the beginning of the decade: an era of national conferences and democratisation has given way to coups and wars. In several countries in West and Central Africa, the myth of democracy has been replaced by 'gemocracies', where power resides in the hands of those who control the production and marketing of diamonds. The civil wars raging across the region have created an opportunity for upstarts to break into the diamond market; the risk is that they may have a vested interest in perpetuating the conflicts.

Diamonds are Africa's second largest export after oil. Unlike oil, that other great igniter of conflict, but more akin to narcotics, gems have a high value/volume ratio; smuggling is easy and highly profitable. Alluvial diamonds can be panned by hand from many African rivers with no significant investment. Diamonds make ideal capital for illicit businesses, run by government mafias and guerrilla movements. Their control is essential in determining which of the two wins the day.

According to western diplomatic sources, diamonds played a part in the attempted coup by a group of drunken soldiers on 28 October in Zambia last year, and Angola was heavily involved. A Zambian colonel claims the MPLA government in Luanda was irritated because it believed President Frederick Chiluba's regime was supporting Jonas Savimbi's UNITA rebels. In an interview with the Cote d'Ivoire's *Le Jour* in mid-November, Savimbi made similar claims.

The stakes are not only political but economic: control of the diamond mines in Angola's Lunda Norte province provides UNITA with the means to purchase its weapons and thereby retain its independence of action and bargaining power. Conversely, MPLA generals are keen to gain access to the country's most valuable resource after oil and to cut off the rebels' lifeline. According to *Diamond International*, UNITA's diamond income in 1996 alone amounted to US$800 million, 80 per cent of Angola's total output. Industry sources allege that UNITA's only remaining route for exporting gems to the world hub of Antwerp was via Zambia. Luanda's involvement in the failed coup attempt, in this light, is not as far-fetched as at first appears.

The extension of government control over gem-rich Lunda Norte and Lunda Sul provinces was a precondition of any new diamond investment by Odebrecht (Brazil), Ashton Mining (Australia), ARS (Russia) and American Mineral Fields International (AMFI, US/Canada). International Defence and Security resources (IDAS) also holds concessions in the area. IDAS is associated with AMFI and also DiamondWorks; its shareholders include Eeben Barlow, former boss of the mercenary firm Executive Outcomes (EO), and Tony Buckingham, ex-UK special forces and manager of Strategic Resources Corporation, which controls EO.

The MPLA commanders Carlos Hendrik Vaz and Luis Faceira are so closely involved in the illicit diamond business that they have been dubbed *garimpiero* (wildcat miner) generals; both are also shareholders in Sociedade Miniera do Lumanhe. According to Angola's official gazette of 12 August 1994, General Antonio dos Santos Franca 'Ndalu', currently Angolan ambassador to the USA, and Angolan armed forces (FAPLA) chief-of-staff, Joao Baptista de Matos, both sit on the board of Teleservice, a company that provides security for the state-owned diamond mining corporation, Endiama, and its Portuguese associate Sociedade Miniera de Lucapa.

In October 1997, in an attempt to salvage the faltering Lusaka Peace Agreement of 1994, the USA helped to broker an agreement between the government and UNITA which gave both parties an equal share in the diamond trade. The plan involved the US export credit guarantee institution, Eximbank, and the chairman of the New York-based marketing giant Lazare Kaplan, Maurice Tempelsman. UNITA was to hand over exploitation in the regions of Luzamba and Luremo to the Sociedade de Desenvolvemento Miniero, a joint venture between Odebrecht, Ashton Mining and Endiama. In return, UNITA's own company, Sociedade General de Minas, was offered a share in the con-

NEWS ANALYSIS: DIAMOND POLITICS

cession held jointly by AMFI, Endiama and IDAS. By mid-October, however, tensions were again increasing in the Lundas as 1,500 troops of FAPLA's Third Motorised Regiment moved from Saurimo in Lunda Sul to the UNITA-controlled area of Lunda Norte.

The quest for control of diamonds and other mineral resources played a central role in Congo-Zaire's civil war. Early in February 1997, AMFI's managing director Jean-Raymond Boulle was one of the first to meet the leader of the Alliance of Democratic Forces for the Liberation of Congo-Zaire (ADFL), Laurent Kabila, in Goma. Kabila used Boulle's leased jet for his frequent trips outside and inside the country until the end of the war. AMFI was rewarded in several ways: on the one hand, by mid-March, its parent company American Diamond Buyers was allowed to purchase the entire stocks of gems then available in Kisangani. One month later, AMFI became the first corporation to strike a major exploration and exploitation deal for the Kapushi deposits of cobalt, copper and zinc in Katanga. The world market leader De Beers, which had done well under Mobutu, dragged its feet before taking sides in the ADFL insurgency and it lost out badly in the final reshuffle. By mid-

Rough diamonds: rich pickings for guerrillas – Credit: Carlos Guarita

FRANCOIS MISSER

Weekend takings in a diamond-miners' bar – Credit: Carlos Guarita

April, Kabila had cancelled the monopoly of De Beers' subsidiary, Britmond, over the purchase of production from Congo-Kinshasa's main mining company, MIBA.

The Angolan army, FAPLA, profited from the confusion in Congo-Kinshasa to pursue its war against UNITA and extend control over the east of the country. FAPLA's forward strategy in the region was crucial in ensuring Kabila's success. In February 1997, Angola airlifted several hundred ex-Katangese gendarmes – part of FAPLA's Twenty-fourth Regiment of Commandos – to Rwanda. Their presence speeded up the Alliance's conquest of Katanga, Western Kasai and Bandundu. UNITA not only lost its sanctuary in former Zaire, its forces were squeezed between the ADFL and FAPLA, enabling the latter to launch their offensive against UNITA's diamond-rich Cuango Valley stronghold.

Oil, in the shape of France's Elf-Aquitaine, played the leading role in recent political changes in Congo-Brazzaville, but gem warfare provided a sub-text. Until the fall of President Pascal Lissouba last October, UNITA used its connections in his entourage, namely with the da Costa brothers and the president's personal secretary, Claudine Munar, to re-export its diamonds through Pointe-Noire airport to Antwerp, via Abidjan and Lomé. Both UNITA and troops from the Cabinda Enclave

NEWS ANALYSIS: DIAMOND POLITICS

Liberation Front (FLEC), which is seeking independence for Angola's largest oil resource at the mouth of the Zaire river, were allowed to train in a Congolese camp previously used by Namibian guerrillas. UNITA had reciprocated by giving gems to Lissouba's entourage. The volume smuggled from Congo-Brazzaville's own deposits are substantial: according to the Antwerp Diamond High Council, exports from Congo-Brazzaville to Belgium from January-September 1997 amounted to 3.1 million carats or US$379 million.

The MPLA intervened on the side of General Denis in Congo-Brazzaville. This deprived Savimbi of his last important diamond outlet and ensured the victory of an old ally, who could be counted on to uphold Angola's claims on the Cabinda enclave. The civil war in Congo-Brazzaville was an instance in which gem and oil interests combined to overthrow an elected government. There is no direct evidence that Elf-Aquitaine financed Sassou Nguessou's militia, the feared Cobras. But it is an open secret that Elf's relations with Lissouba deteriorated after the company refused to finance the former president's 1993 electoral campaign. Lissouba's subsequent decision to accommodate the US corporation Occidental Petroleum, at Elf's expense, contributed to the climate of intense distrust. Elf's activities in Congo-Brazzaville and in neighbouring Gabon are currently under investigation in France following accusations by Lissouba's supporters.

Sierra Leone provides a further example of how a new wave of mercenary firms, linked with diamond interests, gains access to mining resources by enhancing the security of the 'host' government. In 1995, President Valentine Strasser hired Executive Outcomes (EO) to protect the diamond mines and fight the rebels of the Revolutionary United Front. But the government could not pay the US$1.5 million monthly bill for its services. A new agreement, in the form of a 'security equity swap', was instituted. Branch Energy which, like EO, belongs to the Strategic Resources Corporation holding, won concessions at Koidu in exchange for security services provided by one of its shareholders, Eeben Barlow. The initial deal was struck by Barlow's old company –good old EO. ❏

François Misser is a French journalist. His most recent book, written with Olivier Vallée, is Les Gemmocraties *(Desclée De Brouwer, Paris)*

Hate speech

'Sticks and stones may break my bones, but words can never hurt me,' goes the old nursery rhyme. Not true, says *Index*'s editor. All too often and too recently, words of hate have turned into the deeds that kill: genocide in Rwanda and war in Yugoslavia were both incited by media hate speech

National Front anti-Romani demonstrator in Dover, UK, 1997 – Credit: Max Jourdan

URSULA OWEN

The speech that kills

By the time the New York radio station WABC fired its most popular talk show host, Bob Grant, he had spent a good 25 years vilifying Blacks, Hispanics and other minorities with impunity. He described the former mayor of New York, David Dinkins, as 'a men's room attendant', called African-American churchgoers in Harlem 'screaming savages', and advocated 'drowning Haitian refugees'. He was finally sacked because on the day the plane carrying Clinton's Commerce Secretary, Ron Brown, crashed, Grant speculated that Brown (who was black) might be the only survivor, 'because I'm a pessimist'.

And this was finally too much, even for WABC, owned by the vast media conglomerate Capital City/Walt Disney. The shock jock had no difficulty finding another job: he was hired by a rival station only two weeks later.

Hate speech, as Americans call it, is a troubling matter for people who believe in free speech. It is abusive, insulting, intimidating and harassing. And it may lead to violence, hatred or discrimination; and it kills. The USA, as the least censored society in the world, has held firmly to the First Amendment and to Article 19 of the Universal Declaration of Human Rights, which has meant that attempts to make provisions against hate speech have almost all been disallowed by the Supreme Court.

International law appears more contradictory. Article 19 of the International Covenant on Civil and Political Rights says that 'everyone shall have the right to hold opinions without interference' and 'everyone shall have the right to freedom of expression', though this is subject to restrictions necessary 'for respect of the rights or reputations of others' or 'for the protection of public order, or of public health or morals'. But

Article 20 of the same Covenant states that 'any advocacy of national, racial or religious hatred that constitutes incitement to discrimination, hostility or violence must be prohibited'.

None of these statements have stopped the fierce debate on that difficult borderline between free speech and equality of respect. Free speech is thought of as sacred to a democratic society, as the freedom upon which all others depend. But in a world where the effects of speech that fosters hatred are all too visible, there are two difficult questions that must be asked about the defence of free expression: At what cost? And at the expense of whose pain?

It is, of course, dangerous to suggest the possibility of more censorship. The slippery slope argument — if we can censor this, what is to stop someone else censoring that — is hard to argue against. Censorship can kill and maim, for when people draw a cloak of secrecy over their actions, gross abuse may happen with impunity. In the United States, hate speech is typically defended as the price society has decided to pay for safeguarding free expression.

Historically, perhaps the most famous defence of the right to express hate occurred in the case of Skokie, Illinois, in 1977 when a US neo-Nazi group tried to march on a public street in a community populated by many Holocaust survivors. The courts affirmed their right to do so, basing their judgement on the First Amendment. Such a ruling, they believed , was ultimately to the benefit of racial and other minorities, protecting their right to express their own views freely (See p57 Aryeh Neier).

Nevertheless, hate speech and censorship continue to have a troubled relationship. Catherine MacKinnon and Andrea Dworkin's now famous campaign to outlaw pornography was based on their view that pornography is in effect hate speech: it treats women as sexual objects and subordinates them in a vile way to men. Though they did not succeed in persuading the US courts, the Canadian legislature did introduce a severe censorship law. But the first authors to be banned under the new Canadian statute were not those the feminists had in mind. They were prominent homosexual authors, a radical black feminist accused of stirring up race hatred against white people and, for a time, Andrea Dworkin herself. Liberals who had warned against the dangers of censorship felt vindicated.

Censorship backfires: the biter gets bit. The powerful and painful paradox of laws against hate speech is that again and again they have been turned against the very people we would see as the victims of that same hate speech. In Eastern Europe and the former Soviet Union, laws against defamation and insult were used to persecute critics of the Communist regimes. In Turkey the law was used against Ismail Besikçi, Turkish scholar, for his writings on the human rights abuses against the country's Kurdish population. The South African laws against racial hatred under apartheid were used systematically against the victims of the state's racist policies. Even Alex Haley's *Roots* was banned on the grounds that for black viewers 'the polarisation of racial feelings was likely to be intensified'.

Nevertheless, in the 1980s, in the United States, the home of free speech, a new form of censorship was born on college campuses. Alarmed at verbal attacks on women and minority students, some universities introduced so-called speech codes, forbidding remarks that were sexist or derogatory of a particular race or religion. All the great battles for extending liberty in the United States — anti-slavery, anti-segregation, rights of women — had involved parallel battles for the principle of free speech. Yet here were the same kinds of people who had affirmed these civil rights traditions suddenly saying openly they thought free speech was not an absolute right but a contingent and relative one — that speech must be restricted for the protection of vulnerable groups who were the target of hate speech. And with these codes the angry and often tiresome debate on 'political correctness' was born.

PC has been pilloried and argued over for more than a decade now. It is all too easy to see how absurd some of its preoccupations are, though it had a sort of utopianism about it, and a touching, if rather authoritarian belief that behaviour, if properly conditioned, will improve. The problem with the ideal of political correctness is that, like so many censorships, it can turn so easily against what it is meant to protect, encouraging everyone to be on guard against everyone else.

Resistance to PC and its censorship came in a variety of forms. Free speechers such as the American Civil Liberties Union offer hard educative and political work as an antidote. They outlined eight steps to ensure that 'all students may participate fully in campus life, including the adoption of affirmative action', and 'courses in the history and meaning of prejudice'.

Ronald Dworkin believes free speech is what makes people feel human, makes them feel their lives matter: 'Fair democracy requires that every competent adult have a vote in deciding what the majority's will is. And it requires further, that each citizen have not just a vote but a *voice*: a majority decision is not fair unless everyone has had a fair opportunity to express his or her attitudes or opinions or fears or tastes or presuppositions or prejudices or ideals, not just in the hope of influencing others, though that hope is crucially important, but also just to confirm his or her standing as responsible agent in, rather than a passive victim of, collective action. The majority has no right to impose its will on someone who is forbidden to raise a voice in protest or argument or objection before the decision is taken.'

He goes on: 'The temptations to make exceptions to the principle — to declare that people have no right to pour the filth of pornography or race hatred into the culture in which we all must live — may be near overwhelming. But we cannot do that without forfeiting our moral title to force such people to bow to the collective judgements that do make their way into the statute books.'

In 1993, at the time Dworkin was writing his defence of free speech, Umberto Eco was one of 40 European intellectuals who publicly called on all Europeans to be on their guard against the manoeuvres of the extreme right. In an interview (*Index* 1/1994), he says: 'In order to be tolerant, one must first set the boundaries of the intolerable'. What, in his view, was intolerable? 'I see nothing shocking,' he went on, 'in a serious and incontrovertible work of scholarship establishing that the figure for genocide of the Jews by the Nazis was not 6 million but 6.5 or 5.5 million. What is intolerable is when something which purports to be a work of research loses all value by becoming something quite other; when it becomes a message suggesting that "if a few less Jews than we thought were killed, there was no crime".'

What Eco and his fellow signatories were particularly disturbed by was the extent to which dangerous ideas on the Right, including racism and xenophobia, were becoming commonplace — and newly seductive. And it is for just such reasons that it is essential to continue this difficult debate about hate speech.

At the end of the Maastricht summit in December 1991, the European Union's Council of Ministers issued a condemnation of racism and xenophobia, observing that 'manifestations of fascism and xenophobia are steadily growing in Europe'. The report also comments on a paradox

URSULA OWEN

of history: that racism increased as democracy spread through the post-Communist world.

Free speech advocates claim there is little connection between hate speech laws and the lessening of ethnic and racial violence or tension. They argue that what is needed is more, rather than less, attention to the ideas of racial and religious superiority; that they must be confronted to be understood; that dialogue and democracy are more effective tools in understanding the anatomy of hate than silence; and for that reason, freedom of expression is necessary.

Though laudable in principle, it is arguable that these views lack force in the face of much twentieth-century history. They perhaps require us to believe too simply in the power of democracy and decency and above all rationality; in the ability of a long, slow onslaught on racism to have an effect; to believe, in the face of so much evidence to the contrary, that there is always progress, however slow. At the end of our century, we have once again in Europe been faced with an outburst of hatred and destruction based on racial, political and religious differences, which has all but destroyed a country – former Yugoslavia – at least temporarily. It is just half a century since the Holocaust. If that terrifying monument to the dark power of hate speech failed to alter consciousness constructively, what are we to say about the liberal belief in the human capacity to evolve morally?

In the face of such enormities, the political correctness debate has rather muddied the waters, diluting the wider implications of what hate can produce. For the most dangerous threat behind hate speech is surely that it can go beyond its immediate targets and create a *culture* of hate, a culture which makes it acceptable, respectable even, to hate on a far wider scale. Such a culture of hate is not easy to define, and does not necessarily have one trajectory, but its evolution is evident in the circumstances surrounding some events in recent history.

On 4 November 1995, Yitzhak Rabin, prime minister of Israel, was assassinated by Yigal Amir, a 25-year-old law student. But what part was played by rightwing Israeli radicals chanting, 'Rabin is a traitor! Rabin is a murderer!' at Likud rallies? Or by placards showing Rabin's features overlaid with the thin black circles of a rifle target? Or by the mainstream Israeli rabbincal leadership, who for months before the assassination had questioned the 'Jewishness' of Rabin's land-for-peace policies, and solicited the learned opinions of their colleagues around the world as to whether – purely theoretically of course – the abandonment to Palestinian control of West Bank territory divinely promised to the Jews 'might merit the death penalty'. Only one leading rabbi, Yoel Nun, spoke out loudly against the killing. He was denounced by some of the other sages, even had his life threatened, and was forced to resort to an escort of bodyguards to protect himself.

Words can turn into bullets, hate speech can kill and maim, just as censorship can. So, as dedicated opponents of censorship and proponents of free speech, we are forced to ask: is there a moment where the *quantitative* consequences of hate speech change *qualitatively* the arguments about how we must deal with it. And is there no distinction to be made between the words of those whose hate speech is a matter of conviction, however ignorant, deluded or prejudiced, and hate speech as propaganda, the calculated and systematic use of lies to sow fear, hate and violence in a population at large?

One has only to run through newspapers in former Yugoslavia to find examples of hate speech as propaganda. In 1987, the Serbian newspapers published a photograph taken by a Belgrade reporter in Prekale, Kosovo, a Serbian province with a majority Albanian population. Under the headline, 'The Mother from Prekale', it showed a Serbian woman working in the field, surrounded by her children. A gun hung from her shoulder. She needed the weapon, the papers revealed, to protect her and her children from Albanian terrorists, who were torturing and killing Serbs and raping their wives and daughters. The photograph attracted a lot of publicity, and shocked the whole of Serbia. Hundreds of similar photographs and newspaper articles, hours of TV programmes with news of the persecutions of Serbs in Kosovo resulted in nationwide terror and hatred of the Albanian Kosovans. A few years later, the photograph was revealed to be a clever fake, set up by the reporter who had himself supplied the gun on the woman's shoulder. By then it was all over. The propaganda – one can find similar examples from all the protagonists in the war, though the Croats and Serbs seem to have been the masters of this sordid craft – had done its work.

'When the homeland is at stake, I am prepared to lie,' a senior Croatian journalist bravely affirmed. 'I feel no shame in lying if it is in the interest of Serbia and the Serbian people,' said the chief editor of Belgrade Television. 'If it's necessary for Croatia, I'll lie,' said one of the leading commentators of *Vecernji List*, the Croatian daily with the highest circulation. Four years on, no-one on any side has any doubt as to the part played by the media in fomenting the war.

The US philosopher and political scientist Sidney Hook set out starkly his experience of the workings of expressions of hate. 'I believe any people in the world, when roused to a fury of nationalistic resentment, and convinced that some individual or group is responsible for their continued and extreme misfortunes, can be led to do or countenance the same things the Germans did. I believe that if conditions in the US were ever to become as bad psychologically and economically as they were in Germany in the 1920s and 1930s, systematic racial persecution might break out. It could happen to the Blacks, but it could happen to the Jews too, or any targeted group.'

Another important witness to the deadly mechanisms which seem so readily to transform neighbours into murderers is the Serbian novelist and Nobel Laureate Ivo Andric. Here he is, in his epic novel *The Bridge on the Drina*, written in Belgrade during Hitler's war, in the days of the Nazi concentration camp at Banjica, and the public hangings in Terazije, reflecting on what happened to his world after August 1914: 'People were divided up into the persecuted and those who persecuted them. That wild beast which lives in man and does not dare to show itself until the barriers of law and custom have been removed, was now set free. The signal was given, the impediments eliminated. As so often happens in human history, violence and plunder were tacitly permitted, even killing, on condition that they could be perpetrated in the name of higher interests, under set slogans, and on a limited number of people, of a definite name and persuasion.'

If you drive through Bosnia now, you see in the scorched landscape and shattered villages a thoroughly up-to-date model of the pathological mechanism Andric described. Because this was civil war of a kind, its working is revealed all the more clearly. Here the 'Others', whom propaganda hate speech had indicated as the legitimate object of your fears and fantasies, people you must drive away, slaughter, eliminate, are people well known to you – your neighbours, even kin by marriage – now made alien and terrifying by the unreason you have been infected with. The houses, streets and villages from which Muslims or Serbs were driven were not simply ruined by arson and looting; after the fighting they were systematically crushed and destroyed with bulldozers and dynamite. So hate speech results in the end in one of the ultimate forms of censorship: the obliteration of the memory of a place, as if those lives and communities had never been.

Is there a point of necessary intervention somewhere in the continuum between the ugly, offensive but more localised public expression of hatred and the successful establishment in a community or society of a culture of hatred in which the instigators of hatred become its authorisers, become authority itself? And, if so, what is to be done? There are no simple answers, but it's the job of magazines like *Index*, now addressing such a different world from the one in which it was founded, to be a pivotal forum for one of the most important debates of our time.

Finally, to compound an already complicated story, an arresting addendum to the story of Bob Grant, the New York radio shock-jock. What we discover here, in our unregenerate post-modern society, is that hate speech not only kills, it sells. Bob Grant's programme had been hugely successful. Advertisers loved it for its ratings. An ABC producer, on being asked whether Bob Grant's remarks were an example of free speech that must be protected under the First Amendment, or verbal pollution, said: 'If the person has good ratings, a station has to overlook the garbage that he spews out. A radio station always fights for a host's constitutional rights if the show is profitable enough, and Grant had high ratings because he kept beating up on minorities. If his audience had been small, the managers would forget the constitution and declare him a bigot.' He added, 'Radio is the only serious soap box the racists have. Our advertisers are aware that hate sells their products.' ❑

This article is an edited version of the Iain Walker Memorial Lecture.

No port in a storm

What part did the media play in provoking the flight of the Roma from Slovakia and the Czech Republic? Does the press in the British Isles stand guilty of inciting hatred against our new arrivals? Claude Cahn in Budapest, Michael Foley in Dublin and Jeremy Hardy in London pose the questions, and find some uncomfortable answers...

On 4th April 1997, 20 prominent Czechs signed an official complaint requesting a criminal investigation into the activities of one Josef Hajduk between August 1942 and spring 1943. During this time, they asserted, he had participated in the crime of genocide at the so-called 'punitive work camp' for Roma (Gypsies) at Lety near Písek in southern Bohemia.

The complaint stated the known facts about Lety: that before its surviving inmates were deported to Auschwitz, more than 300 Roma had died due to the brutality of the guards and camp director, as well as from the epidemics that thrived in the inhuman conditions of the camp. The complaint also drove home the fact that Lety was established and run by Czech authorities on their own initiative, without assistance, interference or prodding from the German occupying power. As Czech Roma activist Jana Horváthová put it, 'Its planning and organisation came from Czech heads.'

Among the signatories of the complaint is Ludvík Vaculík, formerly one of Czechoslovakia's most prominent dissidents. A signatory of the dissidents' founding document, Charter 77, Vaculík established the first domestic *samizdat* publishing house. He is widely acknowledged to be one of the best living Czech writers.

Vaculík's signature on the complaint was significant: in mid–1991, he had published an article in the leading Czech literary journal *Literární Noviny* in which the Roma figured prominently.

'We have put it into law and taken it as wish and necessity that all

HATE SPEECH: THE MEDIA AND THE ROMA

people are possessed with equal rights. Even Gypsies. In the first class the catechist taught us religion in the following way: "Love thy neighbour as thyself. Repeat it"' We responded in unison. He levelled a finger at someone and asked "Even the Gypsy?" It was a trick question, but the pupil didn't get it. "No, not the Gypsy," he answered from out of his clean conscience. In the higher classes we already knew the proper answer, which did not, however, correspond to our true regard for Gypsies.'

Vaculík went on to explain that Gypsies have little regard for the idea of equal rights with 'us' – the untranslatable pronoun in Czech which signifies the strictly delineated sphere of Czechs, ethnic Czechs, inside which Czech Roma do not belong. He then proposed his solution:

'If Gypsies decide to live among us, it means they must accept our norms (*nás rád*) and if they cause trouble, they will be returned... I seri-

Ludovit Goreij, Romani. Expelled from his native Czech Republic for stealing £3 worth of sugar beet, he was then deported from the Slovak Republic as he was not a citizen. Returning to the Czech Republic he found he and his fiancé were not allowed to work, or to receive benefits. They survive on the charity of a pensioner, Mr Kellich, all three living in a single room. It is this kind of life the Roma are fleeing – Credit: Christian Schwetz

ously see two questions: should we leave them in the already destroyed sections of the city or (better) leave them some piece of earth where they can start, picturesquely, to burn the bare earth? Should we wait for the cultured Rom to stay and improve his community and not run straight to us? If we don't agree on something circumspect with the Roma, one day we may be shooting each other.'

Nineteen ninety one and 1992 were big years in Czechoslovakia: while the country watched the process on television, the Republic moved inexorably toward break-up. The public eagerly anticipated the new democracy and the acceptance of the people's mandate. Different people were mandating different things, but there was one thing on which everyone agreed: Gypsies smell, Gypsies steal, Gypsies are terrible; and graffiti everywhere advocated 'Gypsies to the gas'. Vaculík appealed to the fundamental consensus among his readership: Gypsies are horrible, something must be done.

Gypsies were on the tongues and minds of everyone in those days. Although no-one had ever met one, everyone knew about them: Gypsies appeared in the form of new code words; 'criminality', (by which no one meant the people who were arranging the privatisation of state-owned firms); '*Vekslák*', meaning money-changer (meaning Gypsy). By 1991, the term *Vekslák* had come to mean more than just the old street salesman of illegal cash from communism. It had come to mean the *nouveau riche* who had earned their foreign cars by pimping on Wenceslas Square. It still meant Gypsy. In the go-America spirit of the times there was a film called '*Vekslák*' in which Czech Gypsies acted out a fantasy of underworld US crime in an implausible domestic setting.

During the election campaign which eventually saw victory for Meciar and Klaus, the men who split Czechoslovakia, Czech television played on a new sort of black humour by going out to desperately poor Roma communities in eastern Slovakia and interviewing Roma who claimed they would vote for the Slovak populist.

It was around this time that skinheads appeared on the streets and Roma began to be killed. Non-governmental organisations have documented an estimated 1,250 racially-motivated incidents since 1991 resulting in the deaths of 10 Roma, one Turk mistaken for a Rom and, in early November 1997, a Sudanese student. Government statistics put the figure at approximately 800, with numbers rising steadily every year. Notorious cases include the death in 1995 of Tibor Berki, a Romani

HATE SPEECH: THE MEDIA AND THE ROMA

man, killed when four skinheads broke into his house in Ziar nad sazavou and beat him to death in front of his family with a baseball bat.

Romani activists consider both government and independent figures low. Most attacks on Roma go unreported, and the authorities have been reticent in prosecuting racially-motivated crime. The initial decision in the Berki killing, for instance, was that the skinheads had not acted out of racial hatred because although they had been overheard discussing killing a Rom earlier in the evening, and belonged to a group known to advocate the death of Gypsies, witnesses had not overheard any of the attackers shouting racial epithets at the time of the crime. More recently, a court in Hradec Králové decided that, notwithstanding their proven guilt in an attack on Roma, two skinheads could not be found guilty of racially-motivated crimes against Roma because Roma and Czechs both come from the same 'Indo-European race'. Indeed, at least one Rom has been killed in police custody since 1989 in the Czech Republic, and all of the police officers involved were found innocent of wrongdoing.

For the past seven years, however, the mainstream Czech-language press has either avoided addressing the disturbing rise of domestic racism and racist violence against Roma, or has tacitly abetted it through the use of euphemism, equivocation, racially-stereotyping illustration, or prominent interviews in which racists explain their feelings.

As, for instance, in *Respekt*, one of the top-selling weekly news magazines. *Respekt* ran a review article on Richard J Herrnstein and Charles Murray's *The Bell Curve: Intelligence and Class Structure in American Life*, a book that promotes the thesis that social inequality coincides with genetic factors, specifically intelligence. But what purported to be a review, was run minus any comment and alongside a caricature of a stupefied African-American man with baseball cap perched idiotically on a grotesque simian head.

And there are other examples: after Liana Janácková, a district mayor from the ruling Civil Democratic Party (ODS), offered to provide partial funding for the plane tickets of Roma who wished to leave her municipality and emigrate to Canada, the mainstream daily *Lidové Noviny* provided her with a front-page platform from which she could air her views to a national audience:

'In no way do I consider myself a racist. It bothers me that [Roma] don't follow the laws of this country, and we don't have sufficient power to force them to do so... I don't understand why [people say that] Roma are discriminated against in our country. On the contrary, they keep us down by their inability to adapt... It would be enough if they kept order, sent their children to school, expressed interest in working, but they don't do it... It is unlikely they will ever absorb our way of life.'

In a recent article on the difficulty of establishing exactly how many people have died as a result of racially-motivated attacks, the daily *Mlada Fronta Dnes* printed only two examples of racially-motivated murder, and with the following comment: 'In contrast to state offices, non-governmental organisations are far more categorical in their judgements and consider both the following cases racially-motivated. The death of 17-year-old Jitka Chánová, who together with other Roma attacked skinheads in a tram four years ago, and jumped from the tram while it was in motion and later died from her injuries. The death of a Romani woman who died two months ago as a result of an epileptic seizure after she had witnessed a crowd of skinheads march past her window presenting the Nazi salute, shouting racist slogans, and firing their pistols.'

All the examples above come from the liberal press, the journals read by the urban middle class and the people one would normally expect to oppose racism. The tabloids, which came on the scene in 1992, cater to more sensationalist tastes and manipulate racist stereotypes in more obvious fashion. What is noteworthy in the Czech press, however, is that for the past seven years, there has been no effective counterweight to any of this. In the exaggerated neo-liberal atmosphere, the predominant view has been that any serious opposition to racism smacks of the old Communist order – and is tantamount to censorship.

Some signs of change emerged last year. In May 1997, *Mlada Fronta Dnes* started a campaign against domestic racism, calling for the resignation of Mayor Janácková, as well as Senator Zdenìk Klausner, also a member of the ruling ODS, who publicly advocated ghettoising Roma. But in general, the Czech press has covered seven years of racist violence in the Republic in mindless conformity with the popular view, seeking to justify what the majority of Czech citizens feel. Vaculík articulated the racism widely expressed in private, but it was the act of a non-conformist. The prevailing media practice is to avoid the issue in the hope that the subject will go away.

HATE SPEECH: THE MEDIA AND THE ROMA

It was in this prevailing climate of hostility to the Roma that Czech and Slovak TV were able to show two films that changed a trickle of Roma asylum seekers fleeing persecution at home into a stream to Canada, Ireland and the UK. Both programmes looked like deliberate attempts to entice Roma to leave: the one extolling the benefits of Canada ended with a large Romani man urging. 'Hey! All you Czech Gypsies, get over here!'

Gysies go to Heaven emphasised the financial benefits for Czech Gypsies seeking asylum in the UK. It showed Ladislav Scuka, a Rom who had fled firebomb attacks on his home in Prague, enjoying his state handouts: 'How much money can a Romani family get here?' asks the interviewer. 'We have three children and I get £140 a week. The social services pay our hotel accommodation including breakfast,' replies Scuka happily. 'Can you manage on that kind of money?' 'Perfectly.'

Josef Klima, the TV Nova reporter who made the film, was shown round Romani homes in Dover where refugees praised the schools, the health care and the police in Britain. His film did not refer to the reasons Scuka had left home. (*See Babel, p156*). Was this a film made to entice Roma to leave the Czech Republic? 'Maybe it made the stream of refugees a bit stronger,' says Klima, 'but even without my film it would have been the same; the only difference is that it would have happened later.'

Within days of the film's airing, buses leaving Prague for London were jammed with Roma. No-one knows who put the director up to making the films, but their conspiracy theories are rife. Since 8.5 per cent of the population support an anti-Roma party, there are obvious candidates for funding. ❏

Claude Cahn *is research co-ordinator at the European Roma Rights Centre, Budapest*

Emigration has been engrained in Irish culture ever since the mass exodus from the island during the Great Famine 150 years ago. Former President Mary Robinson lit a candle in her window as a sign of welcome to the Irish Diaspora; Irish in London, Boston, Liverpool and even Dublin sing of leaving Ireland and the sadness of emigration; our sense of national pride is boosted by the success of those who left to make their life in New York or Sidney.

MICHAEL FOLEY

About a year ago, something odd started to happen and a new word entered the language: immigration. People started to arrive in Ireland seeking a new life. It was all very strange. Why were they coming to Ireland? The answer was not far to seek: events in Africa and eastern Europe, coupled with Ireland's new found wealth – the 'Celtic Tiger Economy' of the headline writers – and a successful tourist image of a friendly people, were attracting more than just tourists.

Ireland has always had a small number of refugees. In the 1970s it received a number of the Vietnamese boat people. More recently Bosnians arrived here following agreement with the UN. These were treated by the media with curiosity; their stories were harrowing and often quietly heroic. They became the focus of feature articles on how they settled down and found work; how well their children integrated and even learned Irish at school.

More recent arrivals – such as the Roma from the Slovak and the Czech Republics – have been subjected to something else: an unthinking and often racist media. The reason for such different treatment is complex: the greater numbers; the visibility – many can be seen begging in the street – and the poverty of most newcomers.

Words like 'swamp', 'flood' and 'spongers' started to appear in headlines. The minister for justice warned against organisations who were 'trafficking people' into Ireland. Rosslare Harbour in the south became a 'drop-zone' for refugees who had paid to be brought to Ireland.

Claims by the police were quoted, but rarely checked out, by some sections of the press. 'Refugee Rapists on the Rampage' ran the headline on a story in the *Star*. '*Gardai* (Irish police) have warned women to stay away from refugees after a spree of sex assaults. Prostitutes and minors are the main target of rapacious Romanians and Somalians, according to top *Garda* sources,' the story continued. Certain refugees were said to be 'combing' the city streets and night-clubs for victims. Young girls were being lured from night-clubs by refugees offering parties and booze. A *Garda* spokesman was quoted as saying that 'some refugees have an unusual attitude to women.' But the hands of the police were tied, sympathised the writer, because when picked up, the refugees pretend not to speak English and by the time an interpreter is found the legal time allowed to hold the person is almost up.

Refugees were also 'flooding' Dublin's maternity hospitals, stretching facilities. The *Sunday World* said that there were 5,000 of them and that the 'floodgates open as a new army of poor swamp the country'.

By the time of the general election in June, some politicians were becoming more vociferous. The *Irish Independent* reported that voters were now demanding a 'curb on the tide of refugees'. Joan Burton, a junior minister at the Department of Foreign Affairs, condemned the way in which the arrival of a 'couple of thousand foreign nationals' had been used during the campaign.

Meanwhile, the media found itself under scrutiny. Philip Watt, coordinator of the European Year Against Racism, said that some of the coverage could at best be described as 'irresponsible and at worst outright racist in content'. Other reports were balanced and well researched 'only to be undermined by the application of an alarmist or sensationalised headline or sub-heading'.

Seamus Dooley, regional organiser of the National Union of Journalists, says: 'In a sense, the issues surrounding racism and language are new to Irish journalists. We have much to learn about the nuances of language.' Dooley also raised a concern felt by many journalists when he said the NUJ was not suggesting refugee issues should not be raised in the media. 'Journalists cannot ignore issues of public interest and importance. Where provocative or controversial statements are made by public officials or political figures, they should be recorded. By definition such reports will cause offence. If the media is to be truthful we cannot ignore hurtful comments, difficult situations and complex problems. To gloss over the prejudices of society as a means of avoiding offence would be misguided tolerance.'

There is a feeling that while the initial media reaction was unthinking, insensitive and even lazy, it would be wrong to move towards a form of censorship where immigrants are concerned. Concern chiefly focuses on phone-in radio programmes, frequently cited as the most offensive and racist of all media outlets. What is under attack is the right to continue broadcasting the public expression of views, however hostile.

The issue has already been raised at the European Court of Human Rights which ruled in favour of a Danish radio journalist found guilty under Danish laws of inciting racial hatred by allowing a racist gang to air its views on his programme. He had, said the court, a right and a duty to disseminate viewpoints, however objectionable they might be. ❑

Michael Foley is media correspondent with the Irish Times *of Dublin*

JEREMY HARDY

Britain is proud of its reputation as a haven for refugees, it just doesn't want any to come here, that's all. In fact, the reputation has been tarnished to the point that it is way past being shiny. The clamp-down has been going on for the whole of this century, beginning with the Aliens Act, brought in to stop the entry of dispossessed Ashkenazi Jews fleeing pogroms in Eastern Europe. Shamefully, but unsurprisingly, wealthy Sephardim supported the legislation, because they had just got comfortable in Britain and didn't want a load of dirty peasants spoiling the image of Jews as established citizens.

In fact, until the Holocaust, anti-Semitism was eminently respectable in this country, and the debate about Britain's failure to save Jews from Nazi persecution still rages. Although anti-Semitism is still around, there are now vivid images locked in people's minds which show where the prejudice can lead. And I doubt whether many people today would suggest that Jews trying to leave Germany, Austria or Czechoslovakia before the war were not genuine refugees. That is not just hindsight; persecution was already fierce and there was every reason to expect worse.

Perhaps it's because of numbers that the extermination of the Gypsies is seldom mentioned. Compared to Europe's Jews, the Roma got off lightly, only losing about 500,000. Anti-Semitism is growing again in central and eastern Europe, and its proponents are very much the same sort of people who hate the Roma, but for whatever reason, there are many respectable – even liberal – people who would never dream of being heard to deliver any anti-Semitic utterance, but who are entirely comfortable with being anti-Romani.

Trying to compare one prejudice or atrocity with another always risks diminishing the horror of both, and presenting them as rivals competing for attention. But I'd like to stick with this particular comparison for a while, if only because I think it would be interesting to reprint all the articles in the British press about Romani migration, substituting the world 'Gypsy' with 'Jew', just to see how it looks. Moreover, I think there are some similarities in the way that the two peoples are mystified and feared.

Both nations are scattered and a long way from home. Both are eastern and slightly exotic, and both have members who can pass for a native; so that, although many are physically identifiable, some look like everybody else, and you can never be sure whether you're talking to one or not. Neither people is really viewed as belonging anywhere. Only a

HATE SPEECH: THE MEDIA AND THE ROMA

minority of Jews live in the Middle East and there is no significant movement among Romani to 'return' to India. Jews and Gypsies have always been kicked out of Europe, never fully assimilating anywhere and never being seen as wanting to fit in anywhere. Parts of their culture have remained intact and they've used different languages or dialects from their neighbours. Both are identified with less Christian or less respectable ways of making money, and both are believed to have a knack for it. In short, when it comes to persecution, there are plenty of people who think they've 'brought it on themselves'.

In this country, this is still said quietly about Jews and openly about Gypsies. Only a minority of the articles about the 'tide', 'flood' or 'influx' of 800 people in Dover acknowledged that there is persecution

Dover shoppers applauding marchers of the fascist National Front – Credit: Max Jourdan

of Romani in eastern Europe, and many of the articles that did so also featured quotes from eastern Europeans justifying it. The feature would be balanced: one would read about neo-Nazis abusing, beating or murdering Gypsies with impunity; then there would be a non-Gypsy saying that they make themselves unpopular by being lazy, dirty and criminal. Then we read quotes from solid citizens of Dover saying the same thing about their behaviour here.

To be fair to the local people, they must wonder why a hard-pressed local authority should have to bear all the costs. The numbers are tiny but they are all in the one town and every town has problems because of shortages of local resources. Clearly, immigration is a national responsibility. It is also the duty of central government to face down prejudice and not bow to it.

It was heartening that the National Front spectacularly failed to make capital with their abortive rally in Dover. Most British people are aware that it is a neo-Nazi organisation, or at the very least that it is hostile to black British people who are now broadly accepted. Asian and Afro-Caribbean people in Britain are no longer immigrants. Whether their families came here because of massacres or simply to get better jobs, they are now part of the scenery and part of the culture. Vile prejudice persists but they are here to stay. Brown faces appear at business conferences and even in the Tory Party. It is acknowledged that non-white people have 'made a contribution' in sport, music and (thank God) in cooking.

Ugly stereotyping of ethnic minorities, especially the Afro-Caribbean male, still appears in mainstream newspapers but less and less. It is harder to perpetuate the image of the Yardie when the reader is going to see a pantomime starring a famous black presenter from children's television. And yet denigration of the Romani people has been wall-to-wall in the British media. I think *The Times* was alone in printing Gypsy with a capital 'G', this might seem a pedantic point were not the slight so clearly deliberate.

The use of the lower case not only suggests that this is a lesser culture, worthy of less recognition than others, it involves all the pejorative connotations of the lazy use of the word. Just as a 'jew' is a miser, a 'gypsy' or 'gipsy' is a wanderer, and especially a work-shy vagabond and thief. The government wishes to divide asylum seekers into the genuine and the bogus, the deserving and the undeserving; and the negative imagery surrounding the mythic 'gypsy' is helping them to do it.

HATE SPEECH: THE MEDIA AND THE ROMA

Those journalists who avoided the full extent of the *Sun*'s bigotry ('kick the gypsies out') wrote in more measured terms about abuse of the system and Britain having no responsibility to these people. It's true that none of them have British passports or live in former colonies — not that those criteria are a guarantee of entry anyway. It's also true that they are not citizens of EC countries. There are thousands of EC citizens living and working in Britain, attracting little controversy. Indeed, the government's answer to all problems of need seems to be to get people into work, single mums, the disabled and so on. But when asylum seekers work they are summarily arrested and deported. Racists have never been able to decide whether to attack immigrants for taking jobs or for living on benefits, and the government seems to have much the same problem.

So the British government has used the media here and in the Czech and Slovak Republics, to tell Gypsies that it's no good fleeing poverty, unemployment, homelessness, discrimination and violence there, because they will face more of the same here. And the government can guarantee it. ❑

Jeremy Hardy is a writer and broadcaster

PAUL OPPENHEIMER

In the name of democracy

Germany needs its censorship laws to save face with its friends

You cannot legally purchase new copies of *Mein Kampf* in Germany, nor publish it, nor shout (or whisper) Nazi slogans. You cannot publish and distribute pro-Nazi literature of any kind, nor watch Leni Riefenstahl's *Triumph of the Will* in a public theatre, nor strut (or shamble) in Nazi regalia; not just the obvious symbols such as swastikas, but even less obvious, though trés chic, vintage jackboots and SS helmets.

On the face of it, this seems a puzzling and perhaps disturbing contradiction: one of the world's most liberal democracies banning political books and hate speech in the interests of preserving itself as a liberal democracy.

Yet such is precisely Germany's bizarre and little disputed practice. It pre-dates the breach of the Wall in 1989 by decades, and was practised on both sides of the divide. It was maintained as an unquestioned if not pickled principle of German law after the reunification of the country in 1990.

The paradox seems grimly perverse. It was, after all, Hitler who said that he would use the instruments of democracy to destroy democracy. A present question may be whether a liberal democracy can use the instruments of totalitarianism to prop up democracy. Do not modern German book-banning and film censorship laws amount to a morbid splurge of risky self-indulgence, if not self-delusion? Would it not be fair to say that in the end they are most likely to promote if not incite the very ghastliness at which they are aimed?

Other serious questions arise. Is it not a grotesque irony, one exceed-

HATE SPEECH: THE GERMAN LEGACY

ingly difficult for any free-speech purist to accept with equanimity, that 60 years after the Nazi *auto-da-fé* of books by Mann, Freud, Zola, Proust, Remarque and Einstein in a square opposite Berlin University, the latest twentieth century democratic German government is engaged in the same sort of suppression of free expression, albeit this time of Nazi ideas? May not German history simply be continuing by other means down a familiar constrictive path?

'We need this sort of thing here,' a professor of literature at the University of

German neo-Nazi skinheads – Credit: Cham/Rex

Osnabrück told me two years ago. Things are different here from Britain and the USA.'

What he had in mind was the widely reported storm of countrywide neo-Nazi arson attacks and assaults – over 30,000 and including 30 murders – between 1989 and 1995. The total is still mounting, though the official annual count is now down by about one-third, under 1,600. Few of the most recent neo-Nazi criminal violations of existing laws receive more than scattered attention in the UK and US press. Among democracy-committed Germans, however, their persistence casts a distasteful if not ominous shadow.

One of the things that worried the professor at Osnabrück, and would presumably continue to worry him, is the spotty seductiveness of Nazi propaganda; its lingering appeal to a small but fierce and unyielding minority even half a century after the end of World War II – to the desperate, the nationalistic, the bigoted, the naive and, of course, the evilminded. He was surely thinking then, and would be now, though we did not discuss it, about the necessity of keeping in place laws and court judgements curtailing certain types of speech, or hate speech, in particular anti-semitic and racist speech, and insisting on these restrictions even after two generations of democratic education in the West. In the East, such education in democratic ideals began only after reunification; but contrary to widespread assumptions, most incidents of neo-Nazi violence have taken place not in the economically depressed eastern parts of the country but in better-off western ones.

Along with many other liberal Germans, the professor was not prepared to abandon press controls, or laws criminalising hate speech, at least when it came to pro-Nazi publications and pro-Nazi hate speech. The same stubborn refusal also applied to denials of the Holocaust, which in print and at public assemblies are prohibited under German law (*Ronald Dworkin, Index, 3/95*).

His views continue to be supported by prominent legal authorities. In a more recent interview in 1997, Thomas Lundmark, a German-speaking US professor of Anglo-American law at the University of Münster, observed, 'I have never, in years of living in Germany and talking with numerous people about this issue, found a single German who favours repeal of the prohibitions.'

The laws themselves, however, have been interpreted by the courts as making several interesting exceptions to their own prohibitions. Their

HATE SPEECH: THE GERMAN LEGACY

spirit has clearly been understood as more generous than their letter. In arriving at any fair evaluation of modern Germany's official position on hate speech and book-banning, therefore, it may be sensible to take the exceptions into account. Any condemnation of modern Germany on the basis of its existing censorship laws as a 'special case' in which democracy has failed to plant genuine and firm roots, as some have assumed, may be erroneous. At the very least, the free speech absolutists among us may find it useful to reflect on what is clearly a complex issue.

The court-established rule governing all exceptions seems at first glance Byzantine enough. It has to do with National Socialist propaganda versus what the Federal German Court (*Bundesgericht*) has termed 'information' about National Socialism. While it remains illegal (and can earn up to three years in prison and a hefty fine, though the maximum sentence for violations is rarely imposed) to buy, sell or publish pro-Nazi propaganda, it is legal to buy and sell almost the same thing for the sake of academic curiosity and research purposes. You may not, however, publish this material except as part of your own research. A buyer's motive, rather than the contents of what is bought, has been found all-important in these instances, and the latter is not regarded as automatically propagandistic.

One might, nonetheless, imagine that this very distinction is almost impossible to make. How, after all, can 'propagandistic' editions of *Mein Kampf* be separated from 'informational' ones? In a well known case, however, dating back to 1978, and appealed several times until it was decided at the level of the highest court in the country, German jurists struggled mightily to define the distinction.

The case in point involved an antiques dealer from Fürth, specialising in old coins, who had picked up at an auction, along with all sorts of bric-à-brac, a couple of copies of *Mein Kampf* published in the mid-1930s and early-1940s. He was cited by the police for attempting to sell them at a flea market after failing to sell them in his shop.

What worked in his favour was that he was not a bookseller nor an obvious propagandist. What also mattered was that the books themselves had plainly been published prior to the existence of the Federal Republic of Germany. The court argued that these particular copies of Hitler's notorious testament, as opposed to any that might be published for popular distribution these days, could not possibly be regarded as directed against the post-war, post-Hitler German democratic state.

PAUL OPPENHEIMER

The antiques dealer from Fürth was let off, but not everyone was happy with the decision, the basis of which lay in the court's perception of an absence of a threat to modern German democracy. To many, the very idea of this, at least in respect to press freedoms, seemed self-contradictory. State interests, no matter how democratic the state, had been made paramount over the inviolability of the principle of a free press. Precisely the same sort of reasoning, one might argue (and some have), could be seen as typical of the premises of any totalitarian regime.

Speculation continues to ripple through legal commentaries, moreover, that the real reason for the court's decision was quite different: Germany's gawky position *vis-à-vis* Nazi propaganda. Any other decision might have required the banning of Marxist revolutionary literature too, or even the writings of pro-democracy revolutionaries such as Tom Paine. The court's point was to quash specifically Nazi propaganda. Astonishingly in the eyes of some, a certain amount of waffling on principle has been taken as making easier its practical adjustment to social and historical conditions.

Can such an adjustment in the end be managed without compromising democracy itself? Thomas Lundmark, echoing what is probably a majority view, believes that it can, and that such compromises, though seldom acknowledged, are commonplace in all democracies: 'Each society, in the context of its legal culture, has an obligation to respond to its own history. Impositions on liberty are sometimes appropriate.'

Appropriate, however, to what? When asked whether the deepest reason for the preservation of the censorship laws might not in fact be the continuing irrational suspicions of Germany across Europe and the USA, Lundmark is unequivocal. There is little fear among jurists and legislators, he maintains, of 'the building of a new [Nazi] movement. What they fear is the embarrassment to the rest of Germany, [if censorship laws were repealed]: how Germans would appear to other Europeans and to people around the world.' ❑

Paul Oppenheimer *is professor of comparative literature and English at the City College of New York. He has worked as a foreign correspondent in Germany, where he also held a Fulbright Senior Scholar Fellowship and taught at the University of Osnabrück. His latest books are* Evil and the Demonic: A New Theory of Monstrous Behaviour *(1996) and* An Intelligent Person's Guide to Modern Guilt *(1997), both Duckworth.*

ARYEH NEIER

Clear and present danger

When is hate speech a suitable case for censorship? When there is 'clear and present danger' of the word becoming the deed

In 1977, I helped to defend freedom of speech for a group of American Nazis. There was nothing particularly unusual in this: the American Civil Liberties Union has frequently defended Nazis, members of the Ku Klux Klan and others engaged in hate speech. Yet it aroused great controversy because of the drama of the situation: the Nazis wished to march through Skokie, Illinois, a town with a large population of Holocaust survivors. I thought then, and think now, that it was important to protect free expression even for such a repugnant group.

Two cases that could be considered by UN Security Council tribunals – the prosecution of those who incited genocide on Radio Mille Collines in Rwanda and those who fomented ethnic cleansing through the Serbian media – may appear to raise some of the same issues as the Skokie case. But in the Rwandan case, and perhaps also in the Serbian one, I find myself on the opposite side. Comparing these three situations might help to clarify some of the issues around the vexed problem of free expression and hate speech.

The Skokie case arose in the 1970s because a small group of US Nazis was trying to exploit a tense racial situation in Chicago. In Marquette Park, which divided a white working-class neighbourhood from a predominantly black one, the Martin Luther King Junior Coalition was holding demonstrations calling for desegregation. The Nazi group rented a store-front next to the park and started to organise counter-protests.

ARYEH NEIER

Concerned about the possibility of open conflict, the Chicago authorities demanded that the Nazis post a bond of US$250,000 to repair any damage that might result – a typical ploy then used by US city authorities to restrict free speech and assembly for despised groups. The local office of the ACLU agreed to challenge the bond requirement, but while the lawsuit was under way, the Nazi group was shut out of Marquette Park.

Searching for a way to keep itself in the public eye, the group sent letters to all the suburban communities and towns near Chicago asking to hold demonstrations there. Most of them wisely ignored the request, but Skokie responded with an angry refusal and quickly adopted a series of ordinances forbidding marches with Nazi symbols and repeating the city of Chicago's bond requirement. The Nazi group again came to the ACLU – which takes every case brought to it where it believes freedom of speech is at stake – to ask for representation. The ACLU agreed to file a lawsuit against the town of Skokie.

During the debate that raged nationwide throughout the 15 months of a series of court cases, many people argued that the Nazis should not be allowed to march. Some drew on the doctrine of 'clear and present danger', which the US Supreme Court had invoked on a number of occasions to limit freedom of speech. The doctrine of 'clear and present danger' stems from the period after World War I which saw some 1,900 federal prosecutions for peaceful speech, mostly for statements considered subversive because they encouraged resistance to the draft or otherwise opposed the war effort. Among the notable cases of that era was the prosecution and imprisonment of the leader of the American Socialist Party, Eugene V Debs, which was upheld by the Supreme Court The restrictive force of the doctrine was broadened in 1951 during the prosecution of 11 top US Communist Party leaders, when the Supreme Court ruled that if the climate is right for an evil to occur, the government may imprison people whose advocacy could create that evil at a future point. If the Supreme Court had adhered to this view, which it subsequently abandoned, the government would have had a powerful tool to crack down on all manner of speech that particular officials might find offensive.

Now contrast the circumstances of the Nazis in Skokie, the anti-war protesters during World War I and the US Communists in the early 1950s with that of the hate broadcasters in Rwanda and Serbia. In the

US cases, the groups whose free speech was at issue were minorities representing dissenting points of view. Even if the deeds they advocated were unlawful, everyone had an opportunity to hear contrary views before any crime was committed. Indeed, opposing points of view all but drowned out these minorities. Defending them protected freedom of speech. There was no manifest danger that the violence they might incite would follow so soon that debate could not take place. That is, the danger was neither clear nor present.

In Rwanda, on the other hand, Radio Mille Collines had virtually a monopoly for its hate-filled broadcasts. No contrary view had a chance to be heard. Moreover, once the genocide stated, Radio Mille Collines took over the task of organising it, directing mobs and militias to the places where the Tutsi targets were taking shelter. The violence that was incited was inextricably linked to its broadcasts. Circumstances in Serbia were not quite so extreme, but they were similar. The state television and radio network, RTS, had a monopoly on broadcasting and used it to stir up hate and to mobilise violence.

The Rwandan and Serbian cases show why it is vital to defend freedom of speech even in unpleasant circumstances, as the ACLU did in Skokie. The reason the media were so effective in inciting violence in Rwanda and Yugoslavia is precisely that they had an exclusive capacity to communicate. If a variety of views were being expressed and heard in Rwanda, even the vilest radio station could not have incited a genocide in which 800,000 people were killed during a period of three months. If there had been an opportunity for other voices to be heard in Serbia in the period when RTS and the nationalist press were monopolising communication, the influence of those voices would not have been so extreme. Freedom of speech is ultimately the greatest protection against the kinds of crimes that took place in Rwanda and in the former Yugoslavia, and against the crimes that Julius Streicher was able to incite in Nazi Germany. It is the exclusive capacity to communicate that produces the link between incitement to violence and violence itself. ❑

Aryeh Neier is president of the Open Society Institute, New York

1998 Bath Literature Festival

20 to 28 February

Sir Ranulph Fiennes
Jonathan Dimbleby
Patrick Gale
Irvine Welsh
John Hegley
Kathy Lette
Meera Syal
Jim Crace

Lemn Sissay
Margaret Drabble
Bernard MacLaverty
INDEX on Censorship
Serpent's Tail: Literature, Popular Culture and the limits of taste
Ventures with Words: schools residencies
The Rolling Stones 'Unplugged & Talking' with Max Middleton, Mick Taylor and Harry Shapiro

Brochure Hotline 01225 **463362**

Working hard to get it right

ED VULLIAMY

Tapes of wrath

They see portents in flying saucers and dollar bills: America's militias are preparing for war, and for some it can't come soon enough. Oklahoma City was their calling card

It is a matter of impulse, upon arrival in the mighty American desert: switch off the engine and lights, feel the infinite space around you. Listen a while to the ancient silence under a sky lambent with constellations.

But on the edges of Area 51 air force base in Nevada, the firmament thunders with the creations of man. The desert is alive with the roar of jet engines. A pair of red lights are dancing in the sky, rehearsing a dogfight. The exercise over, they glide towards the ground and the glow of runway lights. Then the empty land is wrapped again in silent darkness. A strange welcome into the high desert.

People call this place 'Dreamland'. The Pentagon says it doesn't exist, but a group of workers suing the US Air Force say they built a prototype for the awesome Stealth bomber here and contracted a horrific strain of skin cancer while doing so.

'Dreamland' is also the epicentre of what Americans call 'Uforia', the now mainstream cult of flying saucers and life in other heavens. Believers say the remains of a crashed UFO were brought here in the 1940s. And so when you check into the only motel in the lonely, trailer-cabin hamlet of Rachel, Nevada, its name is the Little Alie-Inn.

There's a board above the bar reading: 'God grant me the patience to accept the things I cannot change, the courage to change the things I can and the weaponry to make the difference.' It is funny, actually, and motel-owner Pat Travis laughs too. He's more interested in talking about weaponry than Uforia, and from behind the stacks of Ufo-bilia, Pat produces some cassette tapes produced by a radio station in Los Angeles

ED VULLIAMY

Onward Christian soldier... – Credit: Rex

HATE SPEECH: AMERICA'S ENEMY WITHIN

called *Christian Harvester*. 'I think you'll find these REAL interesting,' says Pat, offering five for the price of three.

Next morning, woken by a sonic boom that shook the trailer, I drove north into the Great Basin of empty Nevada and inserted the first tape into the car stereo. By doing so, one takes the first tiptoe-step into a new and wild belief system which holds sway among the armed insurgents on America's fringes – and is now cutting into the mainstream.

This was summer 1994, nearly a year before the bomb which ripped through the Alfred P Murrah federal building in Oklahoma City, killing 169 people, many of them children. I had come across some of the ideas on these tapes the previous summer at a conference organised by *Soldier of Fortune*, the mercenary magazine. The boys had come back to Las Vegas from front lines all over the world and were talking about a new enemy; not Communism abroad, but the government in Washington, puppet of an upcoming 'global government'. They weren't talking about 'commies' or 'niggers' any more; they were talking war in the US heartland.

Ashley Treanor, aged four, was wearing 'little blue jeans rolled up, a denim jacket and shirt,' recalls her mother Kathleen, when she went with Grandma and Grandpa to their appointment at the federal building on the morning of 19 April 1995.

Kathleen and her husband Mike had been high school sweethearts and Mike's parents, Luther and Larue, had 'embraced me right into the family' when they married. Luther and Larue had an appointment at the social security office: Luther was due to retire after working 25 years at Townsley's dairy in Guthrie, north of Oklahoma City. Kathleen's office was just a block away from the federal building, so they all went in together, Ashley clamouring to be allowed to stay with Grandma and Grandpa. 'I'm always happy to leave my little girl with them,' says Kathleen.

'She's a very feminine little girl. She likes having pretty bows in her hair and and I tied a nice big bow for her this morning,' continues Kathleen in the present tense, even though her daughter was blown to pieces that day. 'We're a close family, and close to the Lord.'

A few minutes after 9am, Kathleen saw from the window of her office a red fireball, followed by a billow of black smoke, rise into the prairie-blue sky. 'It was ten o'clock before I realised that they were in there...I saw bits of building sticking into another building. Ashley,' she continues in the present tense, 'is a happy little girl. She smiles at complete strangers. She's just a baby really, she wouldn't hurt anyone....'

After a couple of hundred desert miles of listening to *Christian Harvester* and another station on Pat Travis's tapes, *Radio Free World*, one has undergone a full-immersion baptism in the ideology of a revolutionary movement with an esoteric — some would say mad — but still coherent set of explanations for everything from UFOs to gun control, freemasonry to AIDS, Hitler to Bill Clinton.

Until recently, the 'Patriot' movement that espouses this world-view was regarded by the East Coast liberal establishment as a freak show. Only a few warned that the movement, with its plethora of militias, was both superseding and absorbing the old banalities of the Ku Klux Klan and the neo-Nazi skinheads. With the Oklahoma bomb, the Patriot movement to which the bomber Timothy McVeigh belonged, went centre-stage. At first it seemed that the carnage would stop the Patriots in their tracks.

But a report at the end of last year by the Anti-Defamation League (ADL) confirmed that the traditional Klan and neo-Nazi groups continue to be outflanked by this new movement, which is winning 'rhetorical support' in the broader US society. The language of the Patriots is not hateful on the surface; it is cogent and sympathetic to the cause of individual liberty. It is also apocalyptic, romantic, all-embracing. It is the most potent symptom of what Americans call PMT, or Pre-Millennial Tension.

The first *Radio Free World* tape is called the 'Panic Project' and its cover shows host Anthony Hilder atop Freedom Ridge, overlooking Area 51. Hilder explains how all that 'zig-zagging across the sky' is alien technology, harnessed at Area 51 for a 'crisis-creation programme'. The programme's goal is no less than a 'mock invasion from space', on the eve of the millennium, which will 'panic the planet into accepting global government upon the ashes of American sovereignty.' The mock space invasion will be the climax to many 'created crises', among which figured the Los Angeles earthquake.

The architects of the Panic Project are agents of a 'New World

HATE SPEECH: AMERICA'S ENEMY WITHIN

Order', against which the free citizens of America must urgently prepare, or else face the subjugation of their families, liberty and national sovereignty. 'You are the victim!' says Hilder's voice, 'You are the spoils. They want your home, your family. They want to inject your children with a number!' But who are they? To find out more, you can send off to *Christian Harvester* for a video unveiling the agents of this global conspiracy, and the Luciferian hand behind them. Better, surely, to go to LA and visit Anthony Hilder.

Hilder turns out to cut a debonair figure markedly at odds with the ample-bellied militia leaders who spout his stuff about a New World Order. He is handsome and courteous and sports an expensive blazer. He lives in Beverly Hills and looks after his sick mother. He used to be in the movie business. 'Hollywood,' he begins, is part of the conspiracy, 'a cancer on the haemorrhoid of the ass of the whore of America'. Bear in mind, he cautions, the wands used by Celtic wizards were made out of *holly wood*...

Hilder produces pictures of German-made flying saucers and documents about 'Operation Paperclip', whereby Nazi scientists, whose quest for global government under the Third Reich was thwarted, were spirited off to the US to work on the Panic Project and the New World

Video still taken during the attempted ATF storming of the Waco compound – Credit: Rex

ED VULLIAMY

Order. But whose order, what wizards? Hilder draws a deep breath. The global government conspiracy, he explains, is as old as history; one need look no further than the aspirations of ancient Rome. Its latter-day incarnation is propelled, he says, by the 'Illuminati', an opaque, occult elite, first convened in Bavaria in 1776, which now comes together as the freemasons. The Illuminati's objective was to create such bloodshed and discord that the human race's only hope of survival would be to turn to a single (Illuminati-run) government. The Illuminati came to America, says Hilder, through a 'Faustian financial fraternity', called the Skull and Crossbones Club, in 1832.

Look no further than the dollar bill. In 1934, the Egyptian pyramid, with all its masonic symbolism, was worked into the design and, atop it, the all-seeing eye of Lucifer. Underneath, the inscription *Novas Ordum Seclorum*, or New World Order. There are 13 layers in the dollar's pyramid, 13 stars above the Eagle's head, 13 berries, 13 arrows, stripes and leaves – all the number of Satan. Except for the feathers in the Eagle's wings, which number 32 and 33, the highest orders of masonry. And remember, the Statue of Liberty clasps a torch which, Hilder assures, 'is not the torch of freedom, it is the torch of the Illuminati.' As for the Pentagon, its apex pointing towards the North Star...need we say more?

But what have the Illuminati been up to since 1776, apart from re-designing currency? There is mention of London, the pivot of international capital and, of course, the Rothschilds. After much history – about the Russian Luciferian Helena Blavatsky, who inspired Hitler in his quest for a global government, and the 'Warlocks of Wall Street' – we arrive at the notion that 'National Socialism and Marxism are the same thing.' 'The Anglo-American banking establishment was and is master of both Communism and Fascism, says Hilder. 'The result is Commu-Fascism, or Cashism.' And he grins; and it's quite funny.

The agent of the global conspiracy today is the United Nations, and its servants in the US are the CIA and the presidency of Bill Clinton. The means of subjugation: crisis creation and gun control. The shock troops: the Federal Bureau of Alcohol, Tobacco and Firearms (ATF), as witnessed in the 'holocaust' at Waco. The resistance to this tyranny comes from 'the sovereign people', represented in the militias; the men and women who train in their spare time, who refuse to carry driving licences or pay tax – in the name of the US constitution and the right to bear arms.

HATE SPEECH: AMERICA'S ENEMY WITHIN

Tony Hilder wants me to meet two of his friends. The first involves a drive down to South Central LA, the ghetto, to meet an activist from Louis Farrakhan's Nation of Islam who calls Hilder 'Brother Tony'. Here is a twist to the old hatreds, to cross-burning and church-burning. The two men amicably agree on a well-developed hatred of the government and a dislike of Jews. The second introduction, more intriguing, is made by phone to a man called William Cooper. Hilder counsels to make sure of an appointment before going to Cooper's 'compound' in Arizona: 'he's got all kinds of stuff in there!'

'Don't you ever do this to me again Tony,' says the voice from St Johns, Arizona, on the conference line, 'I don't talk to fucking puke-faced journalists.' Most militiamen and New-World-Order-watchers will do anything for a bit of publicity. The Michigan militia, with which McVeigh was associated, was very happy to don its weekend fatigues and prance around for the cameras with semi-automatic bravado. There was something ominous about Cooper's steadfastness.

Cooper, who claims that two attempts have been made on his life, is revered by militiamen and is the Patriot movement's chief ideologist. He runs an outfit called 'Citizens' Agency for Joint Intelligence', refuses to carry a driving licence or pay taxes and broadcasts his own radio programme. During the McVeigh trial, a militiaman called James Nichols (whose brother Terry is currently on trial as McVeigh's accomplice) said that in the months before the destruction of the Oklahoma building, McVeigh had been a regular and avid listener to Cooper's nightly short-wave broadcast, 'The Hour of the Time'.

Sponsored by Swiss America Trading, which advocates the ownership of silver and gold as opposed to 'corrupt' US dollars, it is an extraordinary show. On 21 November 1994, a few months before the bombing, Cooper issued a call to arms: militias should be ready, he said, to 'fight a war' to restore the US constitution 'within six months'. In October 1995, after the bomb, he told listeners: 'you're gonna need some bullets, you're gonna need some guns.'

McVeigh had been reading a cult book called *The Turner Diaries*, a fictionalised account of the seizure of government by citizens' militias who blow up a federal building and, once in power, begin the subjugation of blacks and Jews. But Cooper's book, *Behold a Pale Horse*, is the one Hilder recommended. It is the Patriots' manifesto.

Cooper's theme is 'the declaration of war by the Illuminati upon the citizens of the United States of America.' The book is a labyrinthine journey through the global government conspiracy: AIDS was created by an occult club, the 'Bilderberg Group', to decrease the population. It is simplistic to label either the book or the movement 'racist': Cooper is appalled to have found out that the 'secret government's' population control programme involved the extermination of 'targeted populations... blacks, hispanics and homosexuals' and, later, 'the old and the infirm.'

Area 51 is epicentral; space aliens are being nurtured by the occult elite to subjugate the earthly masses. When John F Kennedy threatened to blow the lid on the project, says Cooper, he was assassinated; he has 'photographic evidence' to prove it. The New Order will be introduced after a carefully managed catastrophe, with a real-life agency, the Federal Emergency Management Agency, already preparing the round-up of resisters. 'Black helicopters' are buzzing those who are getting ready. 'You must accept,' says Cooper, 'that you have been cattle, and the ultimate consequence of being cattle – which is slavery – is that you must be prepared to fight and even die.' Then you reach something more detailed, spine-chilling and purposeful. Chapter Eight; 'Are the Sheep Ready to Shear?'

It draws attention to an Oklahoma state bill seeking to register rented property for taxation, alongside owner-occupied homes. Cooper calls the legislation 'the test case for the police state'. The legislation (which was dropped) would, he writes, 'make renters into property taxpayers and make life easy for the gun-grabbers'. He quotes a paper called the *Intelligence Advisor*, from as early as 1990: 'If they can pull this off, other states will follow. Big Brother wants to know all and tax all. The New World Order will eliminate all private property...It is time to stand up with a weapon and scream: ENOUGH! It is time to draw the line. It is time to make decisions and carry them out. It is time to resist at any and all cost. The penalty for not doing so is slavery...Pick up a weapon...STAND UP AND FIGHT!!'.

Target Oklahoma had been staring the authorities in the face since 1990. And not only in Cooper's book. Twelve years before the actual bombing, a group of neo-Nazis drew up plans to attack the Murrah building with rocket launchers. It so happened that one of them, Richard Wayne Snell, was executed in Arkansas for a different murder on 19 April 1995, the day that McVeigh's bomb blew up the condemned man's objective. Snell was the first white man ever to be executed in Arkansas for the murder of a black man. As he was strapped into the chair to receive the lethal injection, Snell told the Arkansas governor and President Clinton's successor: 'Look over your shoulder. Justice is coming'. Two hours later, the building imploded.

Details of the earlier plot were confessed to federal prosecutor, Steve Snyder, by one of Snell's accomplices, James Ellison. Ellison was founder of an embryonic Patriot group, The Covenant, The Sword and Arm of The Lord. Accused of racketeering, he turned state's evidence and testified against 14 Covenant co-members, (including Snell, who was already on death row), charged with conspiring to overthrow the government

Interviewed by the *Minneapolis Star Tribune*, Snyder recounted Ellison's testimony. At meetings at a famous neo-Nazi compound in Hayden's Lake, Idaho, it was decided to switch targets from blacks and Jews to federal buildings. Ellison said that Snell had taken him to the Murrah building and told him to go inside to 'gauge what it would take to damage or destroy it'. He had then made drawings of how rocket launchers might be 'placed in a trailer van so that it could be driven to a given spot, parked there and a timed detonating device triggered so that the driver could... clear the area before the rockets were launched.' It was a chilling prophecy of what was to happen on 19 April.

Before Snell's execution that day, the Militia of Montana took up his cause in its bulletin *Taking Aim*. It highlighted the pivotal place the date occupies in the Patriot calendar: the burning of Lexington in 1775 by the revolutionary militia, which the present incarnations claim as their ancestor; and the day in 1995 when the Branch Davidians were burned out of Waco. Ellison also had a debt of conscience to 19 April. Ten years earlier, 200 federal agents laid siege to his armed compound in Arkansas for four days before he was finally persuaded to surrender.

As an objective, the choice of Oklahoma City had a number of other explanations – beyond Cooper's 'test case for the police state'. And each has its own grammatical place in the Patriots' mythic language. The most common is that the National Prison Transfer Centre is based near the city's airport, a hub facility for the transfer of convicts around America. Militia literature is obsessed with the depot, anticipating its use as a 'concentration camp' for true Christians and the patriotic resistance to the imminent New World Order of the Illuminati.

ED VULLIAMY

For a good five years after the founding Patriots targeted the government in general, and Oklahoma in particular, the authorities patrolled the obvious ground. They monitored 'Cyberhate' spewed onto the Internet by the old guard – the Klan, the neo-Nazis and groups such as 'Stormfront' or 'White Aryan Resistance'. There is an acute problem of racial pornography on the Internet; there is a spate of church-burnings across the South; there has been revival of racist murders in Colorado. But these the are old devils.

Last winter, the ADL produced a booklet which confirmed that the ground had changed. The softer language of the Patriots is now far more dangerous than the crude banalities of the struggling KKK, not least because of 'the porousness of the line separating the mainstream from the fringe.' Vehement anti-government rhetoric is now *de rigueur* across western and other states. The ADL cites such incidentals as talk-radio personality Gordon Liddy's instructions on how best to kill an ATF agent: in the groin or head, where he is unprotected. Or the National Rifle Association's likening of the ATF bureau to the Nazi Gestapo. 'When pernicious hate seeps into the mainstream dressed as political rhetoric,' said the report, 'it threatens to legitimise intolerance and exclusion as an acceptable means for social change.'

In a brilliant move, some Patriot militias have put up black Americans to be their public spokesmen. 'Militia thinking has worked its way into general thought and culture,' says Chip Berlet, a specialist in the far right at Boston's Political Research Associates, 'especially as we approach the millennium... It's part of what is called 'millennial expectation' – concern with a New World Order and a search for scapegoats which fits in with old claims that the anti-Christ will arise in the end times.'

Last September, a conference assembled at the Simon Wiesenthal Centre in Los Angeles to consider 'The Changing Face of Hate and Terrorism'. One of the black Patriot leaders, JJ Johnson, was invited and joked: 'If you fear the militias, take steps to defend yourself! The neo-Nazis do not support arms for everyone. In the militia, we do!' Less flippant was Mark Potok, civil rights director of the Southern Poverty Law Centre, which has campaigned on the front line against the old language of hate and is now becoming literate in the new one. 'The old Nazi skinhead groups have become small and ineffectual,' he said. 'But the Patriot groups are gaining ground. They believe what they say, they are opposing what they believe is illegal government meddling in individual rights.'

Pokok has identified 858 Patriot militias in America, as against 'about 100' of the old, overtly racist groups. While an estimated 60,000 people are actual members, polls show an angry stew of five million constitutionalists, tax protesters, 'isolationists', gun-owners and regular folk who have 'sympathies' with their views. 'In a little more than two years,' the ADL claims, 'militias have come to outnumber the membership of the KKK, the neo-Nazis skinheads and other hate groups. The growth of the militia movement does not mean, however, that traditional hate groups are no longer active. It signifies the reconfiguration of traditional hate group activities, in response to trends deep in the broader culture'.

Even in Oklahoma City, Ross Hullet – owner of the Perfect Fit denture company and commander of the Oklahoma State Militia – insists that the bomb was the work of the FBI, just another 'created crisis' by agents of the New World Order. A leader of the national militia movement, Linda Thompson, came from Indiana to address a meeting in which she lambasted the government for its role in the slaughter. Hullet's wife Hazel was particularly conversant with the role of the occult. 'It is from London that the Anti-Christ is coming....'

Seven days after the Oklahoma bomb, relatives, friends and neighbours gathered at the First Baptist Church for the funeral of Dana Cooper, 24, and her two-year-old son Anthony. Dana had worked at the nursery; her son was one of the regulars. We knew the faces in the congregation by this stage from the vigil of hopefuls waiting around the spectral building, which stank of death.

The coffins, one tiny, were carried in by sturdy men from America's prairie heartland, all in tears. The service was interrupted by the crying of a baby at the back, unhappy in the crush of mourners. Reverend Mark Estep, commending the souls of the deceased to paradise, broke his prayer for a long moment.

Then he spoke. 'Could I say to the dear lady over there, let him cry. It sounds like music today.' ❑

Ed Vulliamy *is the Washington correspondent for the* Guardian *and the* Observer.

JULIAN PETLEY

Another year over

And deeper in trouble. Censorship is out; financial pressures, over-cautious and bureaucratic managements, hostile newspapers and the spectre of costly and unpleasant legal action constitute the pressures which throughout 1997 threatened to neuter British TV

JANUARY

Channel 4 shows Peter Greenaway's film *The Baby of Macon*. This features, albeit in a highly stylised fashion, a multiple rape of a young woman and the mutilation of a baby. The film had been passed uncut with an '18' certificate for both cinema and video viewing by the British Board of Film Classification. However, the police are called in to decide whether the film breaks the Obscene Publications Act. According to a Scotland Yard spokesman: 'The Clubs and Vice Unit was called in after a number of calls to police stations from the public expressing concern. We will view the film to decide if there needs to be any further action.' Not altogether surprisingly, none is forthcoming.

FEBRUARY

Having been pulled from the previous November's schedules after C4 suffered a bad attack of cold feet, Chris Morris's new series of *Brass Eye* is set for transmission. However, more troubles are to come. One of the episodes, entitled 'Moral Decline', a savage spoof on TV *vérité* and the media's obsession with the 'entertainment' potential of mass killers, contains a musical sketch about Yorkshire Ripper Peter Sutcliffe. C4 and the programme makers, realising this was a potentially explosive sketch, prepares a substantial defence. But when the inevitable press hysteria starts (led once again by the *Daily Mail*), the channel's resolve falters.

C4 receives calls from families of Sutcliffe's victims who, since they cannot possibly have seen the sketch, must have been prodded into action by the newspapers' antics. At this point, apparently, Grade himself steps in and demands the withdrawal of the sketch. The words 'Grade is a cunt' are broadcast subliminally during the episode.

The Independent Television Commission (ITC) *Programme Complaints and Interventions Report* for April concludes that an episode in the series (in fact the one which caused it to be postponed in the first place), in which a number of MPs are hoaxed into condemning a new and dangerous drug called 'cake' which is allegedly flooding into the country from the Czech Republic, breached the ITC Programme Code in that the MPs were not made 'adequately aware of the format, subject matter and purpose of the programme'.

A further episode, about television treatment of sexual behaviour, breached the code's requirements on taste and decency in that, notwithstanding the pre-transmission warning, the content was unsuitable for broadcasting even at 9.30pm. The subliminal message in the 'Moral Decline' episode obviously ran counter to the section of the code relating to images of very brief duration.

However, the ITC also 'found the series in general amusing and innovative' and had no criticism of the overall programme concept. It acknowledged that risks were attached to making innovative programmes and felt that C4 'should not be discouraged for that reason from seeking to make such programmes'.

It's hard not to be struck by the irony of the situation: a series which savagely points out how easy it is for journalists to get the usual media tarts to sound off moralistically and authoritatively on subjects about which they know absolutely nothing is delayed and sabotaged by the self-same charade.

MARCH

Yorkshire-Tyne Tees Television vetoes the production, halfway through filming, of a documentary about child abuse commissioned by C4. The programme is a re-examination of the 1987 Cleveland child-abuse scandal, the first strand of a three-part series, *The Death of Childhood*, overseen by Diverse Productions. The producer, Tim Tate, is immediately recommissioned by an astonished C4 to make the programme through his own independent company. The programme argues that after a press witch-hunt, led by the *Daily Mail*, against Dr

JULIAN PETLEY

Marietta Higgs and others who, it claimed, misdiagnosed widespread child abuse in Cleveland, many children were sent back to live with parents who, later evidence was to reveal, were indeed child abusers. YTT's decision followed a letter from Cleveland MP Stuart Bell to its managing director, Bruce Gyngell, claiming that there was 'some disquiet in the region about the programme'. He notes that 'since Tyne Tees Television exposed the crisis in the first place ... it might put the station into a somewhat embarrassing situation if there was a programme produced by Yorkshire setting it at odds with one of its own stations'. He also expresses concern that the programme would 'seek to overturn the verdicts of the High Court, the Butler-Sloss report and try to prove that Dr Higgs and her supporters were right and everybody else was wrong'. Bell omits to mention that the selfsame Butler-Sloss report had roundly criticised him for his 'intemperate and inflammatory remarks', which, it said, had worsened an already difficult situation.

JUNE

Jonathan Aitken begins his libel case against the *Guardian* and the Granada *World in Action* programme 'Jonathan of Arabia', broadcast in April 1995. The previous month he had applied successfully for the case to be heard without a jury, a decision upheld by the Court of Appeal. This was the first libel case brought by a prominent politician over his conduct while in office to be heard in such circumstances. It was thought by the judge hearing the case, Mr Justice Popplewell, that the sheer number of documents involved in the trial would have overwhelmed a jury. Writing after dramatic new evidence brought about the spectacular collapse of Aitken's case, revealing him to be both a liar and a perjurer, the *Guardian's* David Pallister states:

'I would have given a souk of Saudi gold for a jury in the Aitken case: especially as it became more and more apparent that Sir Oliver [Popplewell] listened almost without challenge to the egregious deceptions spun by the Rt Hon Jonathan Aitken. Having denied us a jury, Popplewell then went on to rule against us over what our words really meant — a controversial judgement with which a jury would have not necessarily agreed. So certain was he of the judicial capacity to stand aloof from influence or bias, he also remained on the bench when he knew that his former Conservative politician wife might be called as a defence witness'.

OVERVIEW: THE YEAR IN BRITISH TV

After the trial ends, Ian McBride, Granada's managing editor, notes laconically that 'Jonathan Aitken's chosen weapon was a dagger of deceit, not the sword of truth'.

The way has been opened for more libel plaintiffs to win rulings dispensing with juries in future; and Popplewell's attitude to the *Guardian* and Granada bodes ill for a future in which, once the European Convention on Human Rights is incorporated into UK law, judges will play a significant role in matters pertaining to media freedom.

NOVEMBER

In a speech to the Drama Forum, Tony Garnett, Britain's leading drama producer, with a track record stretching from *Cathy Come Home* to *This Life*, forcefully argues that:

'These are oppressive times. We have a government seething with sanctimony. Moves to extend the threshold to 10pm. Moves to stop characters smoking, doing or saying many of the things we all say or do in life. They won't rest until television drama is sanitised in a Barbie Doll world where real human life is unrecognisable. Think 1950s. Think Rock Hudson or Doris Day ...We now, with very few exceptions, have an industry run by managers with the mentality of eighteeenth and nineteenth century mill owners. Where workers are costs, not assets, where slashing overheads is more important than nurturing talent, where fear and loathing are poisoning creativity.'

Garnett's polemic effectively draws together many of the threads running through the year. The programmes cited may have run into difficulties, but at least they got made. Television censorship today is less a matter of outright cuts and bans than of forces which militate against the very making of 'difficult' programmes in the first place. Financial pressures, over-cautious and bureaucratic managements with their eyes fixed firmly on the bottom line, hostile newspapers, a duplication of regulators (the ITC, the BBC Programmes Complaints Unit, the Broadcasting Standards Commission) and, of course, the spectre of costly and unpleasant legal action: together these constitute the pressures which threaten to neuter British television. ❑

Julian Petley *is a lecturer in media and communication studies at Brunel University.*

INDEX INDEX

Paper Tigers

Over the past 15 years, to steal the format of a regular parody of reality adjustment that appears in the UKs satirical magazine *Private Eye*, we may have inadvertently given the impression that the so-called 'Tiger economies' of Asia, with their collective ethos of command capital, rigorous corporate discipline and a no-nonsense approach to libertarian values, somehow provided a role model of capitalist self-reliance that we could all learn from in the twilight years of the century.

Some of our readers may have mistakenly inferred from our articles that, by dint of back-breaking labour and a popular rejection of the real wages, human and civil rights that might otherwise have delayed it, the peoples of South Korea, Indonesia, Malaysia and the Philippines had vindicated the capitalist myth by transforming their countries from malarial rice-paddies into paragons of prosperity, industry and democracy with some of the most sun-kissed real estate this side of Cyberspace.

While a few in the West may have carped at the export of their former means of livelihood to the low-waged in Subic Bay, none could decry the benefits of the globalised economy, when expressed in the Nike trainers, Daewoo cars, Thai mangetout and 10-year bonds, now so central to our lives. Indeed, a recent recreational feature may, unfortunately, have gone some small way toward reinforcing the illusion that the editorial staff were taking a rather 'rose-tinted' view of the long-term prospects for the region. 'Like Taking Sweets From A Baby', our more cogent readers may recall, illustrated some of the cheap and fun things to do with Asian children.

We would like to take this opportunity to reassure our circulation – many of whom may have sunk their savings into the Hong Kong and Shanghai Bank – that such economising with the actualité was never part of our conscious intention. Indeed, our astute business staff have been only too well aware that, for all their apparent robustness, the won, ringgit and baat were nothing more than mildewed pillars held up by high-risk speculation and the kind of 'croney capitalism' so widespread among the tropic races.

Even the Japanese colossus, it appears, has been humbled by the Asian currency crisis. Not so the banks of the US and Europe, whose exposure to the high yields to be had from property and investments during the Tigers short-lived bull run had been tempered by the more mature judgement, greater transparency and sounder accounting practices of the Old World. We have a lot to be thankful for and are profoundly disappointed with those of our readers who doubted for an instant that we saw it all coming all along.

An innumerate Dayak in September could have guessed at big events in the offing from the smoke of his burning forest. Add in the irony of the Kyoto Conference on global warming in December and, with hindsight, the metaphorical stage was set for a different kind of meltdown. Leaving aside the symbolism, a smokescreen of a different order was spewing from the broadsheets even as the monsoon finally arrived. The evasions took two specific forms.

The first was over accountability. The chief executive of a Japanese bank made a bloodcurdling public apology; but from the International Monetary Fund, which has spent over a decade hectoring the governments of Africa on the need to follow the Asian model, nary a peep of humility; a $57 billion bail-out for South Korea, but not a word on how such an inordinate sum of money to its once-favourite pupil was likely to affect the future flow of funds to the 'adjustment' programmes it has foisted on the people of Africa in the 1980s.

More conspicuous by its absence from the debate was any mention of China, newly-linked to the global economy through the absorption of Hong Kong. China is now the new Japan, South Korea, Indonesia, Malaysia and Philippines rolled into one. The smart money may well have escaped the conflagration just in time, but it is just as likely to be lurking in equally flammable Shanghai and Guangdong property.

There will be white faces on Wall Street if China is talked down. ❑

Michael Griffin

INDEX INDEX

A censorship chronicle incorporating information from the American Association for the Advancement of Science Human Rights Action Network (AAASHRAN), Amnesty International (AI), the BBC Monitoring Service Summary of World Broadcasts (SWB), the Committee to Protect Journalists (CPJ), the Canadian Committee to Protect Journalists (CCPJ), Human Rights Watch (HRW), the Institute for Press and Society (IPYS), the International Federation of Newspaper Publishers (FIEJ), the Inter-American Press Association (IAPA), the International Federation of Journalists (IFJ/FIP), Nigeria's 'IFEX's partner in the region' ('IPR'), Institute for the Studies on the Free Flow of Information (ISAI), the UN's Department of Humanitarian Affairs (IRIN), the Media Institute of Southern Africa (MISA), Network for the Defence of the Independent Media in Africa (NDIMA), International PEN (PEN), Open Media Research Institute (OMRI), Radio Free Europe/Radio Liberty (RFE/RL), Reporters Sans Frontières (RSF), the World Association of Community Broadcasters (AMARC), the World Organisation Against Torture (OMCT) and other sources

ALBANIA

On 11 November, claiming they were threatened with bankruptcy, the publishers of nine daily and two weekly newspapers began a shut-down of news publishing until the government lowered taxes imposed on the press. The daily *Koha Jone* resumed publication on 20 November after Finance Minister Arben Malaj pledged newspaper publishers would be exempt from profit tax for at least two years to enable them to invest in new equipment. (RFE/RL)

ALGERIA

The government unsuccessfully attempted to revoke the UN consultative status of Amnesty International and the International Human Rights Federation in October in retaliation for their efforts to initiate an investigation into who is responsible for the continuing massacres. (*Middle East International*)
Omar Belhouchet, director of the French-language daily *el Watan,* was sentenced to a year's imprisonment on 5 November for 'harming state institutions'. Belhouchet's sentence, suspended pending appeal, relates to interviews he gave in November 1995 to the French television stations TF1 and Canal Plus in which he suggested that the state might have been involved in the assassination of civilians. Following the verdict, Belhouchet was questioned by police for 10 hours over two days about an opinion column by **Yasser Ben Miloud** in *el Watan* on 29 October. The column castigated the government and President Liamine Zeroual for shutting down state-owned printing presses for three days in the week leading up to municipal elections on 23 October. Ben Miloud disappeared on 5 November until late 7 November, when he refused to tell colleagues whether he had been detained or in hiding. Ben Miloud, Belhouchet and two other editors spent 8 November under police interrogation. (CPJ, IFJ, RSF)

Recent publication: *Civilian Population Caught in a Spiral of Violence* (AI, November 1997, 37pp)

ARGENTINA

President Clinton implicitly admitted during his visit in late October that the FBI and CIA did not share intelligence on the 1992 and 1994 Buenos Aires bomb attacks on Jewish centres with local security counterparts because of mistrust. Clinton alluded to alleged anti-Semitic groups serving within the security forces. Congressional investigations had revealed that the family of a former police commander was given US$2.5 million one week before the 1994 bombing. (*El País*)
Judges ordered the return of equipment confiscated from the community radio stations FM Del Sol 98.1, FM Illusiones 98.5 and four other stations after they found there was no case against them. The radio stations resumed broadcasting on 14 October. (AMARC)
Economy minister Roque Fernandez accused the media of attempting a 'coup" by scar-

ing electors out of voting for the ruling party in the elections on 26 October. He apologised the following day for this 'unfortunate expression' and said that he had 'unrestricted respect for the freedom of the press' and was just giving his 'point of view' about the lack of objectivity of some media organisations. (SWB)

AUSTRALIA

Commenting on the decision by editors to support a tougher code of practice in the wake of Princess Diana's death, Rupert Murdoch, chairman of News Corporation, urged the world's media on 7 October to resist the move towards tougher privacy laws. He added that his only regret in using *paparazzi* photographs was that he had paid too much for them and he denounced privacy laws as a further privilege for the already privileged. (*Financial Times*)

AZERBAIJAN

On 15 November, Sahavat Kerimov, chairman of a Russian firm, injured **Elman Teymuroglu**, correspondent for the newspaper *Haggin Sadasi*, by driving a steel fountain pen into one of his eyes. Irritated by an article in which he was accused of fraud, Kerimov had been berating Teymuroglu and his colleague Tarana Farjeva in the office of Alesqer Gashimov, the head of the regional govenment of Zangelan in the south of the country. According to the editor of *Haggin Sadasi*, Mirvari Ragimzade, Kerimonov continued to threaten the journalists after the attack, warning that if Teymuoglu lodged a complaint against him, he would put out his other eye. (RSF)

BANGLADESH

The veteran columnist and journalist **Nirmal Sen** launched a fast-to-the-death in Dhaka on 23 November in order to press demands for the payment of wages due to journalists and employees of Times-Bangla Trust publications, the dailies *Dainik Bangla* and *Bangladesh Times* and the weeklies *Bichitr* and *Anando Bichitra*. All four publications were closed down in October in preparation for their privatisation. On 28 November, Sen broke his fast after President Shahabuddin Ahmed said he would advise the appropriate authority to extend the deadline set by the government for the voluntary retirement of journalists and workers. (Law and Mediation Centre)

BELARUS

Parliament passed a new law on 15 October tightening state control over the media. Deputy Prime Minister Uladzimir Zamyatalin, cabinet supervisor for humanitarian issues, told the lower house that 'freedom of speech and the independence of the media are terms for laboratory studies. All the media are dependent and everything is paid for.' The Belarusian Association of Journalists and the Russian Foundation for the Defence of Glasnost both expressed 'profound alarm' at these 'new attempts to impose more limitations on freedom of speech.' A supplement to the law that requires the official registration of all periodicals, even those with a circulation of less than 500 copies, imposes an 'all-pervading control' of printed matter, commented a joint statement. (SWB)

On 10 November some 100 political, cultural and academic figures signed a new manifesto, Charter 97, to promote democracy. Modelled on the Czechoslovak Charter 77, the new group intends to unite opposition to President Lukashenka and press for the establishment of democracy. (RFE/RL)

The arrest on 11 November of Agriculture Minister Vasiliy Leonov and senior agricultural manager Vasiliy Starovoitov for corruption and embezzlement appears to be linked to the murder of **Yevhenii Mikolutsky** (*Index* 6/97). President Lukashenka said that, prior to his assassination, Mikolutsky had intended to inform him of corruption within the Rassvet agricultural complex. Leonov holds pro-market views and has criticised Lukashenka's policies in the past. (RFE/RL)

On 12 November the prosecutor-general notified editors of an independent weekly that its satirical portraits of the president and other government leaders 'besmirch the honour and dignity' of those officials and thus violate the new press law. **Pavel Zhuk**, publisher of the thrice-weekly Minsk

BELARUS

Charter 97

We, citizens of the Republic of Belarus, declare that the actions of the current leadership are aimed at the destruction of inalienable human rights and freedoms. In our country, the fundamental law, the Constitution, has been torn in shreds. The Belarusian people are denied the right of electing their representatives to governing structures. There is a systematic assault on the freedom of speech and the rights of citizens to play a real role in the country. Our national culture and education are being destroyed; there is discrimination against the Belarusian language. The daily price rises and beggarly wages have brought hundreds of thousands of families to the edge of starvation. On the eve of the twenty-first century there is a dictatorship at the centre of Europe. Ten million people are in the grip of violence.

We believe that our motherland deserves freedom and prosperity. We believe that we can achieve this by our common efforts. We are inspired by the example of the free nations who have preceded us on this path. We recall how a group of heroic Czech and Slovak defenders of right and justice signed Charter 77, in which they called for a struggle against totalitarianism in their country and how, after a few year, not a trace remained in eastern Europe of the red dictatorship. The people in those countries gained the chance of freely building their lives and attaining a decent existence...

Everyone who sets out on the path of striving for his rights and human dignity may be assured of our united support. We are hoping for the support of the international community and the solidarity of all forces who understand the danger of the appearance of a new brown-shirt empire in the post-Soviet space. Every splinter of totalitarianism must be removed from the body of Europe... ❑

Signed by 145 leading writers, journalists, scholars and politicians, including three former speakers of parliament (Stanislau Shushkievich. Miechyslau Hryb, Siamion Sharatski), leading personalities of the Belarusian PEN-Centre (Vasyl Bykau, Nil Hilevich. Carlos Sherman), the poet Slavamir Adamavich and TV journalist Pavel Sheremet (both recently imprisoned), trade-union activists, lawyers, Chernobyl relief workers and the entire staff of the newspaper Svaboda.

opposition newspaper *Svaboda*, announced the president had issued a warrant to close down the paper on 20 November. He received fresh warnings from the State Press Commission that the paper could face criminal prosecution for publishing a series of articles which compared the government to that of Joseph Stalin. (RFE/RL)

On 23 November the opposition held demonstrations to mark the first anniversary of the referendum which gave President Lukashenka sweeping powers. ORT journalist **Pavel Sheremet** (*Index* 5/97, *Index* 6/97), who is due to go on trial shortly for 'violating the state border', addressed the main rally, saying: 'We must defend our country, we must defend the press. The authorities are trying to destroy *Svaboda* and are instigating proceedings against the deputy editor of *Imya*, **Iryna Khalip**. If we remain silent, there may be no one left there tomorrow!' (SWB)

BENIN

The High Audiovisual and Communications Authority (HAAC) finally allocated a series of radio frequencies to private operators in November. Chairman Rene Dossa explained that the HAAC had to be cautious in the light of the 'unfortunate experiences' of countries like Rwanda and its Hutu extremist radio station *Radio Mille Collines*. (*West Africa*)

BOLIVIA

Two articles of a bill aimed at reforming the Code of Criminal Procedure pose a threat to press freedom. Article 264 obliges journalists to reveal their sources of information to a judge, while article 427 gives judges the power to prevent the media from covering certain trials. (RSF)

BOSNIA-HERCEGOVINA

Amid a continuing 'battle' over control of the media (*Index* 6/97) and two weeks after NATO troops seized its transmitters, Pale TV resumed broadcasts on 16 October. Officials refused to reveal how they managed to get back on air but observers suggested the Serbs had used a number of small transmitters over a large area, in what they referred to as 'guerrilla action'. NATO aircraft again began jamming Pale's signals on 21 October. The following day, the editorial board invited International High Representative Carlos Westendorp to mediate in the dispute. On 15 November NATO troops fired warning shots to drive away a crowd of Bosnian-Serbs trying to remove barbed wire from the NATO-controlled television transmitter on Mount Trebevic which overlooks Sarajevo. (B92, RFE/RL)

On 29 October Liljana Zelen-Karadzic, wife of Radovan, claimed she was being stalked by SFOR troops as she went about her daily activities. Mrs Karadzic said their actions were an invasion of her privacy. (RFE/RL)

On 11 November Bosnian Federation Education Minister Fahrudin Rizvanbegovic announced that Croatian and Muslim pupils and students will soon study from the same textbooks: they will stress that Bosnia is a single, multi-ethnic state (*Index* 6/97). (RFE/RL)

On 13 November the federal government announced it was launching a probe into the possible embezzlement of some US$30 million in taxes, customs fees and aid money. Carlos Westendorp, the international community's chief representative, said he would make public a list of allegedly corrupt officials' names if the Sarajevo authorities failed to act before 14 November. One week later the *Los Angeles Times* accused the Muslim authorities of diverting millions of dollars to illegal agencies, including an Iranian-trained spy network. Officials denied the charge which European officials have also made. (RFE/RL)

On 15 November SFOR troops disconnected the transmitters of a radio network run by Sonja Karadzic, daughter of Radovan Karadzic(B92)

On 19 November the Ministry of Transport and Communication in Zenica-Doboj county asked Josip Boyavnik, chairman of the local branch of the ruling Croatian Democratic Union (HDZ) in Zenica to remove the antenna booster through which Croatian TV is rebroadcast. In an emergency session, the HDZ municipal

INDEX INDEX

committee argued that the county minister had no grounds for such a decision which places all non-Muslim citizens in an 'information blackout'. On 21 November, the power to the transmitter was cut off. (SWB)

BRAZIL

A bill being debated in the House of Representatives provides no upper limit for financial awards against publishing companies. It also allows awards for penalties of up to about US$ 900,000 against journalists in cases of defamation. (World Association of Newspapers)

On 29 October, journalist **Edgar Lopes de Faria** was murdered in Campo Grande by several men who shot him repeatedly with a rifle. Lopes de Faria's radio and television programmes investigated corruption by local officials. (CPJ)

BULGARIA

On 5 November Georgi Kolev, a deputy from the ruling Union of Democratic Forces, resigned his parliamentary seat two weeks after it was revealed he had been a collaborator of the Communist secret police. He is the second official to resign since the list was made public. On 18 November, 11 citizens became the first persons to read their Communist-era secret police files. A total of 15,000 people have so far enquired about files held on them. The two Bulgarian Orthodox Synods asked on 6 November that the secret police files on the clergy also be opened to the public. A spokesman said this would 'make informers such as [rival patriarch] Maxim and his gang of cops step down and be replaced by real Christians, and not slaves of the socialists.' (RFE/RL)

On 18 November police issued a warrant for the arrest of **Carolina Kraeva**, director and journalist with the newspaper *Istina* (Truth), following a court ruling accusing her of 'abusing and libelling' Georgy Assenov, a local police chief.' The journalist has been forced into hiding. (RSF)

BURKINA FASO

A law was passed in November by the Higher Information Council banning private radio stations from broadcasting foreign programmes. The stations affected include FM Radio and its link with Voice of America; Radio Maria, which is linked to Radio Vatican; NGO Radio and Radio Prichard, both of which transmit programmes by the BBC. (*West Africa*)

CAMEROON

Journalists and reporters were repeatedly harassed and arrested during the presidential elections. *Mutations* journalist **Jean Aime Mballa** was temporarily detained on 11 October while covering an election meeting. On 12 October **Marie Noelle Nguichi** of the bi-weekly *Le Messager* was arrested and detained at a voting booth and later threatened with imprisonment for being a 'spy' for the paper. *Expression* journalist **Alain Bengono** was assaulted in front of another polling booth on the same day. National radio and television station (CRTV) journalists **Barbara Etoa, Philippe Mbawe** and **Hubert Fotso Sobgwi** were forced to read a false communiqué over the air on 11 and 12 October. The document stated that opposition leaders had called on supporters to go out and vote when in fact the opposition had called for a boycott of the elections. (RSF)

On 20 October security forces seized copies of the magazine *Mutations* from news kiosks. This followed the publication of an article in that day's issue alleging that Captain Guerandi Mbara, one of the instigators of a failed 1984 coup, wanted to seize power again. (RSF)

CAMBODIA

Thong Uypang, the publisher of *Koh Santapheap* (Island of Peace), escaped unhurt from a grenade attack on his house on 15 October. While no motive has been established, the newspaper had recently published articles critical of Chea Sim, president of the Cambodian People's Party. Two days before the attack, a reporter for *Samleng Reas Khmer* (Voice of the Khmer People), **Ou Sarouen**, was shot dead by a security guard at a Phnom Penh market. Sarouen had been investigating the illegal payments that guards demand from vendors. (*Phnom Penh Post*)

Antarakum (Intervention), a

Khmer-language newspaper, was suspended in late October after printing a picture of the head of Nhek Bun Chhay, a dissident FUNCINPEC general, superimposed on Prime Minister Hun Sen's body. Publication resumed after the editor apologised. Another newspaper, *Prayuth* (Fight), had not resumed publication after being suspended on 11 November for 30 days for allegedly exaggerating government casualties in recent fighting in the north. Khieu Kanharith, the Secretary of State for Information said the paper was free to resume publication but *Prayuth* staff claim that a government lawsuit was preventing them.(Reuters)

Cambodia has 'one of the freest presses in the region,' claimed Prime Ministers Hun Sen and Ung Huot in response to a UN report on human rights issued on 10 November. Since the coup on 5 July, more opposition newspapers have been published, they wrote in a letter to Thomas Hammarberg, the UN's special representative. The report details 41 extra-judicial killings in the wake of the July coup that ousted First Prime Minister Prince Ranariddh.(SWB)

CANADA

In a landmark case that began in mid-October, Holocaust denier **Ernst Zundel** (*Index* 6/ 1988) is being tried before the Canadian Human Rights Commission for allegedly creating and maintaining a San Diego Internet web-site containing hate literature. Zundel, a renowned revisionist from Toronto, denies he controls the site, but his ex-wife Irene testified that he either writes or approves all the material that goes on it. The case, which has adjourned until December, is the first to apply Canadian human rights legislation to the Internet. (Reuters)

An 86-page decision, issued on 11 November by the Canadian Broadcasting Standards Council (CBSC), left little room to manoeuvre for CHOM and CILQ, the Montreal and Toronto radio stations that carry the **Howard Stern** show broadcast from New York City: either Stern stops violating broadcast standards or the stations take his show off the air. In a swipe at US free speech laws, the CBSC stated in its decision that 'the existence of other standards within other parts of the global village cannot weaken the need to apply home-grown standards .... The bar should not be lowered ... [here] just because it is set at a lower level elsewhere.' (*Montreal Gazette*)

Recent Publication: *Somalia Cover-up: A Comissioner's Journal* by Peter Debarats (McClelland & Stewart, November 1997)

CHECHNYA

It was announced on 10 November that female students and women working in the state sector must conform with the Islamic dress code. Managers who fail to enforce this requirement will face dismissal. (RFE/RL)

Recent publication: *Chechnya, A Small Victorious War*, Carlotta Gall & Thomas De Waal (Pan, Oct 1997, 416pp).

CHILE

The Supreme Court on 11 November refused to hand over to German public prosecutors any information on the secretive German enclave *Colonia Dignidad*, whose founder, former Nazi corporal Paul Schaefer, faces child rape charges. (Reuters)

CHINA

The Foreign Ministry has claimed that remarks made in mid-November by President Jiang Zemin at Harvard University on 'mistakes' and 'shortcomings' in the Tiananmen crackdown were misinterpreted by foreign media and were in no way a 'rewriting' of the official verdict. (Reuters)

Environmentalist **Dai Qing** has accused the government of silencing public debate on the construction of the Three Gorges Dam. Her book *Yangtse! Yangtse!*, a 1989 compilation of essays and interviews criticising the dam, has been banned. (*Independent*)

Pro-democracy writer and dissident **Wei Jingsheng** was unexpectedly released from prison on November 16 where he was serving a 14-year sentence for 'counter-revolution'.

WEI JINGSHENG

Dear Warden Xing...

Dear Prison Warden Xing,

...I haven't been sleeping well for some time now. There are several reasons for this, but the main things preventing me from getting a sound night's sleep is the light that shines in my eyes all night long. My principle is: If Can make do, then I won't bother the people who work here. I know that work of any kind is not easy, and all jobs have their difficulties. That's why I went ahead and fashioned the aluminium foil from a few packs of cigarettes into a shade in order to block some of the bright light that is reflecting off the ceiling and into my eyes.

Who would have known that not only was this prohibited, but when I tried to explain that it wasn't interfering with the brigade leader's work, I was told that, as I didn't 'listen to reason', there was no need for them to be reasonable; they even joked about my age. This left me at a complete loss. I feel that, even in prisons, all actions should be explained. Saying there is 'no need to explain' to those who don't understand your reasons, and explaining things only to those who do, is a bit unreasonable in itself, wouldn't you say?

Dear Members of the Central Committee Secretariat and the Legal Affairs Committee of the National People's Congress,

...I've heard the explanation: a person's incorrect thinking is closely related to the books and magazines he's read and, if you want to reform, your reading materials must be selectively restricted; we can't allow you to read whatever you like. While this hypothesis is somewhat similar to Marx's famous theory that 'man's social being determines his consciousness,' it also bears a close resemblance to that famous view of Goebbels that 'lies repeated a thousand times become truth.' Or, perhaps, this theory is somewhere between the two and might be considered an amalgamation of both. If people's thinking could really be controlled the way you force-feed a duck or teach a myna bird to talk, then there would be few problems in the world and our newspapers wouldn't have to waste so much ink and paper over discussions on the topic of 'how best to undertake political thought work.'...People's thinking always follows the basic rules of human understanding and they will believe what they come up with on their own. The way peasants fatten up ducks by forcing food down their throats can't be applied to humans for it spoils the appetite. Perhaps we should consider this one of the great human weaknesses.

Dear Deng Xiaoping

You might not be able to remember a person you wronged, but it isn't easy for me to forget the one who wronged me. Our situations are very different – you are at the top of a billion people and I am at the very bottom – but life isn't very easy for either of us. It's just that I am not the one making your life difficult, while you're the one making it hard for me. Therefore, when things start looking up for you, you might on occasion remember a person you once wronged. But if my days get better, then perhaps I won't have time to remember all of the people who once wronged me. For the number of people you have wronged and who have wronged me are many.

Even if this letter does manage to make it into your hands, it will most likely have passed through many inspections along the way. All these readers probably have to cover their mouths and stifle their laughter: What a madman! An emperor and a prisoner – how can the two even speak to one another! ❑

Wei Jingsheng, a former electrician at Beijing Zoo, spent all but six months of the last 18 years in prison for his involvement in the Democracy Wall Movement in the late 1970s. Released in November afterg President Jiang Zemin's visit to the US, where Wei now lives, his letters from prison, The Courage to Stand Alone, *were published by Viking in May 1997.*

He was flown to the US for medical treatment. It was Wei Jingsheng's second sentence since 1979; he has spent all but six months of the last 18 years in prison. His first sentence of 15 years was for participation in the Democracy Wall Movement, during which he was co-editor of the pro-democracy journal *Explorations*. (CPJ, Human Rights Watch)

COLOMBIA

Journalist **Francisco Castro Menco**, president of the radio station Fundación Cultural, was shot dead on 8 November. His relatives suspect that he was murdered because he used his radio show to call for peace. (CPJ)

On 20 November journalist **Jairo Elias Marquez Gallego** was shot dead by two gunmen on a motorcycle. Marquez was the editor of the magazine *El Marques*, which is known for its critical reporting on corruption. In the last two years, Marquez had received numerous death threats. (CPJ)

CROATIA

The trial of **Viktor Ivancic**, editor-in-chief of the satirical weekly *Feral Tribune*, and staff reporter **Marinko Culic** was set to resume on 22 December. Both are accused of having 'defamed and insulted' President Franjo Tudjman. They were originally acquitted in September 1996, but the verdict was annulled by the Supreme Court on 5 May (*Index*, 4/96,6/96,4/97). The charges are being applied under an article of the Penal Code that re-establishes 'crimes of the press' and allows for penalties of up to three years' imprisonment. (RSF)

Independent Zagreb-based Radio 101 was granted a five-year licence on 4 November, after a number of delays which the station believe amounted to political harassment. Officials said the licence had been held up by disputes over claims to the ownership of the station. (RFE/RL)

Slobodan Prosperov Novak, president of the PEN Club and a professor at Zagreb University, has lost his teaching job it was announced on 10 November. Novak claimed he was sacked because of his outspoken criticism of President Tudjman. (RFE/RL)

Parents of ethnic Serb students in eastern Slavonia began an education boycott on 10 November, in protest at their children being refused the right to use textbooks written in Cyrillic. After discussions with officials, a deal was agreed in which Cyrillic lettering and the Latin alphabet would be used on official documents, signs and rubber stamps in all schools of the region. Serbian students will also not be required to study Croatian history from 1990 onwards. (B92)

Radio Vukovar resumed broadcasting on 18 November for the first time since the city fell to Serbian forces six years ago. (RFE/RL)

CUBA

Journalist with the news agency Cuba Press, **Ricardo Gonzalez Alfonso**, who had disseminated reports about alleged human rights violations in Santa Clara, was arrested at his home on 16 October by two officials of the interior ministry for reportedly 'no reason'. On 23 October independent journalist **Jorge Luis Arce Cabrera** was assaulted in the street by a former agent of the Interior Ministry. On 30 October, Ricardo Gonzalez Alfonso was detained for several hours for the second time in a fortnight. Police officers warned him he had 'two options: imprisonment or exile'. He had been covering the progress of a strike in Santa Clara by members of a human rights group. (RSF, AI, CubaNet)

The government has obstructed the broadcast of documentaries, produced by the Church, about the Pope and his imminent visit to Cuba, according to a report on 6 November. The Catholic Church in Cuba has expressed dissatisfaction about how the authorities are dealing with their request for access to the media, and has started showing the films in churches and parishes. (*El Pais*)

DEMOCRATIC REPUBLIC OF CONGO

Newspaper editor **Bonsange Yema** was arrested on 18 November and accused of 'spying' for the UN mission. (IRIN)

On 25 November 10 journalists were detained and whipped by police in Kinshasa. This followed their attendance at a press conference given by Z'ahidi Ngoma, the leader of an opposition movement, who was also arrested that day. (RSF)

Detained newspaper editor **Polydor Muboyayi Mubanga** of *Le Phare*, charged with 'spreading false news and inciting ethnic hatred' (*Index* 6/1997), was released on 26 November. (IRIN, RSF, Médias Libres, Médias Pour Tous)

The relaying of foreign radio stations by local stations was banned on 30 November. Information Minister Raphael Ghenda stated that foreign correspondents were engaged in a disinformation campaign against the DRC and that they had 'systematically altered all facts'. As a result, FM transmissions of Radio France International, the BBC and Voice of America are unavailable. (IRIN)

EGYPT

Ahmet Desouki Korali was arrested in mid-October and charged with desecration of the dead after a sculpture by him appeared at Cairo's Ninth Exhibition for Young Artists. The piece incorporated a human leg, a cat's skull and a sheep's spine within a polyester covering resembling an ancient Egyptian statue. (Associated Press)

Police confiscated 41 foreign-licensed newspapers on 23 October on the orders of the Foreign Publications Censor. The government claims its bans are intended merely to bring order to the market, but observers fear the seizures may later extend to popular independent weeklies, such as *al-Destour*, which are also registered abroad. (*Cairo Times*)

President Nasser's former Information Minister Mohammed Hassanein Heikal revealed in mid-November that 'more than 100,000' telephones have been tapped in Egypt. The opposition daily *al Wafd* on 13 November, claimed that 'the government ... spies on journalists, opposition parties, trades unions and all the political players in Egypt.' (*Middle East Times*)

Government efforts to portray the country's Islamic insurgency as vanquished finally collapsed after more than 70 people died on 17 November in a gun and knife attack on tourists visiting the mortuary complex of Queen Hatshepsut near Luxor. The attack came against a background of official assurances that it had defeated the extremist group *Gama'a al-Islamiya*. Fallout from the attack has included the resignation of Interior Minister Hassan al-Alfi. Al-Alfi had been pursuing several libel cases against the Islamist newspaper *al-Shaab* (*Index* 2/1997, 5/1997, 6/1997), which has campaigned for his dismissal for alleged corruption and human rights abuses. Al-Alfi is replaced by the current head of the security forces, General Habib al-Adli, a specialist in counter-terrorism. (*Guardian*, *Middle East Times*)

ESTONIA

On 4 November, by a vote of 44-zero, parliament approved an amendment to the education law whereby 'state language teachers' will be introduced into schools where Russian is the language of instruction. The law was extended on 19 November to require parliamentary deputies and local government officials to prove knowledge of the Estonian language, if they do not have at least elementary education in it. (RFE/RL)

ETHIOPIA

There has been a spate of journalist arrests. Acting editor-in-chief **Solomon Namara** and deputy editor-in-chief **Tesfaye Deressa** of *Urji* newspaper were arrested on 16 October in Addis Ababa. Human rights activist **Garoma Bekele**, also a journalist with the paper, was arrested on 27 October. The recent publication of an article in *Urji*, which questioned the government's account of the killing in Addis Ababa of three alleged OLF members on 8 October, is believed to be the reason behind their arrests. The journalists, who have not yet been charged, are being held incommunicado and there are concerns for their treatment in custody. In addition, *Wonchif* journalist **Gardew Demessie** and *Agere* journalist **Getachew Teffera** were arrested on 28 October. On 13 November co-editor-in-chief of *Meda Welabu*, **Tolera Tessema**, and *Agere*'s **Abay Hailu** were both being held in Central Prison for unknown reasons. The reasons for all the arrests remain unknown. Meanwhile, despite having served their prison terms, it was reported on 13 November that **Sissaye Negussie** of *Agere*, **Samson Seyum** of *Tequami* and **Salomon Gebre-Amlak** of *Mogad* were still being held in Addis Ababa Central Prison. (RSF, AI)

EUROPEAN UNION

A report in early November by the EU's drug monitoring unit criticised the promotion of a drug culture amongst the young by corporate advertising. No specific companies were named but the report described youth-orientated marketing as being 'implicitly or explicitly' drug-related. (*European, Guardian*)
On 10 November EU ombudsman Jacob Soederman ruled that 'officials have a fundamental right to freedom of expression' under Article 10 of the European Convention on Human Rights. The article supports 'the freedom to hold opinions and to receive and to impart information and ideas without interference by public authority.' The decision, which related to a case involving a Swedish EU official, undermines EU staff rules which state that officials 'shall not in any manner whatsoever disclose to any unauthorised person any document or information not already made public.' (*Guardian*)
Justice, the British section of the International Commission of Jurists, expressed concern in late November over EU plans to bring about greater cooperation between member states' security and intelligence agencies. Giving evidence to the House of Lords Select Committee on the European Communities, the organisation warned that the plan could lead to 'extensive and increasing surveillance of individuals.' (*Guardian*)

FRANCE

Photographer **Christian Mouchet** and medical worker **Alain Petigas** were given suspended prison sentences of eight and six months and fines of US$13,900 and US$1,730 respectively on 4 November. In 1995, Petigas took photographs at the scene of a terrorist bombing in Paris using Mouchet's camera. (*International Herald Tribune*)
On 12 November, author **Nicholas Domenach** was ordered to pay National Front leader Jean-Marie Le Pen US$7,000. A Paris court decided that Domenach had misrepresented an interview with Le Pen in his book *Le Roman d'un Président*. In the book, Le Pen was quoted as saying that President Jacques Chirac was financed by Jewish organisations. (*International Herald Tribune*)
An 846-page book documenting the deaths of between 85 and 100 million people under Communist regimes such as those in the Soviet Union, China and Cambodia topped the French best-seller list in late November. Authored by six historians over three years, the *Black Book of Communism* helped bring about heated debate in parliament over the French Communist Party's links with Stalinism. The author of the book's introduction and conclusion, **Stéphane Courtois**, was forced to drop his original title for the work, the *Book of Communist Crimes*, when two contributors threatened to withdraw. (*International Herald Tribune*)

GAMBIA

Ghanaian national **Muhamed E. Seade**, editor-in-chief of the privately-owned *Daily Observer*, was expelled from the country on 1 November. No official reason was given for Seade's deportation, the fifth from the paper since President Jammeh came to power in a bloodless coup in 1994. The first was owner **Kenneth Best** from Sierra Leone. (West African Journalists Association, RSF, Reuters)

GERMANY

In late October the Social Democrat opposition demanded the introduction of 'political training' for army recruits. This move followed the broadcast by television network SAT-1 of a video showing eight German soldiers in Saxony giving the Nazi salute. (*Guardian*)
The Munich-based daily *Sueddeutsche Zeitung* appeared to bow to Iranian diplomatic pressure on 12 November by printing an apology for previous inaccuracies. The paper conceded that its correspondent had supplied the wrong

information in an article on Iran's use of chemical weapons in the 1980-88 war with Iraq. The Iranian ambassador had responded with an angry letter of protest to the story, which appeared on 7 November. (Reuters)

GREECE

On 6 November, a court sentenced a cleric to 22 months in jail for assuming the title of religious leader of a Muslim minority. **Mehmet Emin Aga** was found guilty on three counts of unlawfully using the title of 'Mufti' when addressing the minority and was released pending appeal. (Reuters)

HONG KONG

Two journalists of Hong Kong Chinese based newspapers were arrested in September according to a November issue of the Chinese magazine *Frontline*. **Ha Tai-ning**, associate editor of *Ming Pao* (Daily News) was detained for two days for publishing an insider report, based on confidential documents, on the 15th Party Congress on 5 September. **Li Binghua**, deputy chief of the Chinese newspaper *Ta Kung Pao*, is reportedly under arrest for leaking state secrets and could be given a five-year jail sentence. Both newspapers denied the report. (RSF, Hong Kong Journalists Association)
Two pager companies were warned by the telecommunications authority on 24 October not to censor messages after a complaint by the Democratic Party, which claimed that messages to its members about a protest had been intercepted. (*South China Morning Post*)
A voluntary code by the Hong Kong Internet Service Providers' Association to control obscene and indecent material on the Internet was launched on 27 October to protect young persons and children. The Television Licensing Authority and the Providers' Association pledged it would not be used for political censorship. (*South China Morning Post*)
The newspaper *Apple Daily*, a Beijing critic, has been denied accreditation to cover mainland news and was barred from covering a reception organised by the Chinese Foreign Ministry in Hong Kong in September. (Hong Kong Journalists Association)

INDIA

Mira Nair's (*Index* 4/97) controversial film *Kama Sutra* was not released on 17 October as its distributor had planned because the central board of film certification had not cleared the dubbed version of the movie in Hindi, Tamil, and Telugu. The English version of the movie, titled *Tale of Love*, was cleared by the censor board earlier in the month. (*Times of India*)
The discovery of the headless body of a Catholic priest in the state of Bihar led to calls in late October for the protection of the local Christian community. Father A K Thomas' torso was found 20 kilometres south of the district capital, Hazaribagh, two days after he had gone missing. Although no group has claimed responsibility, church workers and missionaries in Bihar have faced a backlash recently from Hindu fundamentalist groups and upper castes who view them as upsetting the status quo. Thomas was the third Catholic clergyman to be killed in the area in the past two years. (*South China Morning Post*)
On 20 November, the government tabled the Jain Commission's interim report into the assassination of former prime minister Rajiv Gandhi by a suspected Liberation Tigers of Tamil Eelam (LTTE) suicide bomber in Tamil Nadu state on 21 May 1991. The report tends to confirm the long-running suspicion that Muthuvel Karunandhi, leader of the Dravida Munnetra Kazhagam (DMK), helped to shelter LTTE members in Tamil Nadu while he was chief minister there in the early-1990s. After the release of this information, Congress (I)'s backing of the United Front Government in parliament collapsed. Congress (I), allegedly at the behest of Gandhi's daughter, Priyanka, said that it will no longer support the government unless the DMK is ousted from the coalition. After over a week of political gamesmanship, Congress (I) withdrew its support for the government on 28 November. Prime Minister Inder Kumar Gujral's government subsequently collapsed later that day. (Reuter, SWB, *Hindu*)

INDONESIA

On 10 November the information ministry banned two private TV stations, ANteve and SCTV, from broadcasting a live meeting of the People's Representative Council and the Finance Minister. The stations had obtained permission from the Speaker but the ministry claimed that only state-run stations could transmit live from parliament. The law, however, contains no sections which regulate live broadcasts by private-sector stations. (Insitute for the Studies on the Free Flow of Information)

Lynn Fredriksson, an American freelancer covering a ceremony commemorating the 1991 massacre of civilians by the military, was expelled from East Timor on 11 November. She was accused of abusing her tourist visa and 'disturbing public order'. (RSF)

Ahmad Taufik, an Indonesian journalist who spent more than two years in prison for his work, was awarded a Press Freedom Award from the Committee to Protect Journalists on 19 November. (CPJ)

Photographs which allegedly show the torture of Timorese women by Indonesian soldiers may have been faked, a Foreign Ministry spokesman said on 21 November. The pictures, dating back to 1996, were originally taken by army photographers but were smuggled out, according to Andrew McNaughton of the Australia-East Timor Association. (Reuters)

A play called *Marsinah Mengguga* (Marsinah Accuses) by **Ratna Sarumpaet** and the Satu Merah Panggung Theatre was banned three hours before it was due to begin on 26 November in Surabaya. The play concerns the unresolved murder of Indonesian labour activist Marsinah and has been freely performed in seven cities previously. (Institute for the Studies on the Free Flow of Information).

IRAN

The government daily *Jomhouri Eslami* launched a fresh propaganda campaign against the detained *Adineh* editor **Faraj Sarkoohi** (*Index* 6/97, 1/97, 2/97, 3/97, 4/97, 5/97, 6/97) who, after nine months in detention, was convicted in September 1997 of 'slandering the Islamic Republic of Iran'. Exactly one year after his first arrest, the paper carried a letter, purportedly written by Sarkoohi, in which he admitted to having had contacts with foreign embassies with a view to 'putting in place a secular state'. The alleged confession is suspected to have been extracted under torture. On 13 November 1996, at the height of the witch-hunt for Sarkoohi, *Jamhouri Eslami* had written that he was in Germany, when in fact he had been secretly detained. (RSF, PEN)

On 30 October, poet **Simin Behbani**'s speech at the Grand Hall of Art in Teheran was interrupted when the sound system in the hall was disconnected and lights switched off before she could finish. Invited by the Ministry of Islamic Culture to give an address on National Women's day and assured of the freedom to speak freely, Behbani chose to talk about the death in prison of writer Saidi Sirjani and the imprisonment of editor Faraj Sarkoohi. Even after the lights were extinguished, she continued to talk to an appreciative audience. (PEN)

ISRAEL

Journalists from all the major Hebrew dailies signed a 17 November petition calling on the government press office (GPO) to grant press cards to reporters from *Challenge* and *al-Sabar*. The petition, published in *Ha'aretz* on 17 November, was signed by 60 prominent journalists and 20 others. A statement the next day from the GPO was more conciliatory in tone than usual, revealing the recent introduction of an appeals procedure. Previous GPO statements have tried to portray the magazines as organs of the Democratic Front for the Liberation of Palestine. (CPJ, RSF)

ITALY

The Reverend Mario Frittitta was arrested in Palermo on 4 November. He is suspected of performing Mass for one Mafia leader and a marriage for another. (*International Herald Tribune*)

The campaign on behalf of imprisoned philosopher Tony Negri by a variety of intellectuals, including composer Pierre Boulez and political activist Daniel Cohn-Bendit, was taken to Strasbourg and the European Parliament in mid-November. The authorities appear so far unmoved. Negri was charged with collaborating with the Red Brigade in 1979 but cleared. Having fled to France in 1983 he was convicted *in absentia* for being 'morally responsible' for violence which took place during demonstrations in the 1970s. (*Guardian*)

JAPAN

The Ministry of Justice plans to submit a bill during the extraordinary session of the parliament called the Law Against Organised Crime which would allow wiretapping of telephones, cellular phones, fascimilies machines and computers. Although law enforcement authorities will need a court warrant to carry out wiretaps, the bill has been criticised for violating Article 21 of the Constitution which guarantees the secrecy of telecommunication.(*Japan-Asia Quarterly Review*)

JORDAN

Several issues of the London-based Arabic newspapers *al-Quds al-Arabi*, *al-Sharq al-Awsat* and *al-Hayat* and the Lebanese daily *al-Nahar* were seized by the Ministry of Information in mid-October. The confiscations appear to be linked to coverage of Israeli agents' attempted assassination of Hamas chief Khaled Misha'al in Amman on 25 September. Twelve successive issues of *al-Quds al-Arabi* were barred, while *al-Hayat* was stopped three times within two weeks. (*Jordan Times*)
The Higher Court of Justice ruled on 9 November that the government was justified in suspending publication of the weekly newspaper *al-Mithaq* for violating the Press and Publications Law. Amendments to the law introduced in June now require weekly publications to increase their capitalisation from 15,000 to 300,000 dinars ($450,000). (RSF)

Recent publications: *Blaming the Press—Jordan's Democratisation Process in Crisis* (A19, October 1997, 104pp); *Clamping Down on Critics—Human Rights Violations in Advance of the Parliamentary Elections* (HRW, October 1997, 33pp)

KENYA

Palazh Krishnanunni Raja (*Index* 6/1997), an Indian freelance journalist, was ordered by a Nairobi court on 23 October to be repatriated to India. He was also fined Ksh3,000 (US$47.35) and ordered to pay a Ksh20,000 (US$316.20) bond to the Immigration Department. Raja was found guilty of working as a journalist without a permit, being in the country illegally and failing to register as an alien. His arrest on 28 September followed the publication of a story by Raja in the *Rift Valley Times* and the *Times* about the reputed personal wealth of Joshua Kulei, a presidential aide. On 26 October Kulei published a notice in the *Sunday Nation* warning Nairobi newspapers the *East African* and *Expression Today* that he may take legal action against them for publishing articles he claims are false. (NDIMA)
On 21 October almost the entire run of the magazine *Finance* was bought up by people believed to be security officers. Some vendors claimed that they were warned not to buy extra stock. The cover story was on Gideon Moi, son of the president, and draws on allegations made against him by a Central Bank of Kenya lawyer, Philip Murgor. (NDIMA)
On 26 October journalists **Ambura Olira** of the *East African Standard* and **David Ochami** of the *Kenya Times* were attacked by Muslim students outside Garissa Teachers' College. The students claimed that the journalists were biased in their reporting of religious affairs at the college, where there is tension between Christian and Muslim students. (NDIMA)
On 2 November over 200 correspondents threatened to boycott coverage of the general elections, set for 29 December, if they were not paid a risk allowance. They also cautioned their employers against using intimidation. (NDIMA)
Government charges of unlawful possession of firearms, promoting 'warlike activities' and being in possession of seditious documents, brought against the writer, human rights campaigner and presidential candidate **Koigi wa Wamwere**, were dropped on 19 November. Similar charges

against Wamwere's lawyer, **Mirugi Kariuki**, were also withdrawn. (NDIMA)

KYRGYZSTAN

According to the newspaper *Nasha Gazeta* on the 21 October, Colonel A Kayipov, head of the Ministry of Internal Affairs (MIA) for Osh region, filed an action against the Uzbek-language newspaper *Mezon* because of the article 'Who opposes the Mafia?', published on 4 July. The article asserted that 15 MIA employees, all detained for selling narcotics, had been released from custody. 'I consider,' said Colonel Kayipov, 'that the honour of the establishment and consequently also my individual honour has been damaged.' (*Nasha Gazeta*)
An exposé of the shocking conditions in the Belovodskoye Children's Home in the suburbs of the capital, which was screened by Russia's NTV on 12 November during Hillary Clinton's visit, has caused a diplomatic row between Moscow and Bishkek. On 14 November, President Yeltsin's wife, Naina, launched an immediate appeal via the Russian Red Cross for Belovodskoye's 'naked and emaciated' children. One day later, President Askar Akayev condemned the film for undermining 'democratic reforms and Kyrgyzstan's authority on the international scene.' (SWB, Interfax)

MACEDONIA

In another 'flag raising' incident (*Index* 6/97), a local court in Tetovo sentenced Mayor **Alajdin Demiri** and city council president **Vebhi Bexheti** to two-and-a-half years in prison on 14 October, after they refused to remove an Albanian flag from the city hall. (RFE/RL)

MALAWI

Mollande Nkhata, director of news and current affairs at the national Malawi Broadcasting Corporation (MBC), was demoted to chief editor on 17 November for saying that President Muluzi had lost his voice at the Commonwealth Heads of Government meeting in Edinburgh. Nkhata's remarks were reported in the opposition *Daily Times*. He was also ordered to resign from the Malawi chapter of MISA and dissociate himself from other journalists associations or face dismissal from MBC. The source of the story about the president's lost voice, MBC journalist **Irene Banda**, was reprimanded by management on 12 November and accused of not being 'loyal to [the] government' and giving 'poor coverage of the president's trip.' (MISA)

MALAYSIA

The government is considering amending the Printing Presses and Publications Act and the Film Censorship Act in a bid to stem the flow of pornography into the country. Deputy Home Minister Datuk Ong Ka Ting said the ministry had already banned 735 publications.(*New Straits Times*)
The government circulated an order in late-October banning professors, researchers and other academics from discussing in public the effects of the smog which has enveloped the region. (Reuters)
In an interview with the *Star* newspaper on 21 November, Tengku Alaudin Abdul Majid of the Culture, Arts and Tourism Ministry said the the authorities would begin to monitor the internet for inaccurate foreign reports about the country. (AP)

MAURITANIA

The weekly *La Tribune* was censored by the government on 10 November, following the publication of an article in the preceding issue which criticised the policies of President Maaouya Ould Sid Ahmed Taya. (RSF)

MEXICO

Mexican lawyer and journalist at *Excelsior*, **Rafael Perez Ayala**, was found dead in the boot of his car on 25 October. He had been advisor to several politicians. (*El País*)

MOLDOVA

Journalists attending a government meeting on 29 October were forced to leave as discussion on a Revenue Court report on corruption in other state institutions was about to begin. Press law states that all information concerning the public interest should be accessible to the media. (RSF)

In a recent report by Reporters sans Frontières, the state was cited as the region's worst offender against journalists' rights and freedoms, owing to its 1994 press law. (RFE/RL)

MOZAMBIQUE

The main opposition party RENAMO was forced to storm its own radio station in Maputo in order to evict its administrator, according to a report by the Pan-African News Agency on 19 October. Radio Terra Verde, which is seeking to evolve into a viable commercial concern, has said it will sue. (SWB)

NICARAGUA

On 24 October, students at former Instituto Autonomo Rigoberto Lopez Perez, named after the Sandinista fighter who assassinated the dictator Somoza, went on strike after it was announced that the school was to be renamed after a poet. The episode follows a government decision to wipe away the last vestiges of Sandinismo by changing the national symbols. The most notorious action so far has been the replacement of Sandino's image on the banknotes by that of the 19th century general Jose Santos Celaya. (*El Pais*)

NIGER

On 1 November security forces prevented a demonstration against the imprisonment of *Alternative* journalist **Moussa Tchangari** (*Index* 6/1997). Tchangari was jailed for three months in September for publishing official documents. (Reuters)

NIGERIA

Henry Ugbolue, Kaduna correspondant of the independent *News* group, was assaulted by security police and detained on 10 October for writing a report about the sacking of more than 20,000 civil servants. He was released without charge the next day and went into hiding. The *News*' premises have been raided several times since by security agents wanting to rearrest him. (AI, 'IPR')
On 17 October the *News'* **Ademola Adimboye**, and **Gbenga Alaketu** of sister publication the weekly *Tempo*, were detained without charge in the capital Abuja for two days, in connection with a *Tempo* report denouncing recent stands by the armed forces in favour of General Sani Abacha's possible presidential candidature. (AI, RSF)
On 18 October journalists **Tokunbo Awoshakin** of *This Day*, **Wisdom Dike** of the *Week*, **Ola Doifie** of *Post Express*, **Casmir Igbokwe** of the *News* and **Joseph Ollor-Obari** of the *Guardian* were briefly detained for questioning in the town of Ogbia in the Niger Delta. The journalists, who were trying to report on a demonstration by environmentalists against Shell, were released with warnings not to publish anything. (AI, 'IPR')
Soji Omotunde, editor of *African Concord*, has been held incommunicado since 25 October when he was assaulted and arrested for unknown reasons in Lagos by two security men. The newspaper has not been published since July when its Abuja Bureau Chief **Mohammed Adamu** (*Index* 5/1997) was also abducted. Adamu remains in detention. (AI, 'IPR', RSF, Reuters)
Ben Adaji, correspondent for the *News* in the northeastern state of Taraba, went into hiding at the end of October after a tip-off that security officers were about to arrest him. Adaji had written an article in the *News'* 27 October edition about the behind-the-scenes roles of military officers in a local communal war. He was arrested on 17 November after he emerged from hiding in the belief that security had decided not to pursue the matter. ('IPR')
Freelance journalist and assistant director of the Lagos-based Independent Journalism Centre **Ladi Olorunyomi** (*Index* 3/1997, 4/1997) was arrested in the early hours of 3 November by military intelligence officers. She was released the same afternoon after being questioned throughout the day over the whereabouts of her husband, exiled journalist **Dapo Olorunyomi**, and other journalists currently in hiding. (AI, CCPJ)
Military intelligence officers stormed the offices of the *News* in Lagos twice on 3 November, demanding to see managing editor **Bayo Onanuga** (*Index* 6/97), who went into hiding in October.

('IPR')
Adetokunbo Fakeye, defence correspondent of *PM News*, was detained on 4 November while on duty at Army Defence headquarters in Lagos. No reason was given for his detention. ('IPR')
On 8 November **Jenkins Alumona**, editor of the *News*, was arrested as he waited to present a sports broadcast at the premises of the National Nigerian Television (NTA) in Lagos. No charges have been brought and his whereabouts are unknown. Earlier that day, the paper's managing editor, **Babafemi Ojudu**, narrowly escaped arrest by a plainclothes security officer who had approached him on the street. However, he was apprehended as he returned from a press freedom seminar in Kenya on 17 November. (RSF, 'IPR', AI)
Onome Osifo-Whiskey, deputy editor with *Tell* magazine, has been held incommunicado since he was snatched in Lagos by security agents at gunpoint on his way back from church on 9 November. (RSF) *Tell*'s editorial offices were ransacked on 9 November by security agents. All available copies of the magazine were confiscated, loaded into the magazine's distribution vehicle and towed away. ('IPR')
Over the weekend of 8-9 November, squads of security agents besieged the premises of major printing presses in Lagos, warning employees not to print copies of any independent newspapers. The weeklies *News* and *Tell* were not available for sale on Monday.

('IPR')
On 12 November Abia state police declared **Joshua Nnayerum Ogbonna**, publisher of the local weekly *Rising Sun*, 'wanted' for 'criminal defamatory publication'. The allegedly defamatory article has not been identified. ('IPR')
Akin Adesokan, a journalist with the *Post Express* newspaper, was detained on 12 November by security officers at the Nigeria-Benin border. Adesokan, a member of the Association of Nigerian Authors, was returning from Austria where he had attended a four-month writer-in-residence programme. His whereabouts are unknown. ('IPR')
Publisher and editor-in-chief of *This Day* newspaper, **Nduka Obaigbena**, was detained on 14 November in connection with a story the previous week which analysed the strategic importance of four officials in Abacha's administration. ('IPR')
On 18 November, **Rafiu Salau**, administration manager of the *News/Tempo/PM News* group, was detained at military intelligence headquarters in Lagos where he had gone to check on *PM News* journalist **Adetokunbo Fakeye**, detained there since 4 November. On 19 November, the group issued a statement expressing its concern over information indicating that an army officer is on a 'find-and-kill' mission, with editor-in-chief **Bayo Onanuga** as his target. ('IPR')

Recent publication: *Transition or Travesty? Nigeria's Endless Process of Return to Civilian Rule* (HRW, October 1997, 49pp)

NORTH KOREA

The government threatened in mid-November to blow up the South Korean Broadcasting System (KBS-TV) and assassinate the writers responsible for a drama series critical of the north's leadership. 'It's a conspiracy...by low lives of bogus journalism,' Radio Pyongyang claimed. Policeman have been guarding the state-run KBS-TV since the threats began on 16 November. (Yonhap News Agency, *Guardian*)
A label from a can of American beef, found aboard the North Korean submarine which ran aground in South Korea in September 1996, has been kept a secret since it was first discovered by US military personnel. Going public, it was claimed, would hurt Washington's drive to improve relations with Pyongyang as the label indicates a diversion of famine relief to feed the military. Washington reported finding the label in early November. (*Guardian*)

PAKISTAN

On 20 October police in Karachi baton-charged a march by journalists protesting against recent attacks against the press in Sindh province. In the latest series of attacks on 15 October, Hyderabad-based Sindhi language dailie, *Sawal* and *Kawish* had bombs exploded at their premises, and the offices of the daily *Sindh* received a bomb threat by telephone from a member of the so-called 'Front Tiger'. (*Dawn*, Pakistan Press Foundation)

On 28 October, journalists and employees of the Lahore Press Club were beaten up by supporters of the Pakistan People's Party (PPP). On the same day, activists of the *Jamaat-I-Islami* political party ransacked the offices of Pakistan Television (PTV) in Muzaffarabad, Azad Kashmir, to protest against the alleged poor coverage of their party by the state-run broadcaster. (RSF, Pakistan Press Foundation)

Students demanding the right to cheat in their exams forced a university campus at Khuzdar, near the regional capital Quetta, to close on the weekend of 22-23 November. University authorities accused students in the engineering and technology faculty of going on the rampage when their demands were refused. The students had held a rally demanding to be allowed to look at notes and collaborate with colleagues. (Reuters)

Amid a fierce constitutional battle over whether Prime Minister Nawaz Sharif or Supreme Court Chief Justice Sajjad Ali Shah had the power to appoint Supreme Court judges, the Supreme Court, on 29 October, suspended a constitutional amendment that made it mandatory for legislators to vote along party lines. The amendment, passed last July, was aimed at putting an end to the decades-old tradition of vote-buying to get legislation through the national assembly. A three-judge panel led by Chief Justice Shah suspended the amendment, however, on the grounds that it prevented members from voting according to conscience. On 12 November Nawaz Sharif was charged with contempt by the Supreme Court after he said that the court's nullification of the amendment would renew political corruption in the assembly. The political chaos sparked by the contempt charges led to Shah and President Farooq Leghari resigning on 2 December after General Jehangir Karamat, the chief of the army, sided with the prime minister in the dispute. (Reuters, *International Herald Tribune*, *Dawn*)

PALESTINE (AUTONOMOUS AREAS)

Khalid Amayreh, an independent journalist and longtime critic of Yasser Arafat, was placed under house arrest from 26-28 October. The detention was not reported in the local press. Amayreh had just published a report on the torture of Hamas members in Palestinian prisons. (Freedom House, *Independent*)

Police prevented journalists from covering a riot that erupted on 26 October following a funeral in Rafah. Two thousand mourners burned down the house of the governor, a powerful clan leader, after violence broke out at the funeral of a member of a rival clan. Palestinian police used live ammunition to quell the riot, and one mourner was killed. (*Independent*)

Fathi Subuh (*Index* 5/1997, 6/1997) was released on 26 November on bail of 5,000 Jordanian dinars (US$7,500). His release followed the 14 November publication in *al-Quds* of a petition signed by 31 Palestinian academics. (Palestinian Human Rights Monitoring Group)

PANAMA

Journalist **Gustavo Gorriti**'s work permit was finally extended on 15 October, ending the threat of expulsion from that country. US officials said his case was raised with the authorities by Hillary Clinton during her recent visit. (*Index* 6/97). (*International Herald Tribune*)

PARAGUAY

Leo Rubun, host of the programme Al Rojo Vivo, was threatened with death by an unknown individual who 'asked' the journalist to stop criticising General Lino Oviedo. Oviedo, who won the Colorado Party primaries in September and is expected to stand for president in May 1998, staged an unsuccessful coup against President Juan Carlos Wasmosy last April. In a press release on 11 November, the general denied having anything to do with the threats. (RSF)

PERU

On 14 October journalists **Nicolas Lucar** and **Alamo Perez Luna** were cleared of charges of aggravated defamation against airline businessman

Fernando Zevallos Gonzalez. The charges stemmed from two reports broadcast on the TV programme La Revista Dominical, which linked Zevallos to drug trafficking in the 1980s. Lucar and his colleague, reporter **Elsa Ursula Picon**, later had one-year prison sentences, handed down for aggravated defamation of the ex-Army Intelligence Service Agent Leonor La Rosa, revoked. Last June the journalists had reported on La Rosa's romantic attachment to a military official. (IPYS)
After more than five years, the 'faceless courts' were officially disbanded on 15 October. These tribunals, which dealt with terrorism charges, were headed by anonymous judges. As a result, the Global Television case could now be heard in public court. In October 1996, a bomb was detonated outside the installations of both Global and Radio Samoa. Members of the army's intelligence services are accused of having carried out the attack. (AI, IPYS)
Journalist **Roxana Cueva**, who worked at Frecuencia Latina/Channel 2 until its new administration took over (*Index* 4/1997, 5/1997, 6/1997), was called to appear before the Congressional Commission on Defence, Internal Order and Intelligence on 10 November to discuss her sources. **Fernando Viana** and **Gonzalo Quijandria** were also summoned. Quijandria hosted the programme *Contrapunto*, which publicised the illegal wire-tapping of journalists, opposition politi-
cians and government ministers. A congresswoman from the ruling party, Marta Chavez, who presides over the Commission, has informed selected media by letter that she has the power to search the offices and homes of journalists for information. The penalty for publicising classified documents is 10 years. (IPYS))
On 17 November, a security agent at a pharmacy in San Isidro physically assaulted two reporters from the investigative programme *En Persona*, hosted by journalist **Cesar Hildebrant**. **Beatriz Llanos Cabanillas** and cameraman **Sergio Vergaray** were attacked following the transmission of a report on the trafficking of medicines, allegedly with the connivance of a former government minister. On 31 October Hildebrant had reported the theft of computer hard drives from the MCC Computer company which allows *En Persona* to be seen around the world. The police reported that the theft appeared to have been done by the National Intelligence Service. (IPYS)
The investigation into the murder of **Tito Pilco Mori** will be reopened (*Index* 6/97). The decision was made after *La Republica* published in its 16 October edition a report outlining the chronology of events surrounding his death and two eye-witness accounts. Initially, police and the attorney general claimed that Mori had injured his head after falling off his motorcycle. Elsewhere, Jenny Valera, Mori's widow, remarked on the peculiarity
that copies of the 16 October edition disappeared from newsstands in large quantities. Mori was the owner and director of Radio Frecuencia Popular and hosted the programme *El Pueblo Quiere Saber* which he used to criticise local judges and police. (IPYS)

POLAND

On 26 October Fr Henryk Jankowski, priest of President Lech Walesa's Gdansk parish, preached an 'anti-Semitic' sermon, alleging Jewish influence in Polish politics. Bishop Tadeusz Pieronek, secretary of the Polish episcopate, says that Fr Jankowski was 'hard to rein in'. On 4 November Father Tadeusz Rydzyk, director of Catholic Radio Maryja, failed to comply with a summons to answer allegations that he 'insulted state bodies' by saying that deputies who voted to liberalise the abortion law were 'criminals'. On 21 November Rydzyk said that he had received the summons too late to comply, adding that the allegations were part of a 'campaign of unprecedented slanders' by the 'atheistic media'. (SWB)
On 13 November Prime Minister Aleksander Kwasniewski said he wanted to make communist-era secret service files public and that he had submitted a bill to parliament to that effect. (RFE/RL)
On 15 November the daily *Zycie Warszawy* published a list of 23 Russian diplomats – four still in the country – exposed as spies by the State Protection Office (SPO) two years ago.

The SPO explained its refusal to comment on the need to keep secrets. The former head of the secret service, Gromoslaw Czempinski, called the revelations an attempt to 'discredit Polish intelligence'. (SWB)

RUSSIA

On 23 October the private network NTV allowed a 'jury' of viewers to decide whether Martin Scorsese's *The Last Temptation of Christ* should be broadcast. Having cancelled planned airings earlier this year, after protests from the Russian Orthodox Church, the mock trial found in favour of NTV. On 9 November, the proposed day for the screening, about 2,000 Russians demonstrated outside the Ostankino television centre where NTV is based. (RFE/RL, Reuters)

The state Duma asked parliament to investigate the business activities of George Soros and his associate Boris Jordan on 23 October. In a request sent to Prime Minister Viktor Chernomyrdin, First Deputy Prime Minister Anatolii Chubais and Interior Minister Anatolii Kulikov, the Duma expressed concern that the activities of Soros and Jordan could harm Russia's national security. (RFE/RL)

The pilot issue of the daily newspaper *Novye Izvestiya* appeared on 24 October. Chief editor **Igor Golembiovskii** launched the project after being forced out as editor of *Izvestiya* in the summer. Five days later, **Leonid Krutakov** claimed he had been sacked from *Novye Izvestiya* after he published an article in *Moskovskii Komsomolets* criticising Security Council Deputy Secretary Boris Berezovskii. Krutakov claimed Golembiovskii refused to publish the article which alleged that Berezovskii had diverted hundreds of millions of dollars from the state-run airline Aeroflot. Berezovskii is thought to have helped finance *Novye Izvestiya*. (RFE/RL)

The Voronezh Oblast Duma adopted a non-binding recommendation on 30 October, urging teachers not to use an allegedly 'anti-Russian' textbook on 20th-century European history. Deputies claim the book, written by Saratov University professor **Aleksandr Kreder**, is 'unpatriotic and tendentious', both belittling and distorting Russian history, although these claims are not supported by the federal education ministry. The book was financed by George Soros's Cultural Initiative foundation. (RFE/RL)

More than 20 religious and human rights groups formed the All-Russian Movement for Freedom of Conscience and a Secular State on 3 November. The group has been formed in response to Russia's new religion law (*Index* 6/97). (RFE/RL)

On 3 November a movement representing homeless people in Tomsk filed a court appeal after one of its members was denied the opportunity to register as a candidate in the forthcoming Oblast elections. **Peter Kurrennyi** was denied registration by the district electoral commission because he did not have a passport, despite the constitution granting all citizens the right to vote and run for office. (RFE/RL)

On 19 November the Duma approved a draft law establishing government oversight of 'significant expenditures' by private citizens. Under the bill, buyers would be obliged to notify the government of purchases of certain items that exceeded more than 83.5 million roubles (US$14,000). The law would apply to real estate, automobiles, stocks, bonds and cultural artefacts. In such cases, the purchaser would have to present tax collectors with documents indicating the source of the money used in the transactions. (RFE/RL)

RWANDA

Joseph Habyarimana, editor of the magazine *Indorerwamo*, was arrested on 28 October. It is believed this is due to an article published in December that focused on Hutu arrests and called for ethnic reconciliation. (RSF)

SAMOA

The criminal libel trial brought by Prime Minister Tofilau Eti Alesana against two journalists at the *Samoa Observer* (*Index* 8/97) has again been postponed, this time till 3 February 1998, because the Supreme Court has not yet looked at the defence challenge that the law breaches the constitution. Meanwhile, opposition leader **Tuiatua Tupua Tamaese Efi** launched a court challenge on 30 October against the ban on his access to national radio. The government claims he had used the service to 'disturb the peace'. (Pacific Islands News Association)

SERBIA-MONTENEGRO

Eight months after its launch, the cash-stricken independent daily *Gradjanin* hit the streets of Belgrade for the last time on 28 October. (B92)

On 29 October two police officers entered the offices of the Albanian-language daily *Koha Ditore* to inspect the personal identity documents of associate editor-in-chief **Yiber Hysa** and journalist **Fisnik Abrashi**. Both had covered the demonstration by Albanian students in Pristina earlier that day. (RSF)

On the same day **Gordana Igric**, a prominent Serbian freelance journalist, went into hiding after a series of death threats following her report for CBS news about indicted war criminals at large in the Bosnian town of Foce. (CPJ)

In the week beginning 10 November, the Serbian Orthodox Church entered the media world with a pilot radio programme in the diocese of Sabac-Valjevo. The church expects to obtain the necessary licences from the federal government to begin 24-hour broadcasts. Meanwhile, a Muslim radio station in Sandzak has been banned by the government. **Radio Sjenica** was closed down by federal authorities on 7 November, 10 days after it had begun broadcasting, because it did not possess the required licences. (B92)

SIERRA LEONE

Prince Akpu, editor-in-chief of the *Financial Times*, has been detained incommunicado and without charge since 12 October. (RSF)

Jonathan Leigh of the *New Observer* magazine was detained without charge for 12 days accused of subversion. He was beaten severely during his detention. (CPJ)

Francis Akpu, a Nigerian citizen who reports for the local *Financial Times* and owns the newly formed *Alpha Jet* newspaper, was picked up by soldiers on 19 October for subversion. Apparently, the military is unhappy about Akpu's choice of name for the new publication which refers to the aircraft which bombed Freetown in June. He was released without charge on 25 October. (CPJ)

Paul Kamara, editor of one of the most outspoken independents *For di People*, was detained for two days on 17 October, accused of providing reports to the underground radio station 98.1 FM. (CPJ)

Augustin Garmoh, a journalist with the *Point* newspaper, was detained for three days on 17 October by military officers accusing him of collaborating with the Kamajohs, the pro-President Kabbah militia. (CPJ)

John Foray (*Index* 6/97), acting editor of the *Democrat* newspaper, was released without charge on 25 October. He sustained a spinal injury during his detention. (CPJ)

BBC correspondent **Winston Ojukutu** was detained on 5 November, in connection with interviews he held with the public on their reaction to a statement by the ruling Armed Forces Revolutionary Council (AFRC) about its unwillingness to disarm. Ojukutu's whereabouts are not known. (CPJ)

On 12 November the military junta suspended indefinitely the privately-owned magazine *Standard Times* after its editors refused to reveal their sources for a story implicating the junta in a plot to destabilise neighbouring Guinea. The article accused the junta and the Liberian government of supporting the son of a former president in his plans to invade Guinea. (RSF)

Ibrahim Karim Sei, editor of the *Standard Times*, and **Dorothy Awoonor-Gordon**, acting editor of the *Concord Times*, were detained without charge on 21 November. (International Press Institute)

For di People was awarded the Index on Censorship 'Freedom of the Press Award' on 4 December.

Recent publication: *A Disastrous Set-back for Human Rights* (AI, October 1997)

SINGAPORE

On 21 November, the arts ministry lifted the ban on two pro-communist magazines, *Peking Review* and *China Reconstructs*; the *Selected Works* of *Mao Tse-tung*; a novel about Communist Party members, *How Steel is Forged*; and the academic publication, *Journal of Contemporary Asia*, because they are no longer objectionable on 'moral, religious or communal grounds'. (*Business Times*)

The law ministry accused Amnesty International on 17 October of joining the Commission of Jurists in a 'coordinated, partisan propaganda campaign' following the claim in a report that defamation suits taken out by the ruling party against the opposition placed restrictions on freedom of expression. (*Straits Times*)

SLOVAKIA

On 29 October Milos Nemecek, chairman of the Publishers Association, protested at the government's plan to increase value-added tax on publications from 6 to 23 per cent. On 10 November the country's major newspapers cleared half of their front pages alongside the text of a common protest statement, with the size of the blank space increasing until the day of the debate when it would be completely blank. Two days later the press called off the protest after discussions with lawmakers that suggested parliament would not pass the measure. (RFE/RL)

SLOVENIA

On 12 November President Milan Kucan said a proposed law to ban former communists from office was unnecessary as the names of those who had violated human rights were well known and there was no need to punish all former officials for the crimes of a few. If passed, the bill would render Kucan and Prime Minister Janez Drnovsek ineligible to hold public office. (RFE/RL)
On 13 November Justice Minister Tomaz Marusic said that criminal legislation will be changed so that journalists will no longer be prosecuted for disclosing state and army secrets, if their aim is to expose wrongdoing. (RFE/RL)

SOUTH AFRICA

A special parliamentary committee set up on 22 October is to investigate whether Patricia De Lille, a Pan Africanist Congress (PAC) MP, breached her parliamentary privilege when she named several top African National Congress (ANC) members as allegedly having been spies for the apartheid security forces. (Freedom of Expression Institute)
On 28 October a magistrate in the Pretoria Regional Court ruled that all evidence relating to the former government's top secret chemical and biological warfare programme, 'Project Coast', be heard *in camera*. The evidence was expected to be heard during the bail application of the programme's former head, Wouter Basson. *Business Day* and *Sunday Times* newspapers have applied to the High Court to have the decision overruled on grounds that there should be public access to this type of government information. (Freedom of Expression Institute)
The ANC in Mpumalanga province announced on 6 November that it intended to take legal action against journalist **Justin Arenstein** to make him reveal the sources of an article which appeared in the weekly *Mail & Guardian*. The article quoted unnamed members of the ANC's Provincial Executive Committee who confirmed that it had unanimously agreed to withdraw the nomination of Provincial Premier Mathews Phosa for the position of ANC deputy president. (Freedom of Expression Institute)

SOUTH KOREA

The national security agency announced on 19 November that it had arrested six suspected spies last month, one of whom was identified as **Koh Young Bok**, a professor at Seoul National University. Under the National Security Law, anyone knowingly engaging in any act that 'praises, encourages, advertises or supports the activities of an anti-state organisation' can be sentenced for up to seven years. (United Press International)
Human rights campaigner **Suh Jun-sik**, detained in October under the National Security Law (*Index 6/97*) for organising a human rights film festival, was rearrested on 4 November for failing to report regularly to police as required under the terms of his release. Suh is expected to face charges for failing to submit festival

INDEX INDEX

films for pre-screening by the Korea Performance Ethics Committee. Other charges may include violation of the National Security Law for showing films which 'benefit North Korea'. (OMCT, Writers in Prison Committee) According to the Korean daily newspaper *Hankyoreh*, the Ministry of Information and Communication blocked access to the internet site **Geosite** from 19 October, because it contains information on North Korea. Last year a Canadian home page was shut down in similar circumstances. (Social Information Networking Group)

SRI LANKA

The Liberation Tigers of Tamil Eelam (LTTE) announced on 7 November that they would launch a legal challenge in the US federal appeals court against the State Department's 8 October listing of the guerrilla group as a 'terrorist organization'. The decision makes it illegal to fundraise for the LTTE and denies US visas to its representatives. (Reuters)
Police detectives told a Colombo court on 11 November that they would file charges against three policemen suspected of having murdered journalist, human rights activist, and television star **Richard de Zoysa** (*Index* 5/1990, 6/1990, 8/1990, 10/1990, 6/1997) on 18 February 1990. Charges will be brought against Inspector Devasundera, Sergeant Sarathchandra, and Assistant Superintendent Lal Ranchagoda. (*Daily News*, Inform, Reuters)
After almost two weeks of uncertainty, it was confirmed on 26 November that President Chandrika Kumaratunga's government had withdrawn permission for the BBC to film an adaptation of Salman Rushdie's novel *Midnight's Children*. The confirmation came after a month of protests by Muslim leaders against the government's 28 October decision to allow a five-part serial of the novel, renamed *Saleem's Story*, to begin production. (*Daily News*, Reuters, Free Media Movement, *Guardian*)
On 29 November reporters **Sri Ganjan** and **M Dunstan** and the photographer **S Surendran** of the Tamil-language daily *Virakesari* were harassed by police and had their film destroyed while covering the transfer of 223 Tamil detainees from Welikada Prison to a detention centre in Kalutara. In another recent incident, police raided the Colombo hotel room of **Suda Ramachandran**, a Tamil-speaking journalist for India's *Deccan Herald*, seized photographs taken by her and questioned her for hours about alleged connections with the LTTE before she was released. (Free Media Movement)

Recent Publication: *Government's Response to Widespread 'Disappearances' in Jaffna* (AI, November 1997, 16pp)

SUDAN

On 3 November it was announced that journalists not licensed by the state-run National Council for Press and Publication would be banned from working. (Reuters)
The 12 November edition of the independent daily *Al-Rai Al-Akhar* was seized the night before distribution. It is not known why this particular edition was banned, but the paper has already been halted three times in the past for 'publishing false information' and 'erroneous reports'. The paper only resumed publication in June 1997 after having been suspended for a year. (RSF)

SWAZILAND

On 29 October, management of state-owned Swaziland Television threatened to dismiss an employee, **Pasha Mayisela**, for 'being absent from work without permission'. Mayisela, a trade unionist and media freedom campaigner, took part in a nation-wide labour boycott on 13 and 14 October to protest a government-imposed media council. Mayisela gave her employers prior notice of her plans to participate. (MISA)

TAIWAN

Journalist **Shieh Chung-liang** of the international Hong Kong newsweekly *Yazhou Zhoukan* was one of the winners of the 1997 International Press Freedom Award on 23 October. (CPJ)
The Taiwanese American co-founder of the **Yahoo** internet search engine, Jerry Yang,

spoke in Singapore with the Straits Times Interactive on how it bans web pages featuring child pornography or bomb-building. He cited the main reason for censoring the Web as a 'fear of what you cannot control.' (*Straits Times*)

TAJIKISTAN

On 13 November the state-controlled Sharki Ozod printing works refused to publish the daily *Vechernie Vesti* and the weekly *Biznes i Politika* in accordance with an order from President Imomali Rakhmonov. *Vechernie Vesti* was censored because it intended to print an interview with former Prime Minister Abdumalik Abdullojanov. Both newspapers were also going to include an open letter, signed by several journalists, which condemned Shamil Nugayev, the second secetary of the Russian embassy, for his criticism of local correspondents for Russian media. (RSF)

THAILAND

Prime Minister Chavalit Yongchaiyudh in a speech to military officers on 29 October described the *Nation* newspaper as his 'biggest threat'. The *Nation* has frequently criticised Chavalit and called for him to step down. Chavalit said that 'journalists misusing their pens, or commentators misusing their microphones, are no different from soldiers misusing their guns.' Chavalit denied any involvement with the bomb attacks on **Prasong Soonsiri**, a columnist with the daily *Naew Na*. Prasong was unhurt when a bomb destroyed his car in August. The *Siam Post*, another anti-Chavalit publication, was subject to a hoax bomb alert on the 29 October. (ISAI)

TIBET

Details of a 1994 trial of a Tibetan, sentenced to 17 years for collecting information and starting a pro-democracy group, emerged on 7 November. **Lukhar Sham** and two others were sentenced to a total of 45 years. Sham received eight years for purchasing classified documents and was accused of planning to send history and economic books abroad. (Tibet Information Network)

TURKEY

On 22 October **Burhan Aktas** was forced into a car in Erzurum by three men, suspected of being police officers, and driven off. The Erzurum police have denied holding Aktas who is still missing. In 1994, Aktas worked as an unpaid reporter for the Kurdish-owned newspaper *Ozgur Gundem* (Free Agenda) and had been detained twice previously and tortured in 1997. (AI)
On the same day, Interior Minister Murat Baseskioglu announced an investigation into allegations that the Islamist Welfare Party is funding Kanal-7 TV. He says 'Municipalities are not allowed to support any party or ideology. On 23 October Vural Savas, chief public prosecutor of the court of appeals, said that televised remarks by Welfare Party leader **Necmettin Erbakan** will be used as evidence for the closure of the party on the grounds that it is 'anti-secular'. Savas said that a transcript of the remarks will be sent to the constitutional court. (SWB)
Conscientious objector **Osman Murat Ulke** (*Index* 1/97) was convicted of 'persistent insubordination and desertion' by the Eskisehir Military Court on 23 October. He faces five months for each offence. (AI)
The trial of **Yavuz Onen**, president of Human Rights Foundation of Turkey, and three others on charges of 'illegally' reading a report on the 'Susurlu incident' to the people of Kilzilay, opened on 4 November. The unpublished report relates to a car crash on 3 November 1996 in which a former Istanbul deputy police chief, a pro-government Kurdish militia leader and a convicted drug smuggler wanted by Interpol were among the passengers. The accident led to the resignation of former interior minister Mehmet Agar and fed suspicions of collusion between Turkish security officials, organised crime and right-wing assassins. Onen and the other defendants face from 18 months to three years in prison if found guilty. (AAASHRAN)
On 4 November, **Mehmetcan Toprak** and **Vedat Bakir**, the director and manager of Radyo Karacadag, were detained by the anti-terror police following their attempts to report on the

INDEX INDEX

arrests of a group of people at a local bookstore. Police also raided the radio station's office and the homes of both men, confiscating audio cassettes and publications. Toprak and Bakir were released the following day. (CPJ)

On 6 November, at the tenth hearing in the journalist **Metin Goktepe** murder trial (*Index* 2/1996, 1/1997, 6/1997), the presiding judge of the Afyon Court of Assizes, Kamil Serif asked to be taken off the case because of what he described as 'unfair criticism' and pressure from international organisations. Meanwhile, the court ruled that five of the 11 accused police officers were to remain in detention, but no date for the re-enactment of the Goktepe murder has been set. (RSF)

On 19 November Ankara state security court held the second hearing in the trial *in absentia* of PKK founder **Abdullah Ocalan** for treason and 'crimes against the state'. The case against Ocalan and seven others relates to speeches made on the EU-based Kurdish language television Med TV. (Reuters)

On 23 November journalist and writer **Cezmi Ersoz** and journalist **Filiz Kocali** (*Index* 1/97) of the women's weekly *Pazartesi* were among 150 people detained in Istanbul, when police broke up a demonstration in support of university students. (CPJ)

TURKMENISTAN

Yovshan Annakurbanov, an independent journalist, was arrested by police officers at Ashkhabad airport on 30 October. A former stringer for Radio Liberty until death threats forced him to stop work in June, Annakurbanov was due to attend a training seminar in Prague. On 12 November he was released from detention at the investigation prison of the Turkmen Committee of National Security. (SWB, AI)

UGANDA

On 24 October, in Kampala, editor **Charles Onyango-Obbo** and reporter **Andrew Mwenda** of the *Monitor* were charged with publishing false information. They were jointly charged over an article alleging that Laurent Kabila had paid Uganda in gold in exchange for support against ex-president Mobutu Sese Seko. (NDIMA)

UKRAINE

On 15 October the Crimean parliament voted to make Russian, rather than Ukrainian, the official language of the region, and have their clocks conform to Moscow rather than Kiev time. The decision was overruled by a decree from President Leonid Kuchma on 24 October. (RFE/RL)

UNITED KINGDOM

On 22 October the European Parliament supported four Labour MEPs in their refusal to sign a new code of practice proposed by Prime Minister Tony Blair. The code, which forbids public criticism of government policy, was introduced when the MEPs spoke out against Labour's introduction of a closed list system for elections to the European Parliament. They were threatened with disciplinary action if they did not consent. European parliamentary rules state that MEPs shall not be bound by any instructions and shall not receive a binding mandate. (*European, Financial Times, Guardian*)

The Radio Authority overturned its ban on Amnesty International (AI) advertisements being broadcast on commercial radio on 11 November. A High Court ruling in July 1995 had deemed AI 'too political' under the Radio Authority Advertising Code for such forms of publicity. (AI)

Attorney General John Morris gave the go-ahead on 17 November for the prosecution of former MI6 agent Richard Tomlinson. Tomlinson is charged with passing the synopsis of a book about the agency to an Australian publisher. He has subsequently threatened to publish the full text on the Internet. John Wadham, Tomlinson's lawyer and director of Liberty, expressed disappointment that this trial, the first under the 1989 Official Secrets Act, should take place under a Labour administration. (*Daily Telegraph, Times, Guardian, Independent,*

On 17 November home secretary Jack Straw continued to fight a case inherited from his predecessor concerning the right of prisoners to be interviewed by journalists. In December last year, Justice Latham ruled that journalists Bob Woffinden and Karen Voisey should have been allowed to continue visiting prisoners **Ian Simms** and **Michael O'Brien** despite refusing to sign agreements not to publish the details of their conversations. Straw is appealing against the decision. (*Guardian*)

Green Anarchist editors **Saxon Burchnall-Wood**, **Noel Molland** and **Stephen Booth** were sentenced to three years' imprisonment by Judge David Selwood in mid-November for 'inciting their readers to carry out attacks on property and acts of violence.' (*Guardian*).

The single 'Smack My Bitch Up' by pop group The Prodigy became a Top 10 hit on 23 November, despite being banned from the daytime playlists of radio stations throughout the UK. The accompanying promotional video can only be seen on MTV in the early hours. (*Music Week*)

USA

The Mirriam-Webster Collegiate Dictionary's definition of a 'nigger' as 'a black person, usually taken to be offensive' met with an objection in October because the reference to the word's negative connotations appear to have been added as an afterthought. Mirriam-Webster say the oldest meaning is put first and the newest last. (*Guardian*)

A district court in Oakland, California ruled on 19 October that the FBI and Oakland Police Department were not immune from prosecution over the alleged car bombing of **Judi Bari** and **Darryl Cherney** in 1990. The civil rights lawsuit against the law enforcement authorities alleges false arrest, imprisonment, illegal search and seizure and conspiracy to violate their First Amendment right to organise for social change. Bari and Cherney are members of environmental pressure group Earth First! (Earth First!)

A presidential commission concerned with national security and finance recommended on 22 October a US$1billion a year cyber-defence programme. In 1994, a UK hacker gained access to Rome Laboratory in New York and used it as a base for attacking US military sites. In another case, a break-in damaged the computer system which handles emergency calls in the USA. (*Financial Times*)

Supermarket retailers Wal-Mart Stores Inc and Winn-Dixie have been named as two organisations that have in the last year demanded to preview printed material before stocking it on their shelves. The March issue of *Cosmopolitan*, carrying a front page trailer on 'His and Her Orgasms', failed to make the shelves at Winn-Dixie while Wal-Mart banned the June-July issue of *Vibe*, a rap music publication, for being too risqué. (*Wall Street Journal*)

In response to the Oklahoma ruling in June 1997 that banned the film *Tin Drum* for being obscene, academics and artists have grouped to form Oklahomans for Freedom of Expression. Meanwhile, the Video Software Dealers Association has brought a suit against Oklahoma City and Oklahoma Police Department for misapplying the statute on child pornography. (*In Sight*)

URUGUAY

On 14 October an appeals court rejected a suit by President Juan Carlos Wasmony, accusing the editors of the weekly *La Republica*, **Carlos** and **Federico Fanaso**, of slander. The paper had implicated Wamosy's company in direct biddings, over-billing and under-contracting. The court stressed that *La Republica* had merely 'acted as a resonance box for an entire opinion movement.' (SWB)

VIETNAM

Doan Viet Hoat has been awarded the 1998 Golden Pen of Freedom by the World Association of Newspapers (WAN) for outstanding contributions to the cause of Press Freedom. Doan was sentenced to one year in prison in 1993 for his role in distributing the *Freedom Forum* newsletter. (WAN)

The Politburo issued instructions on 24 November for the state media to adhere to Communist Party principles and criticised newspapers for revealing state secrets and for inaccurate reporting. (Reuters)

YEMEN

Brothers/members of the public freedom committee in the House of Deputies...

Re: Investigations in respect of the violations of the Yemeni Minister of Information's (instructions) to the press and personal freedom.

In a very dangerous precedent in respect of personal freedom, the Minister of Information confiscated *Ma'in* from the market on 11 November, banning its publication, discharging its workers in an unambiguous attempt to exert pressure on Yemeni journalists and prevent them from practising their right to criticise and express their opinions, which are secured by the Islamic religion, the Constitution and the Press and Publication Law of 1991. Confirmed in Article 3 of the above law is the right of any journalist to get information, comment and publish without calling them to account about what they write or publish.

The Minister of Information stepped beyond the bounds of all laws and prevailing moral tradition in his dealings with *Ma'in* and its editor-in-chief when he:

1 Confiscated the government-owned magazine from the press market
2 Gave orders to monitor all articles published in *Ma'in*
3 Gave order to ban the magazine and discharge the workers
4 Abused the editor-in-chief in a telephone call
5 His ban led to widespread condemnation of *Ma'in* inside and outside Yemen
6 Wasted government money by confiscating the government magazine...
7 Spread fear and concern among those who work in the national media.

Despite our approach to the minister, which gave him an opportunity to cancel his order and apologise to the editor-in-chief, all attempts to solve the problem met with rejection.

Our approach to the House of Deputies is to inform all members about the silent violations of public press freedom... committed by the minister who, at the same time, is in charge of government newspapers and magazines and also a member of the House.

We call on you to confront these violations and investigate the truth. ❏

Abdul-Fatah Al-Hackeemy, editor-in-chief, Ma'in

YEMEN

Police and agents from Political Security seized 4,000 copies of the 19 November issue of the bi-weekly *Al-Ayyam* before it was distributed in the towns of Al-Mukalla, Seyun and Ahahr in response to two stories about recent government arrests of dissidents in Hadramout governorate. The confiscation follows the banning of two other newspapers. *Al-Haqiqah* was closed down after it published an interview on 4 September with exiled opposition leader Abdel Rahman Jaafri. On 11 October, the official bi-weekly *Ma'in*, which carried an editorial titled 'From the Revolution of the Poor to the Poor Revolution' criticising state socio-economic policies in its 30 September edition, was also closed indefinitely. The chief editor **Abdel Fattah Al-Hakimi**, who wrote the editorial, and his staff have reportedly been dismissed. (CPJ)

ZAMBIA

Up to 89 people have so far been arrested in connection with the attempted coup d'état on 28 October and a state of emergency has been introduced. Dean Mung'omba, leader of the opposition party Zambia Democratic Congress, was arrested under the emergency legislation on 31 October and has been severely tortured. Other detainees, including coup leader Captain Steven Lungu, have also been tortured and denied food and water. Senior broadcast journalists, **Kenneth Maduma** and **Wellington Kalwisha**, were forced to retire immediately. (AI, MISA)
On 31 October Radio 1 announcer **Loveday Haachiyumba** was suspended for allegedly speaking approvingly of the attempt by disgruntled army officers to overthrow President Frederick Chiluba. Zambia National Broadcasting Corporation's management refuse to accept Haachiyumba's explanation that, as one of three journalists who were forced at gunpoint to announce the coup, he acted under duress and in fear of his life. The other broadcasters, **Margaret Chigwedere** and **Evelyn Tembo**, have been lauded by Chiluba for their patriotism. (MISA)
Journalist **Goretti Mapulanga** was dismissed on 3 November for carrying out a 'vox pop' on the coup attempt, even though the interviews included government officials and participants in a pro-government march celebrating its failure. Her husband, **Hopkins Mapalunga**, a ZNBC regional manager, was also dismissed the same day without explanation. ZNBC director-general Duncan Mbazima personally delivered the letters, admitting that the decision was 'beyond' him. (MISA)

Recent publication: *Forcible Exile to Suppress Dissent* (AI, November 1997, 49pp)

ZIMBABWE

Powers that allow the state to ban any publication and impose life imprisonment for civil disobedience have been removed from the revised Public Order and Security Bill, currently being reviewed by the Parliamentary Legal Committee to determine its constitutionality. The new bill, however, makes it a criminal offence for any individual or media outlet to utter, publish or distribute news deemed by the state to be 'subversive'. A definition of subversion is not included. (MISA)

Compiled by: Penny Dale, Lucy Hillier (Africa); Andrew Kendle, Nicky Winstanley-Torode, Peter Beveridge (Asia); Simon Martin, Vera Rich (eastern Europe and CIS); Eli Fénes (south and central America); Rupert Clayton, M Siraj Sait (Middle East); Randip Panesar (north America and Pacific); Andrew Blick (UK & western Europe).

Our home is Russia

Moscow was *en fête* for its 850th birthday party. The church domes were refulgent with new gold and, outshining them all, was the Cathedral of Christ the Saviour, razed by Stalin and rebuilt at a cost of US$350 million in time for the celebrations. The streets had been temporarily cleared of vagrants. But they're back, all 350,000 of them, and come winter, they'll be sweeping them up each morning. Russia is changing – but not so fast that those at the bottom feel the benefits

This file was compiled with Dos'e na tsenzuru, Moscow

On the streets of Moscow – Credit: Olga Khabarova

IRENA MARYNIAK

Sub-zero tolerance

In a low-key insert commemorating the eightieth anniversary of the October Revolution, Moscow's *Nezavisimaya gazeta* remarked that the postmodern Bolsheviks in charge of the new Russia are trapped in a cast of mind which splits the community into those who know about the onward march to reform, and the rest whose nature prevents them from knowing anything at all. 'While Russian society is divided into the enlightened who have 'a future' and people who live in darkness,' *Nezavisimaya* wrote, 'Soviet ideology and history will remain our home.'

The hero of Moscow's 850th birthday celebrations that kicked off on 5 September 1997 was Ivan the Fool. An affectionately held folk-tale favourite, Ivan is the village idiot who unwittingly invites abuse, ostracism and often violent punishment, and just occasionally strikes lucky with a pot of gold or a princess. He clubs his mother to death, and will not be parted from her corpse — which is disturbingly analogous somehow to Russia's recent handling of that waxen manikin with its oddly commanding chin displayed still in Red Square to a steady stream of silent visitors. For all Yeltsin's calls to stop looking back and build Russia from scratch, the country seems as spasmodically caught in the grip of its once idolised father figure, Vladimir Ilich Lenin, as Ivan the Fool is obsessively tied to his mother. The ancestral past will not be consigned to memory.

'Enough buffoons here to last 100 years

Cold comfort in Moscow — Credit: Olga Khabarova

and more,' goes the Russian saying. 'Punch the dunce and make him wise.' For the fool is never spared the rod, and only later comes to be affectionately remembered for representing another, less wordly kind of wisdom. It was after the collapse of the August 1991 coup that Yevgeny Yevtushenko proclaimed on the front page of *Literaturnaya gazeta*: 'Today we're a people – and nobody's fool.'

Moscow's mayor, Yuri Luzhkov, nevertheless finds the fool a congenial figure to promote. Dubbed the city's godfather, with presidential ambitions said to be Russia's best-kept secret, he has adopted a paternal dictatorial style of governance while giving the city a glossy new look, an entrepreneurial image and huge profits. His television chain, TV Centre, will soon begin transmissioon throughout Russia, an autobiography is ready to be filmed, 'Mayor' aftershave is said to be selling nicely. And for journalists in the city, criticism of its mayor is professional suicide.

In metro carriages, advertisement cards display edifying adages for the unenlightened: 'a healthy beggar is happier than a sick king'; 'a greedy

person will always be poor'; 'let everyone dig his own patch'. Around the city, mammoth images of St George lancing the dragon, mounted specially for the birthday, still line the sides of multi-storey blocks. And just who, bolder sectors of the press were moved to ask, might the dragon represent?

As the snow descends, Russia's showcase city is expansively spotlit, gaudy, matronly, voluptuously domed. On Tverskaya Ulitsa, the logo of Mercedes Benz burns like a new polestar against the night sky; and for women, full-length fur coats are not an ethically questionable luxury but an obligatory fashion item. The erection of Europe's tallest building – the 600m Russia Tower – in a new development of skyscrapers overlooking the Moscow River, has just got the all clear. Russia's regions may shudder from the shock of economic transition, but in Central Moscow, where 80 per cent of the country's financial resources are held, the emblems of plutocracy prevail.

The birthday blow-out cost about US$60 million; a fleet of cloud-seeding planes was dispatched to ensure that not a drop of rain fell on all the unveilings and gala events. A new 90m statue of Peter the Great stands on the bank of the river; the 85,000-seat Luzhniki soccer stadium was reconstructed just in time to host the birthday jubilee grand finale; the fabled seven Stalinist skyscrapers have been sandblasted. But everything pales before the looming presence of the Cathedral of Christ the Saviour, that 15-storey marble hulk razed by Stalin to become a swimming pool, and now adroitly reconjured to the tune of US$350 million. Its imprint is there on vodka bottles and souvenir plates – a symbol of Muscovy resurrected.

A true celebration 'with no poverty' was how the mayor described his fest. In May, the city's migration services were given carte blanche to deport refugees and illegal residents. Police operations named 'Regime'; 'Law and Order'; 'Signal'; 'Arsenal' were launched to root out crime and terrorism well ahead of time. In the course of 'Operation Regime', 82,810 people were detained for administrative violations. Darker colouring was a sure invitation to harassment. Prostitutes and beggars were driven away by thousands of extra police. Numbers of sniffer dogs were increased tenfold.

Restaurants were required to have potted trees outside. The 'tree police' came round to check. And when, days before the party began, petrol was short, the media speculated that the mayor might want to clear the roads. The clowns, fireworks, concerts and parades with Jean-Michel Jarre, James Brown, St George and Ivan the Fool went off a treat. The metro carried an estimated 10 million people and finally gave out. No one was hurt but a lot of people had to walk to the suburbs. The event was deemed a success. And

COUNTRY FILE: THE HOMELESS

Moscow emerged consolidated and cleansed. 'Our city,' *Argumenty I fakty* gushed, 'our home.'

The home – according to Theodore Zeldin 'one of the great personal and collective works of art that all humans spend their time attempting to raise up and keep from falling down'– is overriding the personalised images by which Russia has traditionally understood itself. No more Mother Russia: holy, beggarly, deaf, impoverished, sick. Poets of the Silver Age like Aleksandr Blok, Andrei Bely or Leonid Andreyev may have perceived some distinction in these adjectives, but it's not what image makers want for the age of capitalism. The prime minister's block in the *Duma* is named 'Our home is Russia'. Ownership, security and aesthetics are flavours of the month; as the new home goes up, failure is anathema.

And all the while, 80 per cent of Russians live below the poverty line. Outside Moscow, the country is caught in the greatest depression of the century, even according to official statistics. In November, on Sakhalin Island, a man nailed his hand to a wall to protests against months of unpaid salaries. Two of his colleagues threatened to set themselves ablaze if they weren't paid. Reports of hunger strikes and suicides are frequent in more remote regions where factories are abandoned, waters contaminated, fields rotting, children underfed. The welfare safety net has snapped: jobs, education and health care have gone hurtling out of orbit. Patience is being stretched to the brink.

But restraints on travel have been lifted and people are freer to seek their fortunes away from home. Russia has absorbed an estimated 2 million refugees from the former republics since the Soviet Union fell. Many have made for Moscow, along with tens of thousands of others: unemployed, out of luck, former prisoners, young hopefuls, disabled veterans.

The spectre of hunger and distress is knocking on the door of Russia's capital and being rudely ousted. But it persists. On the edges of Red Square, a stereotypical *babushka* intones the traditional appeal: 'Alms for the sake of Christ.' She probably has an arrangement with the militia. At some railway stations it is rather worse: people with limbs contorted and splayed, people with no limbs at all, an elderly woman bent at the hips with the upper part of her body parallel to the ground and a stick for support lest she fold up altogether. All beneath saccharine posters of young love bathed in sunlight with a packet of L&M filters against the New York skyline. 'Meet America'.

'They're stewing in their own slurry,' says Vanya, uniformed, rosy, with a baton. He guards one of Moscow's pristine new night shelters on the outskirts of the city. It has room for 30. The number of people on the streets is variously estimated as between 30,000 – the 'official' figure quoted by foreign news services – and the 350,000 claimed by most of the Russian press. Vanya finds the sight of his visitors chilling: the wolf at the door. 'They should work; or go somewhere else.'

Many have. A presidential decree adopted in July enabled city and regional governments to detain vagrants and beggars in social rehabilitation centres for up to a month, and empowered the police forcibly to remove the homeless from Moscow. In the first five months of 1997, well over 16,000 people were deported from the city. More than 200 were sent to unspecified 'treatment centres'. Soup-kitchen volunteers admit to rumours of a camp in Yaroslavl. According to some reports, Luzhkov plans to initiate legislation which would criminalise vagrancy – rather as in Soviet times, when prosecution for begging and other forms of 'social parasitism' could mean imprisonment for up to 10 years.

Living in the capital is virtually off-limits to non-Muscovites. Registration rules are strictly enforced and can serve as pretexts for police extortion, brutality and the destruction of documents. The *propiska* or residence permit is a Soviet-era stamp in the internal passport intended, once, to track people and restrict the flow of the rural population into cities. Everyone had a single place of residence; the *propiska* gave the right to work, education, a marriage licence, medical care, state benefits and so on. It remains in force today, despite the prohibition of arbitrary restrictions on freedom of movement in international and domestic legislation, partly as a result of bureaucratic inertia, but mostly because of its capacity to generate personal revenue: fines and bribes. It also gives legitimacy to the exclusion of 'undesirable' ethnic minorities from schooling, jobs and housing.

Propiskas get lost, sold, stolen or given away in response to threats, for drugs, vodka, or dodgy get-rich-quick schemes. They can be invalidated by debt, imprisonment, war, dysfunctional relationships, disability and insanity. To lose a job, get sick, divorced, pregnant, or orphaned, to sell a home to racketeers can be a call to the streets.

Irrespective of stipulations in the Russian Constitution, the Moscow city government sells permanent *propiskas*. The price is US$55,000. An average monthly salary is US$130. Temporary permits are much cheaper but renewable every 45 days. Fines are levied at the whim of the militia. The first is notionally US$20-55. After that it's US$275 or deportation from the city with all the trimmings: raids, interrogations, threats and beatings.

COUNTRY FILE: THE HOMELESS

Outside the Kursky Station, discreet between a couple of dilapidated buses marked *Médecins sans Frontières*, volunteers from the St Seraphin Brotherhood ladle out *kasha* and bits of meat to an inconspicious group of about 40 NFAs – citizens of No Fixed Abode – or, in Russian, BOMZH. There is talk of an ethnic Korean from Uzbekistan, a translator with English and Chinese, who was beaten to death by OMON troops in the courtyard where he slept. His companion, who was beaten too, and spoke about what he had seen, subsequently disappeared. A teenager, sharp featured and insistent, says he was evicted from a disused basement with his five fellow squatters by militia who beat them, then threatened to gas and kill them. 'They kicked me in the groin; that's sacred isn't it? I never hurt anyone. It's just the way things worked out. I know I have a sinful soul, but you see I help out in Church.' An older man who sleeps at the station says, in a matter of fact sort of way, that the truncheons come out as soon as you try and get into the warm: 'There's a shaft where warm air comes out, that's where it happens.' Since when? 'It's about a year now. Since the jubilee preparations began.'

There are an estimated 4 million homeless people in Russia according to independent research. This winter, in temperatures as low as -30C, they will seek out hot pipes in stairways, basements, attics, landings, dumps and stations. They will display their stumps and sores, hold up boards with extravagant appeals for help, do a bit of loading at train stations, sell bottles, tins, sausage and clothing retrieved from dustbins. They will steal and mug. In out of the way regions such as Kalmykia or Eastern Siberia, some may find themselves confined to camps guarded by local agricultural managers and used as slave labour. In cities, many will pass through 'filtering stations' where they will be held for a while, treated for lice, given a notional identity and then 'sent home'. Thousands will die. An estimated 60 per cent have tuberculosis. Statistics are mostly unavailable, but in the winter of 1992, 150 were found dead in Moscow's Kazan Station alone. In 1994, 3,500 BOMZHs died in St Petersburg. In Russia, to be homeless is to mark time on death row.

Public rejection, hostility or indifference is well rooted. The popular perception remains that beggars are a sham and BOMZHs untouchable. It has been reported that St Petersburg hospitals dump amputees in the streets after operations with plastic bags wrapped around their stumps. In 1995, the Moscow press was blaming lack of legislation enabling police to screen and detain the homeless for the TB epidemic in the city. Until the clean-up operation began, the authorities tended to ignore the problem – unless epidemics or severe frost called for extra funds to gather the bodies.

Viktor was a BOMZH for eight years and now works as a cleaner in the Vastrykovo night shelter, about 20km south of Moscow. He is nervous, and at times on the verge of tears. 'The worst thing is when you're asleep and the *sistema* find you. They can disfigure you in minutes. They've got pistols and knives. They're all about 16. It's like in the military. They cut off part of my ear. It's no good going to the militia. They say it's your own fault. It was your flat. You lost it. It's your problem. You've no papers. You don't exist.'

In the late nineteenth and early twentieth centuries, thinkers like Dostoevsky, Musorgsky or Berdyaev looked to the time-honoured tradition of 'wanderers of the Russian land' for the key to their nation's identity. Holy Fools, as they were known, were familiar figures in towns and villages up to the 1917 Revolution and beyond. They were treated with a mixture of veneration and ruthlessness. Ivan the Terrible credited his victory over the Tatars in 1553 to his personal Holy Fool, and built St Basil's Cathedral – that multi-coloured, tent-roofed, onion-capped edifice in Red Square – in his honour. Thirty-six fools have been canonised. They featured in the work of Pasternak and in the essays of Chernyshevsky. Equally they were prey to verbal abused, physical attack and arrest. They were the dissenters of Tsarist Russia: dispossessed of rationality, position and interest, ascetic, homeless. 'They had real freedom of expression,' says Andrei Ar'ev, editor of *Zvezda*, 'everyone else was afraid to speak out. The homeless have lost their status. No-one listens any more. Without that mystical glow, they're rejects.'

While reviving the Muscovite tradition – big, extravagant, intemperate – mayor Luzhkov has also espoused the more puritan aesthetic of order and cleanliness. The old, quasi-religious role of poverty and the coxcomb has been relegated to the carnival. For, if the work ethic and market forces are to prevail, that is where the Fool belongs.

Besieged by the dislocated, the sick and the malnourished, Moscow is succumbing to what Neil Ascherson has recently called the western 'fear of those who move'. ❑

Irena Maryniak

MIKHAIL GORBACHEV
Look to the people

Russia's politicians have reconstructed themselves behind the same Kremlin walls as their Communist predecessors and are beginning to take on the same dictatorial characteristics

The time has come to gather stones. Nowadays I wouldn't try to impose strict divisions between parties like the social-democrats, the socialists or 'Yabloko'. They are all committed to democracy, social and market economies and good government. Given that we are watching a succession of attempts to foist a minority ideology on the country, what we need more than anything else today is a unifying idea that crosses the nation, and a broad platform for unity.

The President said this year should be a year of consensus, and was given a mandate to implement this. Even if the accusations of vote-rigging were not entirely without foundation, all in all he gained the support of the Russian people.

Where are things going? His activities are aimed solely at saving this regime and his presidency. His government is repeatedly engaged in fire-fighting operations, practising various new forms of shock therapy; now it revises pensions, now, once again, it raids pensioners' purses.

How is this a recipe for consensus? Up at the top there is a struggle for ownership: a fight over the distribution of property, goods, industry. There is a queue for the sweetest slices of the cake: land, oil, gas, metal. These will be the contested areas. That's what the state has focused its energy on. If only they were carrying out this privatisation of public enterprises to balance the budget, to pay teachers, doctors, scientists. But they are not. That budget will be balanced out of the purses of pensioners and apartment owners, and previously state-owned resources distributed in such a way as to guarantee support for the government and to strengthen the regime.

It is not through agreement with the people that the regime is seeking

MIKHAIL GORBACHEV

Mikhail Gorbachev – Credit: Novosti/Rex

to gain support, not through democratic channels, not through dialogue. What sort of dialogue is possible if newspapers, television and all the means of mass information are to be among the most important items to be divided up and distributed? At one of his regular meetings with editors, first deputy prime minister Anatoly Chubais stated: 'It's just a matter of time. The time for free flight is over.'

The time of free flight is over: the mass media must have their bosses. Once again it won't be the people or the nation or society that control the means of mass information; once again people will be unable to find out what's really going on in the country, let alone influence it.

The government I led was accused of cowardice; people said we had promoted the idea of *glasnost* (transparency) but were ourselves afraid of it. Yes, we were cautious, but not out of cowardice. I myself was only afraid of one thing: of burying all our projects, all the fundamental democratic transformations. It is not easy to live as a free man; without democratic institutions and rules, freedom often becomes its opposite.

Even so I am not disillusioned with the people as others are. To complain about one's people, let alone condemn them, shows political and intellectual bankruptcy. The people are the guardians of wisdom, they understand everything. And they get things right much more often than we give them credit for.

We are living through a difficult and dramatic period, but what is happening to us is necessary. The main thing is that we are now open to relations with the rest of the world. And the whole world is faced with problems. No frontiers, whether they be state or national, can isolate us.

Take, for example, the crisis in the global economy the world is about to face. As for the spiritual and intellectual spheres, they are already falling apart. Humanity is menaced by a general crisis. No single ideology is capable of resolving our present problems. Neither socialism nor liberalism nor anything else can solve the problems on which the survival of humanity depends.

Our civilization has been based on the principle that man is the lord of nature. Man has dominated nature, transforming it and at the same time attempting to transform himself. As a result, our technological civilization has given us a world in which one third of the inhabitants live in comfort and two-thirds suffer social, educational and cultural deprivation. In short, two-thirds of humanity live in poverty. This is the civilization that has brought us to the brink of a global crisis. And, most visibly of all, to an ecological crisis.

Because we confront ecological problems on a day-to-day basis – air, water, health – people are at last beginning to deal with these problems as best they can. Everyone can see that forests are retreating, rivers becoming polluted. The reasons are obvious – people rule the earth but they are not looking after it, only making demands: give me cotton, give me wood, give, give, give. We have to manage things differently.

You will remember that at the start of *glasnost*, ecology sprang to the top of the agenda immediately. Unfortunately it has taken terrible tragedies to spark off ecological initiatives.

We closed down 1,300 enterprises in order to protect the countryside and defend the environment. On the basis of their own experience, people understood how far we had gone in our conflict with nature; understood that nature had already begun to fight back.

MIKHAIL GORBACHEV

Nowadays I understand all this better. I am involved in the creation of a planetary non-governmental organisation, 'International Green Cross'. We are moving cautiously, increasing the number of participants systematically step by step. Japan, Russia, Germany, the USA, France, the Netherlands, Sweden and Korea are among the 12 countries already involved.

In the autumn of 1992, 1,500 scientists gathered in Washington, among them 101 Nobel prize-winners. They established that, given the present trend of development, especially in the developed industrial countries, in about 30-40 years time irreversible changes will have taken place in the biosphere, destroying the conditions that make life possible. We must consciously and voluntarily adopt another quality and way of life, other modes of consumption.

We once tried to commit the Central Committee of the Communist Party of the Soviet Union to a transnational attitude to ecology. Today, the memory of that amazes me, makes me smile. It is typical of the *nomenklatura's* way of thinking, the Soviet grasp of the world. The *nomenklatura* can do anything they want. A national ecological policy? Fine! Turn rivers back? Fine! We were seriously contemplating turning back rivers! And I played an active role in that saga!

It is unimportant that the Soviet Union has actually fallen apart. The main thing is that the collapse has already occurred and that one cannot glue it together again 'as it used to be'. But the responsibility for the collapse remains. Our general blindness, including my own, played a large part. We were all under the influence of utopian illusions. But utopia is highly dangerous. One such utopian illusion was the legend of the internationalism of the Soviet people. In 1982, at the Sixtieth Anniversary of the Union, Andropov spoke of the total conquest of national differences. That is how it seemed at the time. And I believed it, sincerely. People rarely doubt utopias, that is their hidden peril. Who could have believed in the collapse of the Union? Right up to 1991, neither we nor anyone else believed the Soviet Union would fall apart.

Perhaps if I had insisted more forcefully upon a new treaty of union I might have convinced people and clarified the situation. But nothing more. Arrests of conspirators, military attacks on separatists – these are false solutions. We acted constitutionally, offered a new form for a new Union. But the intelligentsia remained silent and gave no support; sat quietly as if paralysed or hypnotised. No doubt it was their disillusionment that lay at the heart of their indifference to the fate of the Union.

The intelligentsia was disillusioned with Gorbachev and set its hopes on Yeltsin simply because he was my opponent. Yeltsin used the intelligentsia and, because the intelligentsia stuck with him, the outcome was a foregone conclusion – collapse and fall.

That is our shared drama. The people justifiably felt that Gorbachev had one weakness – faith in the intelligentsia. I haven't changed my mind: I still pride myself on that weakness. Without its thinkers any society is doomed. They are the yeast of a nation and without yeast you obviously can't bake bread. This makes the utopian illusions and deceptions of the intelligentsia all the more dangerous. They end up in disintegration.

But I am not pessimistic. All over the world the last dictators are leaving the political scene; attempts to impose dictatorship are ridiculous. Only one thing can protect us from such attempts – freedom of speech. That's why any defence of freedom of speech is so important. Without it we could find ourselves once again caught in the trap. ❑

Interviewed by the editors of Dos'e na Tsenzuru. *Translated by* **Michael Molnar.**

The acclaimed bestseller . . .

"*The best informed account of Gorbachev's political views and strategies between 1985 and 1989*"
Orlando Figes, TLS

"*Richly researched, easily readable . . . It should be studied at once in every diplomatic service worthy of the name . . .*"
Michael Foot, Evening Standard

. . . available in all good bookshops, £10.99

OXFORD

SVETLANA ALEKSIYEVICH

A prayer for Chernobyl

On 26 April 1986, at 01.23 hours and 58 seconds, a series of explosions destroyed the nuclear reactor and building of the fourth power generator unit of Chernobyl atomic power station.

During World War II, the German fascists destroyed 619 Belarusian villages along with their inhabitants. As a result of the Chernobyl disaster, the country lost 485 villages and hamlets. During the war, one in four Belarusians lost their lives. After Chernobyl, one in five Belarusians, 2.1 million people, are living in contaminated territory. Seven hundred thousand of these are children.

Ongoing low level radiation results in a year on year increase in the number of Belarusans suffering from cancers, mental debility, neuro-psychological disorders, and genetic mutations.

'Chernobyl' volume of the Belarusian Encyclopaedia, *Minsk, 1996.*

These extracts are not about the Chernobyl disaster, but about a world of Chernobyl of which we know almost nothing. They are history that never got written.

People I was interviewing were having to articulate everything, to put it into words, for the first time ever. Something had happened for which neither our eyes, nor our ears, nor our language are adapted. We are made for seeing, hearing, touching. In the world of Chernobyl none of that is possible. The feelings are quite new.

Two cataclysms coincided: one social as a vast socialist continent disappeared beneath the waves; the other cosmic – Chernobyl.

People want to forget Chernobyl. We had hoped to beat it, but recognising the futility of our efforts, we fell silent. It is difficult for us to

COUNTRY FILE: A PRAYER FOR CHERNOBYL

defend ourselves against something which we, and mankind, cannot get a grip on. Chernobyl propelled us out of one historical period into another. Now all of us have to face a new reality.

MONOLOGUE ON A LUNAR LANDSCAPE

Within days of the accident, books on radiation, books about Hiroshima and Nagasaki, even books about X-rays vanished from the libraries. The word on the street was that Authority had ordered them withdrawn to avoid panic. We had no medical advice, no information. Those who could got hold of potassium iodide pills (not on sale in the pharmacies of our town; you needed very special connections to obtain them). Some people swallowed a whole handful of the pills and chased them down with a tumblerful of spirit. The ambulance men had to pump out their stomachs.

People discovered a test, and everybody started looking out for it. While there were sparrows and pigeons in a town or village, it was habitable for human beings too. You would be travelling along in a taxi, and the driver would wonder why birds were flying into the windscreen and getting killed, as if they were blind or had taken leave of their senses. As if they wanted to commit suicide.

I began asking myself why no one was talking about Chernobyl. Why were our writers writing so little: they went on writing about the war, and the labour camps, yet seemed to have nothing to say about Chernobyl. If we had overcome the threat of Chernobyl, if we had even been able to understand it, more would be being said and written about it. We don't know how to start making sense of

Inside Chernobyl – Credit Fotobank/Rex

this horror because it is impossible to measure it against our experience as human beings, or even against our human timescale.
Evgenii Alexandrovich Brovkin, lecturer at Gomel State University.

A HUMAN VOICE, SOLO

I didn't see the explosion itself, just the flame. Everything seemed to be lit up. The whole sky. A tall flame. Soot. Terrible heat. Still no sign of my husband: I waited and waited. The soot came from burning bitumen. The power station roof was coated with bitumen. He said it was like walking over tar. They beat the flames. They kicked off burning radioactive graphite with their feet.

They set off without protective tarpaulin suits, just as they were, in their shirt sleeves. Nobody warned them. They were called out to attend an ordinary fire.

Seven o'clock. That was when I was told he was in hospital. I ran all the way, but the police had already cordoned it off and would not let anyone through. Only ambulances. After that it was Moscow, the Acute Radiation Sickness Clinic, for 14 days. It takes 14 days for a man to die of radiation sickness.

I was with him through life and I was with him when they laid him in his coffin, although what sticks in my memory is not the coffin but a big polythene bag. That bag. They asked me in the mortuary, 'Do you want to see what we are going to dress him in?' I did. They put him in dress uniform, with the peaked cap on his chest. They did not put shoes on his feet, though. They couldn't find any big enough, because his feet had swollen so. They had to cut the uniform too, to get him into it. The body wasn't intact any more, it was just one big wound. In the hospital, those last days, if I lifted his hand the bone in his arm would be hanging there; his body had come away from it. Bits of his lungs and his liver came out of his mouth. He was choking on his own innards ... I would wrap my hand in a bandage and push it into his mouth to fish all that stuff out of him. I can't describe it. It can't be written about. It was all so dear to me. I loved it so much. They just couldn't find any shoes big enough to fit his feet. They laid him in his coffin barefoot.

Everybody came for the funeral, his parents, mine. They bought black headscarves in Moscow. We were seen by a special commission who told everybody exactly the same thing: they could not give us back the bodies of our husbands and sons. They were too radioactive, and they would be buried in a special way in a Moscow cemetery, in soldered zinc coffins, under slabs of concrete. And there was this document we had to sign. If anybody started getting angry and wanting to take the coffin back home, they got told these were heroes and didn't just belong to their families any longer. They were state people; so they belonged to the state.

We sat in the funeral bus with the coffin, us relatives and some military people, a colonel with a walkie-talkie radio. They called him over the radio: 'Await further orders! You will have to wait!' For two or three hours they kept us driving round the Moscow ring road, then we came back into Moscow. Over the radio we heard: 'Permission to enter the cemetery not granted. The cemetery is being attacked by foreign journalists. Continue waiting.' Us relatives said nothing, mother in her black scarf ... I could feel myself losing control. I became hysterical. Why do you have to hide my husband? What is he? A murderer? A common criminal? Do you know who we are burying?' Mother said, 'Take it easy, little one.' She stroked my hair. The colonel said into his radio, 'Request permission to proceed to the cemetery forthwith. The wife is hysterical'. At the cemetery we were ringed by soldiers. We walked on under guard. And they carried the coffin. They didn't allow anybody else to come near. We were completely alone. They filled the grave in straightaway. 'Quickly, quickly!' the officer ordered them. We were not even allowed to hug the coffin; and then we were put straight back on to the buses. Everything was really underhand.

All the power station people live near me: the watch, we call them. They have worked at the atomic power station all their lives, and to this day they go there as watchmen. Many of them have terrible illnesses, disabilities, but they won't abandon the power station. Who needs them, where are they needed today? A lot of them die, instantly. They will just be sitting on a bench, and then they fall over. Or they leave home, they are waiting for the bus, and then they fall down dead. They are dying off, but nobody has asked them properly to tell their story, what we lived through. People do not want to hear about death and things that are frightening.

Ludmilla Ignatenko, wife of Vasily Ignatenko, a fatally injured fireman.

THE SOLDIERS' CHOIR

Our regiment was scrambled. Only in Moscow, at the Belorussian

Station, did they announce where we were being sent. One lad, from Leningrad I think, protested. They threatened him with a court martial. The commanding officer said in front of the whole parade, 'You will go either to prison or before a firing squad'. I felt differently. Just the opposite. I wanted to do something heroic.

Before we got there I felt fear, just for a short while. But once we got there the fear vanished. I really wanted to take a look at this terrifying thing. Orders. Work. A job to be done. I wanted to look down at the reactor from a helicopter, to see what had really happened, what it looked like, but that was forbidden. They wrote down 21 roentgens on the record card as my radiation exposure, but I don't believe that's right. The way they worked it out was very simple: you flew to Chernobyl, the regional capital (which by the way is just a little provincial town, nothing like as grand as I'd imagined it). There was a dosimeter operator stationed there, 10-15 kilometers away from the power station, to measure background radiation. His measurements were then multiplied by the number of hours you had notched up in a day. I took off from there in a helicopter and took a look at the reactor: I flew there and back, and made passes in both directions; today the radiation might be 80 roentgens there, tomorrow 120. I circled the reactor for two hours at night. They were filming with infra-red sensitive film. Lumps of graphite which had been thrown out showed up on the film. You couldn't see them by day.

Before we were sent back home we were all called in by the KGB and strongly advised never to tell anyone what we had seen. When I came back from Afghanistan, I knew I was going to live, but in Chernobyl it was all different. It was after you had come home that you got killed.'

'It was all 10 years ago. By now I could be feeling none of it had ever happened if I had not fallen sick. I could have forgotten all about it.

Serve the motherland! Service to the motherland is your sacred duty! They issued underwear, foot wrappings, boots, epaulettes, a cheesecutter cap, trousers, a field shirt, belt, kitbag; and sent you on your way. They gave us a tipper truck. I was transporting concrete. Nothing to worry about. Everything was going to be just fine. Young lads, unmarried. They carried their respirators around with them. No, I remember one man: a middle-aged driver. He always wore his mask; but we didn't. The traffic police were out there with no masks. We at least were inside the cabin of the truck, but they were standing in the fallout for eight hours a day. Everybody was well paid: three times over the odds plus a daily allowance. Everybody was drinking. Vodka really helps. Reduces stress. You would see a drunk policeman fining a drunk driver.

Do not write stuff about marvels of Soviet heroism. There were some. Real marvels. But mostly there was incompetence and irresponsibility; the marvels took second place. They flung us in there the way they threw sand on the reactor. Every day they posted a new 'battle bulletin': 'going about their work manfully and selflessly'; 'we shall endure and we shall win!'

For my gallantry I got a certificate and 1,000 roubles.

We are loners now. Outsiders. We even get buried separately, not like normal human beings. Like aliens from outer space. I would have done better to die in Afghanistan. I can't pretend I don't think that kind of stuff. Death there was straightforward. You knew where you were. .

THE FOLK CHOIR

I am a schoolteacher of Russian language and literature. It must have been early in June, because the examinations were taking place. The headmaster suddenly called us together and announced, 'You are all to bring spades to school with you tomorrow.' We discovered we were to remove the top layer of contaminated soil from around the school buildings, and then the army would come and cover everything with asphalt. Somebody asked, 'What kind of protective clothing are we going to be issued with? Is someone bringing special suits and respirators?' The answer was no. 'You will take your spade and you will dig.' Only two young teachers refused, the rest went out and dug. We felt bad, but at the same time we felt we had done our duty. Very Russian. Holding the line, defending the motherland. Had I ever taught anything other than that to my schoolchildren? Go out, throw yourself into the thick of the fray. Defend, sacrifice! The literature I taught was never about life, it was about war. Only those two young teachers refused, but they belong to a new generation. They are different people.

All the livestock from the evacuated villages were herded along to us in the regional capital, to special reception points. Crazed cows, sheep, piglets running through the streets. Anyone who wanted could catch a few. Trucks took the carcases from the slaughterhouses to Kalinovichi railway station and from there they were sent to Moscow. Moscow refused them. The wagons were like charnel houses by this time, and they came straight back to us, whole echelons of them. The carcases were buried here. The stench of rotting meat plagued us at night. 'Is this what atomic war would smell like?' I wondered. The war that I remembered smelt of smoke. The first few days they evacuated our children at night-time so fewer people would see what was going on. They wanted to keep the disaster out of sight, but people found out all the same. They brought out churns of milk and buns they had baked to the road, to our buses. The way people did in the war. What else can you liken it to?

There were suddenly programmes on television. One report showed a woman who had milked her cow pouring the milk into a bottle. The reporter came over with a military dosimeter and passed it over the bottle. The commentary was to the effect that as you could see everything was completely normal, and that this was only ten kilometers away from the atomic reactor. They showed the River Pripyat, with people swimming in it or sunbathing. In the distance you could see the reactor with smoke billowing above it. The commentator said voices in the West were trying to sow panic, spreading what they knew perfectly well to be lies about the accident. Then we again saw the dosimeter monitoring a plate of fish soup, a bar of chocolate, doughnuts in an open-air kiosk. It was all a trick. The dosimeters the army had at that time were never designed for checking produce. They only measured background radiation.

The unbelievable amount of sheer lying with which Chernobyl is associated in our minds can only be compared with what went on during the war.

In factories in the villages workers from the Communist Party's regional committees made speeches, travelling around, meeting the people. And not one of them was capable of giving a sensible answer to such questions as: what is deactivation? how should we protect children? what statistical information is there on the rate at which radionuclides are passing into the food chains? Alpha, beta, gamma particles; radiobiology; ionising radiation; radioactive isotopes: all these things were way above their heads. They gave lectures on the heroism of Soviet people; exemplary instances of military courage; the mischief-making of western intelligence services. When I tried to voice doubts about this approach at a Party meeting, I was told I would have my Party card confiscated.

COUNTRY FILE: A PRAYER FOR CHERNOBYL

THE CHILDREN'S CHOIR

'I was in hospital. It hurt so much. I said, 'Mummy, please, it's too sore. Can you kill me?'

'We were loaded into a convoy. The little ones were shrieking and dirtying themselves. There was one adult to twenty children. All the children were crying, 'Mummy! Where's my mummy? I want to go home.' I was ten. Girls my age helped to calm the little ones down. Women came to meet us on the platforms and made the sign of the Cross over the train. They brought home-baked cakes, and milk, and warm potatoes.

We were transported to Leningrad province. There, however, when we were approaching stations people would make the sign of the Cross over themselves and keep their distance from us. They were scared of our train; at every station we came to they hosed it down for ages. When we jumped out of the carriage at one stop and ran to the station buffet they would not let anyone else in. 'There are Chernobyl children in there eating ice cream,' they said. The buffet lady was saying to someone over the phone, 'When they leave we'll wash the floor with bleach and scald the glasses.' We heard.

We were met by doctors. They were wearing gas masks and rubber gloves. They took our clothes and all our belongings away, even envelopes, and pens and pencils. They put them in cellophane bags and

Chernobyl's legacy – Credit: Sutton-Hibbert/Rex

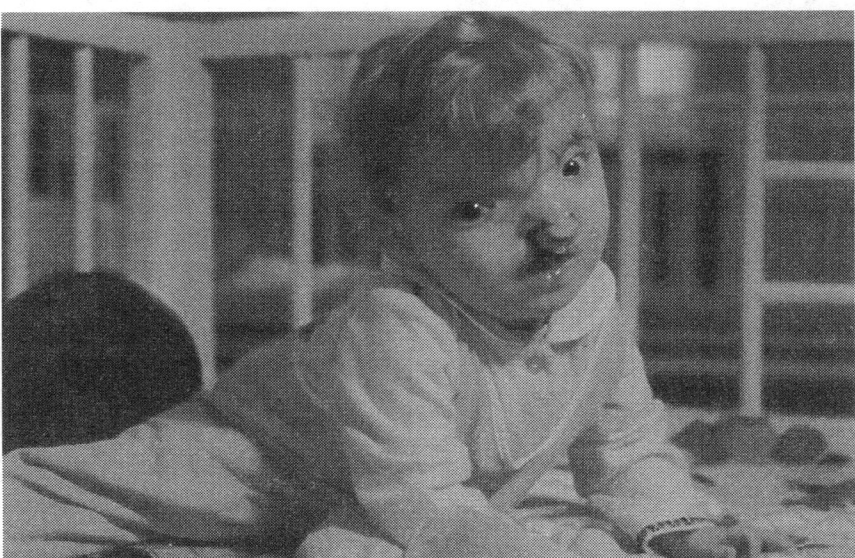

buried them in the woods.

We were so frightened. For a long time after that we were waiting to start dying.'

'I was little. Six. No, eight, I think. Yes, eight. I've just counted it up.

I remember there was so much to be afraid of. I was afraid of running barefoot on grass. My mother frightened me by saying I would die if I did. I was afraid of everything – swimming, diving, picking berries in the woods, picking up a beetle. After all the beetle crawled over the ground and that was poisonous. Ants, butterflies, bumble-bees, they were all poisonous. The garden was all white and glassy.'

'A year later we were all evacuated and they buried our village. My dad is a driver. He drove there and told me. First they dug out a big pit five meters deep. Then the firemen would come along and wash a house from the ridge of its roof to its foundations in order not to spread radioactive dust. The windows, the roof, the door: they washed the lot. Then a crane would pull the house up from where it stood and put it in the pit. There would be dolls and books and jam jars falling everywhere. The digger would fill the pit in and then everything was covered with sand and clay and rolled down hard. In place of a village you had a flat field. They sowed our one with spring wheat. Our house is under there; and our school and village hall; and my herbarium and two stamp albums. I really hoped I could go back to get them. And I had a bicycle.'

'I am twelve and I am disabled. The postman brings two pensions to our house: one for me and and one for my granddad. When the girls in my class found out I had leukaemia they were afraid to sit next to me or touch me.'

'The teacher said, 'Draw radiation'. I drew yellow rain falling. And a red river.' ❑

Svetlana Alexiyevich's *documentary books on World War II (*War's Unwomanly Face*), the Soviet conflict in Afghanistan (*Boys in Zinc*) and the turmoil of perestroika (*Bewitched by Death*) have gained her world renown as an uncompromising truth-teller. She bases her work on eyewitness accounts of historical events and their repercussions on the lives of ordinary people. Svetlana Alexiyevich lives in Minsk, Belarus.*

A prayer for Chernobyl *was published by Ostojie, Moscow. It is not available in Belarus. This selection by* **Elena Obnokina** *of* Dos'e na Tsenzuru *translated by* **Arch Tait**.

Dos´e is one of the few publications in Russia currently able to speak openly about the fact that freedom of speech is absent in Russia.

Ekaterina Degot
Kommersant Daily

Dos´e na tsenzuru

Index on Censorship in association with the Glasnost Defence Foundation publish *Dos´e na tsenzuru*, the new Russian-language magazine concerned with human rights and freedom of speech. Each quarterly issue includes articles and reports by writers and journalists from the region, as well as articles translated from *Index*.

The current issue of *Dos´e* features:

*an interview with Mikhail Gorbachev – on the failures of *glasnost* and the new order in Russia.

*a report by Alexei Simonov on the threat to media freedom posed by litigation over 'dignity and honour'

*the hostage diary of Olga Bagautdinova, a journalist kidnapped in Chechnya.

*articles from *Index* and an expanded Index Index

Dos´e na tsenzuru is essential reading for anyone concerned with media and democracy in Russia and its neighbours.

To subscribe
A one year (4 issues) subscription costs £22/$35.

Index accepts payment via cheque (in pounds sterling or US$, payable to Index), by credit card (Visa, Mastercard or Am Ex), by bank transfer (account number 0635788 at Lloyd's Bank, Hanover Square Branch, 10 Hanover Square, London W1R 0BT) or by National Giro through the post office (account number 574-5357 Britain).

 33 Islington High Street, London N1 9LH
Tel: (44) 171-278-2313   Fax: (44) 171-278-1878
e-mail: indexoncenso@gn.apc.org

A8D01

OLGA BAGAUTDINOVA

Diary of a hostage

Alexander Utrobin, photo journalist for *Chelyabinsk Worker* and *Satkin Worker*, and Olga Bagautdinova, a reporter with *Satkin Metallurgist*, were taken hostage in Chechnya in mid-March 1997 and held for 53 days. The excerpts below are from Olga Bagautdinova's hostage diary with her notes added after their release.

It was the devil's day, that Sunday 16 March. We had been a week in Grozny, and we didn't move anywhere without protection. Salman Raduyev, the Chechen rebel leader, had personally chosen our bodyguards. We could move freely around the town, and drive out to the villages. 'Raduyev's bandits' turned out to be perfectly normal boys: one could sit in a café with them and in the evening, when our work was over, wander round the ruins of Grozny. Some of them were even rather good guides. As the days passed, the edge of our vigilance wore off. Why should it have been otherwise when we were surrounded by sympathetic people who wished us well and took care of our every need...?

Utrobin and I were wandering slowly over a bridge one day, when we heard the sound of sporadic shooting below. Our professional reflex outweighed our instinct for self-preservation, and we rushed to the rails. 'Take cover! Are you tired of living?' a voice shouted at us. A wedding procession was making its way under the bridge, and every guest considered it his duty to fire his automatic weapon into the air. The chance of being hit by a stray bullet was high.

The concerned voice produced an MVD (Ministry of the Interior) document and said his name was Ruslan. His ID confirmed he was a member of the 'organs' and, since he said he had helped journalists in the past, and since every day in Grozny began with the search for transport, we took up his offer to be our guide more out of necessity than anything else.

Up to the last, he was polite and considerate. He showed us the places where there had been fighting, took us by car to the legendary GUOSH – High Command of the United Staff. Utrobin took pictures, I dug around in the rubble hoping to find something interesting. Then we drove to the wreck of the oil institute. We said farewell to our new acquaintance, only to meet him again in completely different circumstances. Five weeks later, he turned up with a smile and asked how we were!

The kidnappers caught up with us in a Volga when we were strolling back along the deserted highroad. Their car braked and two men got out and moved on us. They looked like twins, big and strong, identically dressed in camouflage fatigues and with identical weapons. When they showed their MVD Special Assignment Forces ID (which, as I found out later, were genuine), we didn't have a shadow of doubt: they lookd exactly like the Speznatz. One of them, Usman, could have been taken for a model for a poster proclaiming, 'I am in service for the free Empire!', or 'Guarding the state of law'. He had an open face, bright eyes, a neat 'military' haircut and was all spruce and self-confident.

To be brief, the SAF men asked for our documents and, with good reason, asked why we were alone. (MVD minister Makhashev had recently published an order, forbidding journalists to work without protection.) We explained that we had let our bodyguard go only half an hour ago. Usman took our accreditations and said that we had to go to the MVD. I got into the car with a feeling that we had got caught up in an unpleasant story.

There were two more people in the car and so they made me sit on Utrobin's knee. We were squeezed between our guards. When the 'Volga' sped past the promised building of the MVD, my palms became wet with sweat. When there were clear signs that we were on the outskirts of the city my heart started beating crazily. And when the driver turned off first onto an earth road, and then right into the forest, I became alarmed.

The car finally stopped among some trees, a sort of orchard. Usman announced, 'Here's the story, you've been taken hostage by us...'

We were taken out one by one to be searched, they threw out the contents of my bag on the bonnet of the car, and took all the documents and a clasp-knife. They didn't do a personal search on me, although they did on Utrobin, they didn't search my pockets and didn't touch me. (In Chechnya searching women is not accepted; they acted the same at the border post and at Raduyev's headquarters.)

When, it got dark, they made us put on camouflage fatigues over our clothes: jackets, trousers and caps. They ordered us to pull our caps down over our faces, and me to take off my glasses... The car finally stopped and we we were made to run up a staircase in the pitch dark The flat they pushed us into had a massive, iron doorway and a tiny square window.

We spent the first 18 days of incarceration behind this door...

No-one had explained the reason for our being taken hostage; in the forest, while we were waiting, we had tried to talk sense to the hostage takers; tried to persuade them they had taken the wrong people: we represented small provincial newspapers, not large agencies. Now I thought they would just want to get shot of us as fast as possible....

At night they handcuffed us. A young man came to us, wearing black jeans, a black shirt and a white mask, and said: 'Please forgive me, for God's sake. This isn't my idea. I tried to convince them that you didn't need to be handcuffed, but they insisted. I'm sorry.'

I was bewildered by his courtesy: but the cold of the metal on the wrists was real enough. However, when the man in the mask had gone away, I discovered that I could easily get my hands out of the manacles and I finally went to sleep unencumbered. In the morning I had to shackle myself again, but then we started shouting for our guard to free us.

A little later, the 'man in the mask', whom we nicknamed 'the Intellectual', admitted that he'd done this as a gesture of solidarity.

We spent the second night of captivity in handcuffs put on for real. It was painful and our hands went numb. After five in the morning Hasan came, and secretly freed us. He sighed and shook his head when he touched the bright-red scars on my wrists...

On the third day I began to move fairly freely around the flat, to go out to the kitchen where at least there was daylight; our window was covered in masking tape as well as being blocked by a cupboard. Despite being forbidden, I occasionally crept up to the balcony door. In the guards' room we saw a whole arsenal: grenade launchers, flame throwers, automatic weapons...

COUNTRY FILE: HOSTAGES

Given that we were journalists, one of the worst things was that we had no news. It made us appreciate how much we relied on the media without even giving it a thought.

A couple of days after our capture, our guards told us that the central TV channels often mentioned us. We knew they were bluffing, trying to raise our morale: don't worry, they're looking for you, everything's OK. For them, media interest was important: the amount of a ransom is directly related to public concern.

We reckoned we could ask our captors for at least a radio (there was no question of a television; not many people in postwar Chechnya had such a thing). To our surprise and joy, they brought us an old, battered Chinese cassette radio. Reception was restricted, and we mostly listened to 'Mayak' and 'Radio Russia'.

We were in for a shock: our colleagues in the Moscow radio-stations had either not heard anything about us or were not in the least upset by our disappearance. We clutched hungrily at news from Russia, especially the fate of Nikolai Zagnoyko, Yuri Arkhipov, Nikolai Mamulashvili and Lev Zeltser, who had been abducted two weeks earlier. We began to wonder exactly what the meaning of 'journalistic solidarity' meant.

On 2 April, we were stunned by the news on Molodyozhny Radio: The presenter said we had been abducted but, without any questioning or comment, simply repeated the words of minister Makhashev: 'I have absolutely no knowledge of any Chelyabinsk journalists, they didn't register at the ministry of the interior and didn't get accreditation. They've probably done a deal with the bandits to share the ransom.'

It was a monstrous lie: we'd met him on the first day of our arrival in Grozny and shaken hands with him. I was bitter and bewildered that a journalist could so glibly repeat words that impugned the honour of colleagues who were in captivity. Radio Russia simply stated the fact of our abduction.

Occasionally we heard our names mentioned on the radio; we knew we were being searched for and that people were thinking of us in Chelyabinsk and Moscow. We now know that news was also coming through on TV, mostly on RTR and NTV (Independent TV channels). ORT, the official state channel, was silent on our case, mentioning only their four Moscow colleagues. The contempt and 'capital snobbery' of the official channel bewildered people: 'Aren't you the same as them, carrying out your duty?'

The group reacted swiftly to the news by moving us to another flat where the conditions were terrible. They didn't take back the radio but carefully delivered it to the new address. It wasn't long before we were once again reduced to despair by a report stating that someone unknown with a Caucasus accent had 'phoned the chief executive in our city, and demanded US$2 million'! We knew no-one would ever pay that for our release. The ransom was later reduced to US$600,000; even that, we knew, was just as far out of reach for our papers...

By the end of April, we had given up hope of ransom or rescue and Utrobin started to work out an escape plan.

The only way to freedom was from the big window in our room. Our guards were convinced it was securely nailed, but Utrobin discovered a lower frame that could be opened.

At night we tore a big, strong sheet into two. We intended to lower ourselves from the balcony on this makeshift rope. If we got down successfully Utrobin was going to run down the road, and I was going to hide in one of the neighbouring doorways.

It all seemed so simple but as I imagined the precarious descent, I panicked... Utrobin decided to escape on his own.

I decided our best hope lay with the Speznatz 'twins': they were over-confident, slack, smoked marijuana. Hasan and 'the Intellectual', who had been on duty the evening before, had come festooned with automatic weapons, daggers and grenades, as though they were specifically prepared for an attempt to storm the place. The other guards – Emil, Hizir and Timur – came on guard with their girlfriends who guarded us far more zealously than the bandits themselves. I had no doubt that the escape should be made during Usman and Movladi's shift.

It was five in the morning of 6 May when Utrobin silently removed the fabric which substituted for a shutter, opened the frame and jumped like a cat onto the balcony... He got caught in the damned vine, but reached the ground successfully.

I hunched in my bed and waited... Events began to unfold before nine in the morning. Someone banged on the metal door, and the crashing continued for about five minutes. I rushed round the room, but then decided to conduct myself naturally and went out looking sleepy into the hall and said: Can't you hear, someone's knocking at the door!' Usman, looking desperate, was already standing there. He ordered me with a gesture to go back and hide.

Then it happened! The crashing became thunderous: the Special Assignment Forces were storming the flat from both directions! Crashing, noises of boots, breaking glass... I grasped that the Special Assignment Forces were already in the flat and wondered whether they were going to open fire or not? Should I lie on the floor as in the films, or not?

Finally there was a gap in the door, and first there was the barrel of a machine gun thrust through, then the flat suddenly was filled as if by locusts, with people in camouflage fatigues. There were dozens of them. From the neighbouring room shouts were heard and the noise of a struggle.

'Where are the weapons?' One of the rescuers came bounding up.

'On the left behind the door in the cupboard on the wall! Grenade launchers and flame-throwers!'

Usman and Movladi were already standing there in handcuffs.

'Who are you?' The rescuers finally remembered I was standing there.

'I am a journalist.'

'Then get ready.'

'And who are you?'

'We're from the MVD and National Security Services.'

I went out of the house down a living corridor of snipers. (Before this I had only seen such a thing in films about the Italian Mafia.)

I met up with Utrobin later in the day at the National Security Service headquarters...

In the first hours of our freedom there began a series of incredibly numerous interrogations. The Prosecutor's investigators gave way to Militia operatives, and them to the Security Service representatives. I couldn't work out who was who, I wasn't up to that, except I spotted the KGB man immediately although he didn't introduce himself: he wasn't interested in the abduction but my activity at home.

Utrobin immediately entered into trusting contact with the investigation. For him it was simple: collaborate with the authorities in the discovery and punishment of our abductors and anyone even remotely involved.

But I couldn't forget Maskhadov's order: hostage-takers have the choice between capital punishment or life imprisonment – with the odds heavily stacked in favour of the former.

I was far from idealising the bandits, and I didn't observe in myself any of the hostage syndrome where the victim becomes one with the terrorists. But I had got to know the people with whom I spent two months at close quarters.

Hasan, the same age as me. He had to look after a wife and two hungry tiny children (the youngest one his wife gave birth to in Grozny, under the bursting bombs of the August storming of the city). He had no work, no other source of means...

Islam. He said that he wouldn't even touch 'that dirty money', that is the ransom. He himself had to pay the Federals a ransom, when they offered him the headless body of his brother for 10 million.

The young Surkho. He had not been involved with fighting yet, and once admitted that he had two wishes in life: the first that the whole people would be happy in a free Chechnya; and the second to die for this cause in a Holy War.

Usman, captured by the Speznatz. Before the war he had graduated from a technical college. He was studying to be an economist. Instead of books he took up an automatic weapon. However Usman pronounced the aphoristic phrase: 'It's easy to take up arms, but it's difficult to lay them down.'

Maskhadov once remarked that the laws of the Shariat can only be applied in a settled, well-fed, successful country. When many people have nothing to buy bread with, you can't cut off the hand of a hungry little thief. When the war mutilated souls, swept aside moral norms and devalued life, you can't punish with murder.

I didn't take the course of 'active giving of evidence'.

Our homecoming – or rather our meeting with our own Special Services – happened while we were still in Grozny, at Severny airport. General Chernyshev and the executive representative of the President of Russia in Chechnya, I Rybkin, met us almost lovingly: they fed us, gave us a change of clothes, heated up the water for a bath and let us sleep. The MVD people were equally cordial and invited us to their place. They had a whole collection of drinks, including quite a good cognac – produced in the local factory which federal troops had gone through when they were storming the city – and dry wine in plastic bottles. Utrobin and I were invited separately: him first and me next day.

This 'informal contact' was used to soften us up. In their version of events, Utrobin did not escape but was released or given the opportunity to escape. Everything was arranged by them; the storming of the flat was entirely due to the men of the MVD.

At GUOP (State Directorate for Public Protection) in Moscow, they continued to din into our heads that we were freed not thanks to the heroic action of Alexander Utrobin, but as a result of a successfully planned operation. Clearly, they felt compelled to justify the vast resources spent on keeping a Russian MVD presence in Grozny. ❏

First published in Dos'e na Tsenzuru.
Translated by Richard McKane

ALEXEI SIMONOV
A matter of honour

Media freedom is sacrificed to the honour and dignity of Russia's governing elite

In 1995, the courts of the Russian Federation heard 3,500 cases in defence of 'honour and dignity'. The figures are not yet available for 1996, but on the evidence of recent years, there is no sign that the number is going down: in 1990 it was 1,140 cases, in 1994, 1,793.
Here's a paradox; given the undiminished rise in poverty, red-tape and civil disorder, in today's Russia, on what is the new-found self-esteem of our citizens based? And when the words themselves have lost all meaning – to the point where the 'honour' of office has only negative connotations and 'dignity' (*dostoinstvo*) is invoked almost exclusively in financial transactions – why have these virtues become the last bastions for which Russians, in a completely uncharacteristic way, are prepared to go to court? Are we witnessing a last stand on the bridge of vanishing moral values? Who are these brave warriors who hunger and thirst after justice? And who has offended?

The sense of personal honour in our country has long disappeared and loss of dignity barely raises a blush, let alone a sense of shame. Lying, practised publicly and blatantly by the head of state, parliament and local governments, entails no loss of votes nor dumb-struck horror, but evokes only a delighted, 'Well, he got away with it!'

My concern here is with the media, one of the principal defendants in these cases. Since the Glasnost Foundation first began to monitor abuses of the press and attacks on journalists in 1993, we ignored cases brought against the press; as defenders of press freedom, we didn't think it our business to look into charges against them. When we realised that litigation against the media was part and parcel of the same forces that are determined to tame the unfettered press, we started to include these cases in our register of violations. Our 1996 handbook was called *Conflicts with the media* to reflect this; earlier issues had been called *Persecutions* (1993-94) and *Breaches of the law* (1995).

Our handbook for 1996 records 415 breaches of the media law. Sixty-five per cent of these were criminal encroachments on journalists and editorial boards, prevention of their legitimate activity, restrictions on access to information, breaches of the professional independence of editorial boards, and so on. But 35 per cent were offences in which the media themselves were incriminated or charged. We have recorded 138 such cases – by no means the full picture; our correspondents work in 10 of the Federation's 89 regions – 71 per cent of which were charges brought against the media for derogation of honour and dignity, professional reputation, and defamation and insult to the person. In 1995, the proportions were 85 and 15 per cent. Were the media especially unbridled in 1996? On the contrary, they were noticably more cautious, yet the proportion of cases won by the plaintiffs has risen from 60 to 70 per cent.

Now for the next batch of statistics. Around 40 per cent of the cases in which the media were the plaintiffs were settled out of court; cases in which the media appeared as defendants, 97 went to court. In other words, when the media attempts to defend its rights, our rusty law-enforcement machinery is revealed in all its lumbering slowness. When it comes to 'screwing the scribblers', the machine springs to life and works like a well-oiled mechanism!

A final statistic: those who thirst after justice in defence of honour and dignity are chiefly those who govern us, defend us, judge us or those whom we have elected; as litigants, they outnumber we simple citizens 10 to one: their honour and dignity is infringed 100 times more often than ours.

The media, it goes without saying, is not blameless. At the centre and in the provinces, their one-sided and partisan reporting leaves a lot to be desired. Journalists' skills are grossly inadequate: they frequently lack the ability to express an idea or present facts in an irrefutable manner. Editorial boards, in search of sensation and sales figures, top inoffensive stories with outrageous headlines. The media are politicized beyond belief: up to 80 per cent of their column inches or screen time is devoted to the interests of their owners or sponsors. Journalists themselves are not experts on the law and editorial boards are too poor to retain staff lawyers to advise on potentially actionable copy; there are virtually no lawyers qualified in the subject; and not a single law school in the country to train them. Far from being burdened with 'information overload', the average rank-and-file journalist has far too little data; many have no proper knowledge of their rights and duties; few have command of standard Russian. But none of this is a reason for taking them to court; none of it justifies what is being done to the media in the name of honour and dignity.

Becoming a politician, an official, an elected member the world over is like entering show-biz and suffering the crossfire of the critics.

The sole newspaper in the Kalmyk republic to point out that presidential elections there conformed with the old Soviet formula according to which God brought Eve unto Adam and said to him, 'Elect thy wife!' became an enemy of the people, and was all but finished off by the sole candidate's hitmen.

The Procurator stirs up some case against the journalist who comments on the pranks of the minister of defence and he is sentenced to a year's corrective labour for an 'insult to dignity'. A year later, the minister has ceased to be a minister, the insult has evaporated and the appeal court overturns the verdict.

In addition to the prosecutions in defence of honour and dignity that come before the courts, all the organs of repression from the civil police and public health inspectors to the tax police initiate prosecutions.

The examples go on. Not that the number of cases is the whole story. The achievements of our newfound and tenuous 'democracy' are being turned against itself and we are losing one of its few gains: we are losing the freedom of the press. And one of the most potent weapons driving things backwards are prosecutions in defence of 'honour and dignity'.

The motives which inspire them centre on the lack of financial, moral and administrative responsibility. Having once paid a few pence in tax, as far as the plaintiff is concerned, the sky is the limit for damages. If these warriors for truth were obliged to pay a deposit of even 10 per cent of the sum specified in the suit, the number and scale of the prosecutions would drop dramatically. That the court knocks a few zeroes off the awards is nothing to do with justice; even the judges are embarrassed by the plaintiffs' greed. In the minority of cases – 30-40 per cent – the plaintiff loses, no moral approbrium attaches to him and no investigation of the abuse alleged in the offending publication is ever undertaken.

The other motive inspiring such cases is nothing more than political expediency. When a department feels it has been insulted, all its officials launch individual prosecutions against the offending paper in defence of their personal honour and dignity on instruction from those at the top. Attacks on the press become mass-produced and continuous – literally every issue of every paper that mentions the belligerent department ends up in court. For example, in the city of Vladimir, over the last four years, *Pryziv* (The Call) has been prosecuted 104 times; and honour and dignity are beginning reach down to smaller operations when the main publication has its hands full.

The most malicious perpetrator of infringements of the right of access of journalists to information is the judiciary itself: in violation of the laws on the mass media and the courts, judges have journalists turned out of open hearings, or refuse to let them bring in tape-recorders. Many judicial decisions in civil honour and dignity suits, or in criminal cases of insult and defamation are, to put it mildly, legally flawed. The two most typical errors are putting into action claims for compensation for moral damage brought by departments or organisations and, contrary to law, holding journalists responsible for the accuracy of information already in the public domain.

The excessive sense of civil dignity we see among our VIPs confuses the dignity of the individual with the dignity of office; their suits are an attempt to paper over their offences and keep them out of the public eye. The legal system cannot handle them properly. While they continue, they are a real and constant threat to the freedom of the word. ❏

Alexei Simonov *is chairman of the Glasnost Defence Foundation and editor in chief of* Dos'e na Tsenzuru

ANATOL LIEVEN

New Russia: what the people think

Russia's changing, but not as fast or as far as some imagine

> 'There was always opposition to the state among the [Russian] people; owing to the excessive geographical space, however, it was expressed in flight and the shunning of obligations which the state imposed on the people, but not by effective opposition and not by struggle'.
> (Nikolai Kostomarov 1817-85, Russian-Ukrainian historian)

The war between Russia and the Chechen separatist forces, which lasted from December 1994 to August 1996, may be seen by future historians as a key moment in Russian and perhaps world history; not because of its consequences, which are likely to be limited, but because of the stark light which this war has thrown on one of the most important developments of our time: the end of Russia as a great military and imperial power.

The reasons for the Russian defeat in Chechnya go far deeper than the specific problems of the Russian armed forces in the 1990s: they reflect both the weakness of the contemporary Russian state and, perhaps more important, longstanding and deep-rooted changes in Russian demography, society, culture, and mentality.

Rather than making comparisons between the Russia of today and either the Soviet Union or the Russia of the Tsars, it would make more sense to look for parallels and models for understanding Russia today in the 'liberal' states of southern Europe and Latin America in the late-nineteenth and early-twentieth centuries, and among developing countries in other parts of the world today – with the key difference that while their populations are growing, that of Russia is falling steeply.

But as political developments in Russia contemporaneous to the Chechen War – especially the presidential elections of June 1996 – have demonstrated, while the Russian state today is weak, like many such states, it is probably relatively stable. The coming years may see considerable political instability among the ruling elites, local mass protests, possibly even coups d'état. Unless, however, the new elites prove so greedy and incompetent that they drive a majority of the population to sheer desperation, they are unlikely to see either a complete failure of the state, or its transformation by some revolutionary force and the recreation of Russia as a great military, expansionist and ideological power. It is time to abandon the belief that the Russians – not just particular Russian states, but the Russian people and Russian culture – are deeply and perennially imperialist, aggressive and expansionist. Every opinion poll in Russia in recent years has put great-power status very low on the scale of ordinary Russians' priorities, far below fear of unemployment, crime, and civil war. (*What the polls say, over*)

> 'Abandon the belief that the Russians... are deeply and perennially imperialist, aggressive and expansionist'

Russian politicians of course often make open or veiled imperialist remarks, but these need to be taken with a massive pinch of salt. As a close reading of his *A Last Bid For the South* shows, even Vladimir Zhirinovsky, despite his wild expansionist rhetoric, gives some evidence of ambiguity in his attitude to war, or at least war in the sense of real Russian military sacrifice. This is partly because he has never troubled himself in the slightest about ideological, moral or even logical consistency, but also because for all his foolery, he has often shown an acute sense of what many ordinary Russians feel in their guts (*Index* 1/1994).

Zhirinovsky has been equally inconsistent on the recreation of the Russian Empire: he has called for the reconquest of the Transcaucasus – but said that Russia should leave the Caucasians alone to kill each other, meanwhile closing Russia's borders against 'Caucasian cockroaches'. He has spoken of Russia's vital geopolitical role in Tajikistan – but told the media, on a parliamentary visit to Dushanbe, that 'above all, we must make sure our boys get home safely'. It would be wrong to think that

Continued on page 146

WHAT THE POLLS SAY

In answering the open-ended question, 'What is the single most serious problem facing the country?' in an opinion poll of April 1996, 56 per cent of respondents pointed to various economic problems, 17 per cent to ethnic conflicts, eight per cent to crime and corruption and less than one per cent issues related to national security and similar issues.

It is true that polls have always shown a strong desire for the restoration of the Soviet Union, but this has also been true among many Ukrainians, Caucasians and Central Asians; the key reason, especially among the elderly, is a desire not for empire and glory but for a return to security. Furthermore, most Russian politicians as well as the vast majority of ordinary Russians stress that reunification must be voluntary or at least peacaeable. According to polls conducted in 1996, fewer than 10 per cent of Russians were willing to contemplate the use of force either to recreate the USSR or to 'reunite' Russia with Russian-populated areas beyond its borders.

The lack of real will and determination which underlies the desire for a Soviet restoration is reflected in the fact that according to opinion polls, in the years from 1992 to 1996 a desire to return to the Soviet Union grew steadily (in eastern and southern Ukraine as well as in Russia); but in the latter part of that period so too did the belief that such a restoration is in fact impossible. Thus a December 1996 poll by the Russian magazine *Itogi*, linked to the NTV news show, showed only 11 per cent of respondents saying that the Belovezhskaya Pushcha agreement that ended the Soviet Union had brought good for Russia, and 65 per cent saying it had brought harm (24 per cent could not reply one way or the other). Forty-six per cent said the Union could not now be restored. This mass attitude supports a saying common among the Moscow intelligentsia: 'Whoever does not want to restore the Soviet Union has no heart. Whoever thinks it is possible to restore it has no brain'. A majority of Russian officers share this view.

As to specifically Russian national goals, a poll during the December 1993 parliamentary election campaign (the high point of Vladimir Zhirinovsky's popularity, as it turned out) by members of the Universities of Keele and Glasgow showed 49 per cent of Russians believing that some parts of neighbouring republics – ie Crimea and northern Kazakhstan – should in principle belong to Russia, but only 25 per cent willing to threaten military action to defend the rights of Russians in these areas.

Even more strikingly, when a number of opinion polls on the Russian involvement in Tajikistan were taken in the summer of 1993, after a Russian outpost had been wiped out in an opposition attack, large majorities of those polled spoke in favour of Russian withdrawal – even though both the Yeltsin administration and the parliamentary opposition, and indeed every major Russian politician, with the exception of General Alexander Lebed, was speaking of the absolute need for a continued Russian involvement to defend Russia's vital interests in Central Asia.

Fourteen months later, in a poll of April 1995 (ie after the start of the Chechen War and during Ukrainian moves drastically to restrict Crimean

PUBLIC OPINION: CHECHNYA AND EMPIRE

autonomy, only 9.6 per cent of respondents were willing to support the use of the Black Sea Fleet or the army to 'defend the Russians of Crimea' — even though 40.6 per cent had agreed that 'Russia should work for the return of Crimea to the Russian Federation', 23.8 per cent had said that Russia should 'guarantee the rights of the Russians in Crimea' and, only 18 months later, in September 1996, 70.4 per cent agreed with Moscow mayor Yuri Luzhkov that 'Sevastopol is not part of the Ukrainian state'.

Even before Russian casualties began to mount, a poll of 16-20 December 1994 showed only 30 per cent of respondents favouring 'decisive measures to restore order in Chechnya', whereas 36 per cent were for a peaceful solution and 23 per cent for an immediate withdrawal of the Russian army. The following month, January 1995, no less than 77 per cent of respondents to an opinion poll said that they opposed the bombardment of Grozny, with only 12 per cent in favour; 53.8 per cent were now claiming that they had *always* been against sending in the army.

The only signs of Russian majority enthusiasm for the war came in the immediate aftermath of the hostage-taking in Budennovsk in June 1995 which most Russians saw as terrorism. By February 1996, 46 per cent of Russians were agreeing with the Chechen separatist demand that Russian troops should be withdrawn immediately; only 33 per cent said they should be withdrawn only after the 'restoration of order'; and by March 1996, 52 per cent were in favour of immediate withdrawal.

According to another poll, of April 1996, after Yeltsin announced peace talks with Dudayev in March 1996, only five per cent of respondents were against talks with Dudayev; 15 per cent said they were wholly in favour of peace; 20 per cent expressed support for the statement, 'I am not convinced that this is the best path, but it is still better than a bloody war'; 30 per cent said they did not believe Yeltsin's plan was sincere; while 11 per cent knew nothing about the subject. Only a year earlier, 3 per cent had been against talks and for a 'forceful solution'; 22 per cent had been for a 'reasonable compromise', while 50 per cent had said that they would like a compromise, but doubted it was possible.

By September 1996, after the defeat that August and the Lebed-Maskhadov peace agreement, 39 per cent of respondents gave their approval to the proposition that the Russian government should ensure full compliance with the agreed ceasefire, 32 per cent that Russia should agree to free elections in Chechnya, and 46 per cent that Russian officials responsible for starting the war should be punished. Only 14 per cent said that the Russian army should recapture Grozny and 11 per cent that under no circumstances should the Russian government allow Chechen independence.

By November 1996, 33 per cent were agreeing that the Chechens should be left to make their own decisions and 26 per cent that they should have independence if they wished. On the other hand, 23 per cent were for establishing strict border controls and 22 per cent for keeping Chechnya in the Russian Federation.

Russians who voted for him were doing so out of a real desire to go out and conquer other areas; what the vote for him reflected was an inarticulate howl of pain from the poorest and most uneducated parts of the population at wrenching economic and cultural change.

An interesting and important example of the gap between Soviet nostalgia and the desire for a militant programme of Soviet restoration was the public response to the Communist-led vote in the Russian Duma in March 1996 declaring the Belovezhskaya Forest agreement [the 1991 agreement dissolving the USSR and creating the Commonwealth of Independent States] illegal and calling for the restoration of the Soviet Union.

The Communists obviously reckoned that this would gain them additional support; but nothing of the sort happened. On the contrary, the barrage of criticism and alarm from Russia's neighbours seems to have convinced a good many wavering voters that a Communist victory would bring a danger of war – something relentlessly repeated by Yeltsin's propaganda. In consequence, they voted for Yeltsin or Lebed, or stayed at home.

Yeltsin himself may have made a similar mistake in launching the Chechen War, if, as has been reported, his staff thought that a victorious war against the hated Chechens would increase his popularity. (Colonel Sergei Yushenkov, Chairman of the Duma Defence Committee, says that when he protested to Oleg Lobov, then Secretary of the Russian Security Council, about the intervention in Chechnya, Lobov replied, 'Don't make too much noise. The President needs a small victorious war, like the USA had in Haiti'.

The plan misfired: though Yeltsin won the election, repeated opinion polls showed how little taste the population had for the war – even before casualty figures started to arrive. They fail entirely to show a population obsessed with Russian prestige or even territorial integrity, let alone imperial glory, when faced with real costs.

History is full of examples of the folly of attributing fixed and unchanging national characteristics. All nations change over the years, and many in the course of history have abandoned warlike cultural attitudes and nationalist obsessions. Hungary is a good example. Having lost two-thirds of its territory and millions of ethnic Hungarians after World War I, Hungarians swore never to accept this as a determining element in Hungarian politics and culture. After the East European revolutions of

1989, Hungarian politicians, and even ministers, made noises suggesting that this sentiment was still very much alive; but from 1991 to 1994, when Serbia's involvement in the wars in Croatia and Bosnia, its international pariah status and its expuslion of ethnic Hungarians gave Hungary a chance to attack Serbia and recover the Vojevodina, Hungarians showed no inclination for war.

Their ancestors would have cursed them and called them apathetic, materialist, fat, lazy and decadent. By the same token, Russia today is one of the most materialist and cynical societies on earth; and such societies do not go to war if they can help it. ❏

Anatol Lieven *is Budapest correspondent of the* Financial Times. *From 1993 to 1996 he was a correspondent in Russia and the former Soviet Union for* The Times *(London). His next book,* Chechnya: Tombstone of Russian Power, *is to be published by Yale University Press this Spring*

Out of the depths

Stories and images from the streets of Moscow. Photographs by Olga Khabarova

ANDREI DEDOV'S TALE

Komsomolskaya Pravda has announced that the homeless are to be fingerprinted. My fingerprints have already been taken. Because I am homeless. When I asked: 'Why?' they answered me up front at the militia station: 'So that you can be identified when you die.' It's a happy prospect.

You lose everything swiftly. Czar Peter's friend, Alexander Menshikov, also lost his palace, became homeless, and went away to Berezov. It was simpler for him. In our times the homeless don't even get to go to the countryside. The villages have emptied, the inhabitants are suspicious and meet any newcomers malevolently. You also need capital and connections.

A homeless person can only survive in a big city. Only there does the fugitive or person deprived of registered accommodation succeed in somehow hanging on.

Once the Jews were guilty of everything; now it's the homeless as well. The mass media have surrounded us with a ghastly aura, and we are pretty well the basic evil in society. The homeless person can be accused of anything. *Kaleidoscope*, for instance, tells of a fight between embittered homeless and people seeking treasure in the sewers round Vitebsk station. A well written but completely fabricated article.

To keep up its circulation, *Komsomolskaya Pravda* ran an article about homeless Borya, who got married to a four-year-old girl. The names and family names were not included nor the place where it happened. Everyone reads with horror: if it weren't a pity to waste bullets on them, these homeless should be shot. What can you say after that? The militia report a robbery – and some homeless person was at the scene of the

PHOTO STORY: FROM THE DEPTHS

Homelessness takes its toll on physical and mental wellbeing – Credit: Olga Khabarova

crime. It's compulsory for a homeless person either to have been on the spot or taken part.

Most people simply can't imagine what it's like to have lost everything; how much worse it is than living in a train. If you're robbed clean, they'll all kick you sooner or later; you'll get drunk, lose your documents, sink lower and die.

Homeless people are always dirty. People try to keep up their appearance, but when they're spending the night on stairs, sooner or later they let themselves go. The homeless are always harassed, they get undeserved traumas, no one supports them – neither the Orthodox Church nor the authorities. You can be a criminal; but don't on any account be homeless.

A dog carries its clothing with it, needs no shoes; no-one sees if it's washed or not; it doesn't need much space to go to sleep at night. We pity homeless dogs, but we've stopped pitying the homeless.

I've not been tried, I don't have a criminal record; more than that, I've tried to act positively in life. Can I not break out of this myself? Twice I've been given authority for accommodation and twice I was given the run around. I'm hoping for a third authority for accommodation. I want to go up to A V Ponidenko and ask him: 'What's going on?'

It's the same everywhere. I worked in a church. Those who weren't homeless were paid workers. But they couldn't put me on their books and pay me legitimately because I had no residence permit.

I can stay calm only because, in my time, I went on a lot of walking trips, drove round the shores of the Black and Caspian Seas, walked round the Crimea and the Caucasus from the Danube to Batum. I organised tourist centres. Anyone who does not have that sort of preparation, or at least the experience of walking long distances, is doomed in the homeless zone. They can only last a year or two.

Society is unkind. I have the suspicion that many people experience pleasure because someone is worse off than they. This is why the homeless person crosses the boundary into crime: because they are tortured. Or they are dying and hole up in a basement and don't come out. They find them and can't identify them because they haven't got their fingerprints on file.

I got interested in the stories of the homeless; I talked with them and saw how they fight for life. They may live in communal flats and rent rooms, but they are always at the limit of human powers.

PHOTO STORY: FROM THE DEPTHS

Burning trash provides a momentary comfort – Credit: Olga Khabarova

Two Ukrainians lived with me under the eaves. They had got stuck in Petersburg and couldn't find work, and they went to work a bit on the market. They were given a bit of money for drinks and used up all their time. One died, the other, who was stronger, is still alive. Three years of living in basements got to him and he lost his humanity. Before my eyes he turned into a virtual animal.

Many have the philosophy: another day's gone, thank God. Today I earned a bit, holed up in a hole, drank some solvent and for a few hours felt good.

I try to keep variety in my life. I wander round the town, read a lot, some museums let me in for free as a homeless-intellectual. I often call on people – a terrible shock for my acquaintances. I arrive with the greeting, 'Homeless Andryusha's here!' Strangers invite me to visit them, and those who lived with me at the flat consider me a fool. My former friend says indignantly, 'You had everything!' So I bring a certain pleasure to the intelligent, who live in their flats.

I really did have enough. I realised that the more you have, the more you have problems. For 20 years I tried to keep my places on the Black Sea and in Leningrad, worried myself with unending probationary periods at work, got up to all sorts of tricks. Now I live a completely calm life, I'm practically resting.

I'm in my third year. I look on the former 20 years of my life with horror, and am amazed that I bore it all. All the time you're rushing about, the rat race, the rat race. In the end I didn't do it any more. No-one envies me now.

I'll go to Moscow, sit by the memorial to Karl Marx. It'll be a bit of a paradox, he and I with our beards and me selling *The Depths*. I think I'll be wildly successful.

VLADIMIR KARELIN'S TALE

I'm a down and out. Everyone tells me so. I have so many hard luck stories.

I robbed the neighbour and was put in prison. I don't know why I robbed her, she was a good woman; she used to give me the keys and I took her money. I returned the money in a week. She asked after me in tears at the militia station. But they put me away for four years anyway.

PHOTO STORY: FROM THE DEPTHS

For many, soup kitchens are a lifeline – Credit: Olga Khabarova

VLADIMIR KARELIN

I worked in a company called Larissa. They had taken over our factory and offered jobs. They paid us quite well. Then the factory broke the contract. The boss let me stay because I had been working there for seven years and had the highest qualification as a machinist. But I failed the medical commission. I could have worked in the company without the medical commission certificate, but not at the factory. I tried to explain that I don't have any bad effects from high blood pressure; I'm used to it – but they didn't let me work at the machine anyway. I left. I could have had a pension within a year.

When I was released, I found out that the building I lived in was up for capital repair. I was fighting for a year to get a room. I lived there for a year or two and decided to do an exchange. But it was some kind of an exchange based on selling and buying. I had no idea what was going on.

In Gatchina they showed me a room. I agreed to take it and handed over all my papers in exchange for a temporary residence permit. They promised the permanent one in a year. Then the owner arrived. He said he knew nothing about me, that the temporary year was over and that I had to move. Where he'd been before, I don't know. I returned to my room on Fontanka; the neighbours wouldn't let me move in although no-one was living there. I couldn't work out what on earth was going on. What's more, the agency had somehow disappeared. All my stuff, wardrobe, sofa, etc. was left behind in Gatchina.

It's not a question of being down on my luck. There are a lot of swindlers around, and no-one tries to catch them.

Now I don't even have any permanent place to live. You sit on the local train, sleep for three hours, then one hour in the waiting room at the station and then return.

On warmer nights I sleep in the open somewhere on the embankment. ❑

First published in Nadye *(The Depths), St Petersburg.* Nadye *has been started with the support of* The Big Issue, *UK*
Olga Khabarova *is a Moscow-based freelance photographer.*
Translated by **Richard McKane**

PHOTO STORY: FROM THE DEPTHS

Prejudice against the homeless starts young – Credit: Olga Khabarova

Babel: the Roma

Roma in Dover, their point of entry, explain why they came to Britain and citizens of the town voice their problems. Roma and neo-Nazi skinheads back home in Slovakia and the Czech Republic paint a picture of the life that drove them out

VOICES FROM A DOVER SHOPPING CENTRE

'I would put them all on a boat and send them all back to where they came from.'

'Because, well, we can't look after our own people, can we?'

'They're scrounging off the country. but not only that. They're doing a lot of shoplifting and everything, aren't they?'

'No, I haven't seen it. But I've heard about it.'

'Most of them are here just to see what they can get out of the system. Of the 800 who are listed in Dover, I'd say that only about 50 to a 100 are genuine asylum seekers, so they should be allowed to stay, but the others, no.'

DAVIPE CERVENAK, A ROMA FROM PISEK, CZECH REPUBLIC

'One afternoon in autumn four of us had gone to a small park on the island to exercise. We were there for about five minutes when about 20 skinheads started shouting at us: 'Black swine! We'll kill you.'

MILAN BRAT, MEMBER OF A CZECH SKINHEAD GANG

'We didn't attack them. Three of us boys went over to them just to shout and somehow the violence broke out and I wouldn't like to go into any details.'

DAVIDE CERVENAK

'They kept on shouting that they would kill us. They were waving baseball bats and chasing us. We didn't know what to do. So we just had to jump into the water. There were some people passing in a canoe. We

BABEL: ROMA

National Front protestor in Dover – Credit: Max Jourdan

shouted for help and tried to get on their boat but they just left us.'

DASA DANIHELOVA

'The skins were running from both sides and kicked back into the water anyone trying to get out. Every time our boys climbed out, they were pushed back. It was hopeless. [One of the boys, Tibor Daniel, got too tired to swim and managed to climb out of the river.]

DAVID CERVENAK

'When he got on the bank, they kicked him and hit him with baseball bats. He fell back into the water and didn't come out again.'

DASA DANIHELOVA

'We all felt like we were dead. It was a terrible blow because he didn't make it to his birthday [his family were preparing his eighteenth birthday party when they heard of his death]. Everything came to an end. Even today we haven't got over it. We are still totally destroyed by it.'

MILAN BRAT

'I didn't even know that he was drowning. I only found out the following day that he had drowned. I didn't do anything to him so I had no reason to have it on my conscience.'

DAVIDE CERVENAK

'Here in Pisek I don't go out at night any more. At seven when it starts to get dark, I go home and if gypsies do go out, they don't go alone and they arm themselves.'

MILAN BRAT RECIEVED A SUSPENDED SENTENCE FOR RACIST VIOLENCE; THREE OTHERS GOT THREE YEAR SENTENCES FOR ORGANISING THE ATTACK

LADISLAV SCUKA, SEEKING ASYLUM IN DOVER

'My home in Prague was firebombed My daughter was burning. If I hadn't saved her she would have burned to death in front of my eyes. There was a group of skinheads and somebody threw a petrol bomb in my window. I have three children and I was so confused that I didn't know which child to save first.'

BABEL: ROMA

PETR FRICER, MEMBER OF CZECH SKINHEAD GROUP. THESE OFTEN HAVE CONNECTIONS WITH BANNED OR SEMI-BANNED POLITICAL PARTIES SUCH AS THE PATRIOTIC FRONT OR HAMMERSKINS. THESE HAVE CONNECTIONS THROUGHOUT EUROPE, INCLUDING THE UK

'I like this kind of fashion. I respect what it stands for: dictatorship and a pure white world. I've been part of this movement for five years now since the gypsies killed my friend's brother. That's how I got into it. And then when I see what the gypsies are doing, how they live on our money, steal, carry out prostitution and such things, I don't like it at all.

'We get together a group of skinheads in town and we agree on some kind of action against them. When the gypsies do something, we just get together, have a chat and organise the same against them. We do to them what they do to us. We don't beat up small children. We may scare them off sometimes but we don't beat up small children.'

BLANKA ZUZLOVA, CARE ASSISTANT AT THE TOPOLCANY SPECIAL SCHOOL, SLOVAKIA. MOST OF THE PUPILS ARE GYPSIES, MANY OF THEM MENTALLY HANDICAPPED

'It was at quarter past seven in the evening. It was already dark. We were going out this way. We were getting the children into line. I was at the front, my colleague was walking at the end. As we were doing this I noticed a line of skinheads waiting a few steps away. They had baseball bats and baseball caps turned around. We didn't say anything to the children but we already sensed that something was about to happen.

IVAN, DENISA, KATKA, BRANO, PUPILS

'They first only watched us and as we walked further they started shouting at us. "Gypsies to the gas chambers." Things like that.'

'We were running and they were running after us with chains and knives and screaming: "Gypsies we'll kick you around".'

'They were carrying knives and chains and chains around them instead of belts. They were shouting at us: "Gypsies we'll beat you. We'll kill you". And we started running away. And two boys ran away and one of them ripped his jeans.

'They tripped me up and kept kicking me in the leg and the face.'

'They grabbed us and beat us up. With chains. Like that.'

BLANKA ZUZLOVA

'It's not possible for so many skinheads armed with baseball bats and chains to be otherwise gathered at the stadium at the same time. So it must have been prepared in advance. They haven't been adequately punished. And if they were, it was only two or three of them and the others got away with it.'

THE GANG BEAT THE BOYS UP SO BADLY THEY HAD TO GO TO HOSPITAL. IVAN HAD TO HAVE HIS FRONT TEETH REBUILT. FOUR SKINHEADS GOT SUSPENDED SENTENCES

MIROSLAV IACKO, ROMA ACTIVIST

'This is Sichow in Presov, one of the largest districts in Slovakia. Just back there is the block of flats where I live – more than 2,500 Roma live here but they rarely leave this ghetto; and in this walkway someone's written this graffiti: "Burn the niggers."

And: "Gypsies to the gas chambers." Over on the other side, we can see where someone's written: "White Race." And: "White Slovakia."'

LUBA HACELOVA, ROM FROM THE VILLAGE OF HONTIANSKE NEMCE, SLOVAKIA

'A group of villagers came in the middle of the night carrying petrol cans. We watched as the house was burning and we were afraid and shocked. We didn't know what to do. Children were screaming. And while we were still in the house, the thugs threw rags soaked in petrol into the house. They lit them and threw them through the windows into the house into the same room where we were. And we threw the burning rags back through the windows because by then the flames were even spreading to the part of the house where we were with the children...

'Most of us climbed out of the back windows. But my brother Josef was beaten back with a concrete post as he tried to get out. The flowers mark the spot where we found his charred body.

'The whites who did this were shouting that they didn't want any Romani here and that they were Hitler's followers and that Hitler killed Romani and that they were going to do the same.

MIRO, A VILLAGER WHO WAS PRESENT AT THE ATTACK

'We went there to have a bit of excitement. To shout a little bit at those gypsies. It was quite exciting. We threw stones at them and they threw stones at us. I wanted to get inside the house but it wasn't possible so my friend and I kicked the door in and they smashed my head. That was the end of it. We went home. Well, we went to the local bar because that's what we call home. (Laughs) So we went to the bar. I put something on my head but it was still bleeding. Then the following day, the police came after me saying that the house had been burnt. But I was part of the second group. There were three groups. I was in the second group and it was the third group who set the house on fire.

'At first I laughed. I didn't care at all. But I stopped laughing when the police came to get me but you know how it goes, I didn't feel sorry.'

LUBA HACELOVA

'When we go shopping the thugs chase us. They throw us out of the shops. They throw stones and they say we smell. It's not our fault we are black.'

NO ONE WAS EVER CHARGED WITH ANY OFFENCE IN CONNECTION WITH THIS ATTACK. NOR DO THE AUTHORITIES CONSIDER IT RACIALLY MOTIVATED

DOORMAN AT BAR TANGO, TO MIROSLAV

'Citizens of Romany origin are not allowed in. I'm sorry it's not my idea. Unfortunately that's how it is. I didn't make the rule...Don't ask me why. That's simply the way it is...Just like we ban drunks.'

GARY TONG, DOVER BUTCHER

'I must have sent 20 or more petitions [protesting at local taxpayers footing the bill for Roma asylum seekers in Dover], all full of signatures. You know, it's just the general feeling, no-one wants them here.' ❑

Voices compiled from 'Nowhere to run', a **World in Action** *programme produced for Granada Television, UK*

DAVID BANISAR & SIMON DAVIES

The code war

As the Internet and other communications systems reach further into everyday lives, national security, law enforcement and individual privacy have become perilously intertwined. Governments want to restrict the free flow of information; software producers are seeking ways to ensure consumers are not bugged from the very moment of purchase

The US is behind a worldwide effort to limit individual privacy and enhance the capability of its intelligence services to eavesdrop on personal conversations. The campaign has had two legal strategies: the first made it mandatory for all digital telephone switches, cellular and satellite phones and all developing communication technologies to build in surveillance capabilities; the second sought to limit the dissemination

Encryption and Free Expression: the basics

1) The cyphers
Cryptography is the scrambling of information into an unreadable language that only the intended recipient can understand. It has been used by individuals and governments to protect communications since ancient Egypt. In the computer age, cryptography is the primary technique for protecting confidential communications from eavesdroppers; the authentification of identities for electronic commercial transactions; and the prevention of the spread of computer viruses or the illegal copying of

NEW MEDIA: ENCRYPTION

of software that contains encryption, a technique which allows people to scramble their communications and files to prevent others from reading them.

The first effort to heighten surveillance opportunities was to force telecommunications companies to use equipment designed to include enhanced wiretapping capabilities. The end goal was to ensure that the US and its allied intelligence services could easily eavesdrop on telephone networks anywhere in the world. In the late 1980s, in a programme known internally as 'Operation Root Canal', US law enforcement officials demanded that telephone companies alter their equipment to facilitate the interception of messages. The companies refused but, after several years of lobbying, Congress enacted the Communications Assistance for Law Enforcement Act (CALEA) in 1994.

CALEA requires that terrestrial carriers, cellular phone services and other entities ensure that all their 'equipment, facilities or services' are capable of 'expeditiously...enabling the government...to intercept...all wire and oral communications carried by the carrier...concurrently with their transmission.' Communications must be interceptable in such a form that they could be transmitted to a remote government facility. Manufacturers must work with industry and law enforcement officials to ensure that their equipment meets federal standards. A court can fine a

software. Its most common manifestations are in automated teller machines, home security systems and digital cellular phones.

There are two basic types of encryption: symmetrical (private key) and asymmetrical (public key). In symmetrical encryption, the same key is used both for encryption and decryption. The problem with the system is that the parties who wish to communicate privately have to first find a secure way of exchanging code-books so that they can read each other's messages. The most popular system of symmetrical encryption is the US Data Encryption Standard (DES), introduced in 1977.

DAVID BANISAR & SIMON DAVIES

company US$10,000 per day for each product that does not comply.

encryption technology was 'born classified'

The passage of CALEA has been controversial, but its provisions have yet to be enforced due to FBI efforts to include even more rigorous regulations under the law. These include the requirement that cellular phones allow for location-tracking on demand and that telephone companies provide capacity for up to 50,000 simultaneous wiretaps. While the FBI lobbied Congress and pressured US companies into accepting a tougher CALEA, it also leant on US allies to adopt it as an international standard. In 1991, the FBI held a series of secret meetings with EU member states to persuade them to incorporate CALEA into European law. The plan, according to an EU report, was to 'call for the Western World (EU, US and allies) to agree to norms and procedures and then sell their products to Third World countries. Even if they do not agree to interception orders, they will find their telecommunications monitored by the UK-USA signals intelligence network the minute they use the equipment.' The FBI's efforts resulted in an EU Council of Ministers resolution that was quietly adopted in January 1995, but not publicly released until 20 months later. The resolution's text is almost word for word identical to the FBI's demands at home. The US government is now pressuring the International Telecommunications Union (ITU) to adopt the standards globally.

> In asymmetrical, or public, key cryptography, there are two keys: a public key used for encryption, and a private key used for decryption. It is not practically possible to derive one key from the other, so someone with only the encryption key cannot decrypt messages, and vice versa. The public key can be published anywhere – an electronic phone book or on a web page. Anyone who wants to communicate can do so knowing that only the recipient can read the message. Public key cryptography can also be used to create digital signatures.
>
> Digital signatures provide the same legal assurances as handwritten signatures do. The most popular system of public key

The second part of the strategy was to ensure that intelligence and police agencies could understand every communication they intercepted. They attempted to impede the development of cryptography and other security measures, fearing that these technologies would reduce their ability to monitor the emissions of foreign governments and to investigate crime.

These latter efforts have not been successful. A survey by the Global Internet Liberty Campaign (GILC) found that most countries have either rejected domestic controls or not addressed the issue at all. The GILC found that 'many countries, large and small, industrialized and developing, seem to be ambivalent about the need to control encryption technology.'

The FBI and the National Security Agency (NSA) have instigated efforts to restrict the availability of encryption worldwide. In the early 1970s, the NSA's pretext was that encryption technology was 'born classified' and, therefore, its dissemination fell into the same category as the diffusion of A-bomb materials. The debate went underground until 1993 when the US launched the Clipper Chip, an encryption device designed for inclusion in consumer products. The Clipper Chip offered the required privacy, but the government would retain a 'pass-key' – anything encrypted with the chip could be read by government agencies.

Behind the scenes, law enforcement and intelligence agencies were pushing hard for a ban on other forms of encryption. In a February 1993

> cryptography is RSA, named after three researchers at the Massachusetts Institute of Technology who invented it in 1977. Two very long prime numbers are chosen at random and these yield the public and the private keys. The cryptanalyst's problem of finding the private key from the public key can only be solved by factoring the product of the two primes – without knowing either. The best-known methods would take current computers millions of years for keys several hundred digits long, although mathematical study of primes may one day yield new techniques. *DB&SD*

document, obtained by the Electronic Privacy Information Center (EPIC), they recommended: 'Technical solutions, such as they are, will only work if they are incorporated into all encryption products. To ensure that this occurs, legislation mandating the use of government-approved encryption products, or adherence to government encryption criteria, is required.' The Clipper Chip was widely criticised by industry, public interest groups, scientific societies and the public and, though it was officially adopted, only a few were ever sold or used.

From 1994 onwards, Washington began to woo private companies to develop an encryption system that would provide access to keys by government agencies. Under the proposals – variously known as 'key escrow', 'key recovery' or 'trusted third parties' – the keys would be held by a corporation, not a government agency, and would be designed by the private sector, not the NSA. The systems, however, still entailed the assumption of guaranteed access to the intelligence community and so proved as controversial as the Clipper Chip. The government used export incentives to encourage companies to adopt key escrow products: they could export stronger encryption, but only if they ensured that intelligence agencies had access to the keys.

Under US law, computer software and hardware cannot be exported if it contains encryption that the NSA cannot break. The regulations stymy the availability of encryption in the USA because companies are reluctant to develop two separate product lines – one, with strong encryption,

2) The information

In 1992, Phil Zimmerman, a US computer security consultant, custom-built an encryption software application for use by human rights groups. It allowed users to generate their own public and private keys and maintain a 'key-ring' of signed certificates in a web-of-trust. Any Internet user could now send and receive e-mail, impenetrable to the most skilled cryptanalysts. It was Pretty Good Privacy (PGP).

As Zimmerman prepared to release his initial version in April 1993, the US government announced its own plan for the Clipper Chip. He released it anyway and published the full text for domestic use and another, with weak encryption, for the international market. Several cases are pending in the US courts on the constitutionality of export controls; a federal court recently ruled that they violate free speech rights under the First Amendment.

The FBI has not let up on efforts to ban products on which it cannot eavesdrop. In mid-1997, it introduced legislation to mandate that key-recovery systems be built into all computer systems. The amendment was adopted by several congressional committees but the Senate preferred a weaker variant. A concerted campaign by computer, telephone and privacy groups finally stopped the proposal; it now appears that no legislation will be enacted in the current Congress.

While the key escrow approach was being pushed in the USA, Washington had approached foreign organisations and states. The lynchpin for the campaign was David Aaron, US ambassador to the Organisation for Economic Cooperation and Development (OECD), who visited dozens of countries in what one analyst derided as a programme of 'laundering failed US policy through international bodies to give it greater acceptance'.

Led by Germany and the Scandinavians, the EU has been generally distrustful of key escrow technology. In October 1997, the European Commission released a report which advised: 'Restricting the use of encryption could well prevent law-abiding companies and citizens from protecting themselves against criminal attacks. It would not, however,

of the programme as free software. He was investigated for 28 months for breaking the ban on disclosing encryption technology to foreigners. But Zimmerman never personally exported PGP; one of his friends had posted it to an Internet discussion group, which distributed the information across US borders.

His motive for creating PGP was political, according to Zimmerman's testimony to a Senate committee (http://www.pgp.com/phil/phil-quotes.cgi). He believed that the susceptibility of digital communications to automated mass-surveillance was an unprecedented invasion of civil liberties and wanted to provide a secure means of communication. The totally prevent criminals from using these technologies.' The report noted that 'privacy considerations suggest [that we not] limit the use of cryptography as a means to ensure data security and confidentiality.'

> 'The US government and some of the world's largest corporations, notably Microsoft, are on a collision course'

Some European countries have or are contemplating independent restrictions. France had a long-standing ban on the use of any cryptography to which the government does not have access. However, a 1996 law, modifying the existing system, allows a system of *tiers du confidence*, although it has not been implemented because of EU opposition. In 1997, the Conservative government in the UK introduced a proposal creating a system of trusted third parties. It was severely criticised at the time and by the new Labour government, which has not yet acted upon its predecessor's recommendations

The debate over encryption and the conflicting demands of security and privacy are bound to continue. The commercial future of the Internet depends on a universally-accepted and foolproof method of on-line identification; as of now, the only means of providing it is through strong encryption. That puts the US government and some of the world's largest corporations, notably Microsoft, on a collision course. ❑

---

programme is now in regular use by human rights monitors in countries with repressive regimes – but also by criminals and terrorists eager to cover their tracks.

Under a computer law, decreed by Burma's State Law and Order Restoration Council (SLORC) in September 1996, the possession of an 'unsanctioned' modem is punishable by up to 15 years in prison. Rights groups such as FreeBurma, base their communications facilities across the Thai border, where government reaction to their activities ranges from the 'less than cooperative to downright hostile'. PGP encryption is crucial, both to communicate with sympathisers outside South East

David Banisar *is an attorney at the Electronic Privacy Information Center (EPIC) in Washington, DC and deputy director of Privacy International (PI). He is co-author of a new book on encryption policy:* The Electronic Privacy Papers: The Battle for Privacy in the Age of Surveillance. **Simon Davies** *is director general of PI, the author of* Big Brother *and a visiting fellow at the London School of Economics. More information on EPIC, PI and encryption issues is available at* http://www.privacy.org., www.epic.org, www.gilc.org/crypto/, www.ispo.cec.be/eif/policy/97503toc.html, www.oecd.org/dstiiccp/crypto_e.html

Asia and to protect data on hard disks, particularly those that detail their sources.

Security analysts recently reported that Singaporean contractors are building a 'cyberspace warfare centre' to help SLORC crack down on illegal modem use. Even so, spotting data leaving a country is one thing; interpreting it is something else. 'Thanks to encryption,' said an un-named source in South East Asia, 'an unprecedented amount of information is getting out. There's no stopping it.' *MG&FF*

ALEX REYNOLDS

Asian values and all that

7 August 1997

In the dining room of the Atlanta Hotel, Bangkok, there's a curious old photograph of Louis Armstrong and Benny Goodman sharing a jam session with the King of Thailand on saxophone. What sets this picture apart is the smiling figure of George Bush; not playing, but sitting cross-armed in the background. After all, this is a photograph from the era of the Domino Theory; taken at a time when America needed a friendly border and a few whorehouses for GI Joe after some heavy-duty arson in 'Nam. I wondered if Bill Clinton went to have a jam session (on tenor, the King on alto) when Thailand secured a US$17.2 billion credit package from the International Monetary Fund. One expects the IMF's director, Michel Camdessus, to take a tough line with Thailand at a time when the baht is sinking at a faster rate than the Titanic. Perhaps the King has booked his place with the band as she goes down...

What bothers the IMF is the fear that what is happening in Thailand could infect the economies of others in the South East Asia region. In a country already contemptuous of *farangs* (foreigners) the intervention by the US-dominated IMF has sown uncertainty in Prime Minister Chevalit Yongchaiyudh's government. Thailand fears a domestic crisis similar to Mexico's where output levels fell by 7 per cent, real wages fell by a quarter and social-sector provision collapsed. Over one million jobs were lost in Mexico and average incomes have still not recovered. It's not suprising the Thais seem wary of an IMF package that will increase poverty levels and only benefit domestic and foreign currency speculators. People are praying in temples all over Bangkok to brace themselves for the inevitable crunch in the economy.

DIARY: THAILAND

8 August

The Thailand I wanted to see was the Thailand of the 1927 movie *Chang*: a land full of innocent people protecting their homes from a horde of rampaging elephants. Today, the people of Siam are flogging hard-bargained fake Versace to the haggling young whiteys who have come out here on the trail of Alex Garland's novel *The Beach*. On observation, it seems these people are too busy to peep their noses up from their much-fingered paperback to notice the 'tiger' crisis of newly industrialised Thailand. For the influx of tie-dyed long-hairs the misery of the indigenous population does not stand in the way of having a good time. Meanwhile, the people of Thailand starve.

No, for the *farangs* it is as good a time as any to visit 'the land of the free', the literal translation of Thailand. Never mind the sinking baht and cap-in-hand gestures of the present government to the IMF. They don't hear the rumblings from the army. General Chetta, a dead-ringer for Panama's Noriega, is unhappy about cuts to his budget, a delay in the road-building programme and the renewed slump in the economy. To many Thais, it seems to be an adequate recipe for another military coup, in spite of Chetta and chums promises to the contrary. For the long-hairs in tie-dye, this does not get in the way of following Mr Garland's fictional footsteps *à la recherche du Kerouac perdu,* down to the islands to get wasted at the annual full moon party.

9 August

I was here to find the spirit of Siam as I knew it. *Muay Thai* (kickboxing as *farangs* call it) is an ancient form of combat which has evolved into a national sport. Two men fight under the command of a bell to kick, knee and punch their way through five painful three-minute rounds for little reward, save honour. I had a list of clubs to check out. One of them took me into a whitey ghetto, off the Khao San Road in downtown Bangkok. Walking down an alley I came upon a gym with a pigmy-sized ring and a disclaimer for any injury sustained 'during training' hanging proudly above the entrance. Bangkok was not the place.

But along my path to the gym I could not help bumping and tripping over the *farangs* that come to study more obvious pleasures: prostitution and drugs. The land of the smile is what they call Thailand; and who can blame the smiling Thais for doing so in disdain at the hapless legion, filthy foreigners with bells on their toes and rings through their noses.

11 August

I journeyed to Chang Mai, the rose of the north. The Lanna Muay Thai camp, run by a woman called Pom, boasted two champions and a reputation for 'matching' *farangs* with the local talent. I started training there and made friends with a Thai who had blonde hair and lipstick who fought out of Lanna as a light-welterweight. After a couple of days the coach pulled me to one side and said that he had matched me with a middleweight from the local army barracks in a bout two weeks away. I said my companion wouldn't let me have a tear-up while on holiday. The kid with lipstick then said in broken English, 'It sound like my girl-friend.' But the coach, a mean old snake with 200 fights behind him, shook his head and laughed, 'Get rid of woman and come fight for me. I can make lots of money with white *farang* in stable.' But instead of fighting I was designated as sparring partner for all the others who were entering the ring. When asked where I was from in *ang grit* (England) I said, 'Oh, you probably wouldn't have heard of Liverpool.'

'Liverpool,' said Com, the coach, 'I love Liverpool: McManaman, John Barnes,' he began to list in broken English. He was much impressed. Scousers are very popular in Thailand, as are Mancunians and other people from the Premier League.

15 August

The coach, Com, took me to where all his boys fought; at the Bar Beer on Moon Muang in Chang Mai. A full-sized ring where the local talent, precocious *farangs* and fighters from other districts fought for the drunken amusement of tourists, prostitutes and trans-sexuals (pre- and post-op). Many of these took bets and played Harry Carpenter (colourful UK boxing commentator) in the crowd with the hookers they'd rented for the evening. I had read that many tourists had been poisoned, killed or robbed in the company of such ladies.

One tourist, an obese bourgeois in safari suit at the ringside, said after the first bout, 'It's not quite the standard of Bangkok.' He yawned and continued to offer more wisdom. 'It's not as good as there, you know.'

DIARY: THAILAND

Com knew enough English to know when he'd been insulted. 'Maybe you'd like to fight with my *farang* here,' he said gesturing towards me. 'Oh no, no, I didn't mean it like that," said the other *farang* with his (now) laughing prostitute on arm. 'You talk much like lot *farang*,' said Com, 'maybe you full of it.' The safari-suited know-it-all from Bangkok disappeared into the crowd with his Thai date. 'You know,' said Com, 'that *farang* not know that his woman is a *man*.'

'Where there's muck there's brass'; panning for gold in the sewers beneath Bangkok - Credit: Vision Press/Rex

18 August

In Ko Pha Ngan for the infamous full-moon party on Hat Rin beach.

There are swarms of cops and soldiers on the island to police the event as numbers of those who come swell each month. At Hat Rin, many tourists of European origin stumble about in druggy dazes still looking for magic mushrooms, LSD, Ecstasy.

Although Hat Rin beach was filling up with cops; the assorted white trash were content to wander, stoop and puke their way through the seething crowd in a techno-music-trance of reality indifference. The full-moon party is the equivalent of Butlins for the alternative set. Posses of bored bourgeois brats and assorted eco-friendly kids (back home, maybe) litter the beaches with beer bottles, ripped Rizla packets and their presence. They are a major problem for the Thai authorities. Back on the mainland at Surat Thani, the mental hospital has to keep half a dozen beds free for the acid casualties that come their way after the party.

One soon-to-be rave casualty was wandering around the beach talking about 'vibes reaching him from the dogstar Sirius'. Then he spun into a druggy monologue about vibes from 'infinity' entering his body 'via osmondis'. 'Hadn't they split up?' I asked. Whatever happened to Donnie, Marie and little Jimmy? But no, he meant *osmosis* and proceeded to tell us about a form of 'alien intelligence coming through my brain... telling me to spin my turntable to create a happening vibe for the people to enjoy'. And it was the aliens who had told him 'to cut off my dread-locks out of respect for Jah and the twelve tribes of Israel'.

I looked at Mr Osmosis-through-the-brain-via-Sirius and figured that he'd probably end up in the snake pit back on mainland Surat Thani. I imagined him writhing about the floor in a straitjacket shouting for 'nanny' on the peak of a bad trip.

20 August

After the ordeal of modern Thailand it was time to go back to what it was like before the haggling *farang*, white trash and currency speculators came along. It was off to Sukhothai, the place of the rising of happiness, Thailand's first capital and symbol of its civilisation. The Sukhothai Historical Park is a reminder to foreigners that Thailand had a culture, continuity and spirit that cannot be obscured by the material problems of the present day. Sukhothai was built by a benevolent despot and ruled in a climate of peace until its zenith in the late fourteenth century; it does not help a capital city to be landlocked; slowly and inexorably it fell into gentle decline. Sukhothai's still sitting Buddha images look so lifelike that I expected them to stand up Ray Harryhausen-style to chase me out of the brick and stucco ruins of the winding *wats* and spires. I supposed that they'd only reserve that pleasure for the likes of George Soros. Thailand's economy might be bleeding, the haggling *farangs* will come and go; but Sukhothai stands as a reminder to all outsiders that Thailand is Buddha's jewel. Whatever happens to Thailand in the present crisis, the Buddhas of Sukhothai will always be watching.

30 August

Walking into a restaurant in Bangkok I notice an assembly of Brits watching the news on television. It is the BBC. As a nervous newsreader rambles about shock and tragedy a caption flashes on the screen: '*Diana, Princess of Wales is dead.*' What happened? I ask of the balking Brits, did she step on a landmine? No. She had died in a car crash. I look about the restaurant. In the back of the room I catch the eye of a Thai man busy in the kitchen; he looks at me, gestures a driving motion with his hands and laughs; he laughs because in Thailand a cockroach dies and comes back a princess. Life is cheap in Thailand and the logic of reincarnation dictates that no matter what happens you always die and you always come back; be it as a cockroach or be it as a princess with an 'O' level. While the Brits gawp and whimper, the Thais laugh at us because they sense our need for life when death is our common disease. They recognise that it is our remorse that makes us inferior to them, in spite of our authority to exploit or consume.

If the Princess does come back as a cockroach she'll discover there are worse places to be than in a Thai kitchen where they know enough about death to laugh at it. ❑

Alex Reynolds *is a freelance journalist based in London.*

BBC WORLD SERVICE
Worlds of Difference

I am disabled due to polio in my infancy. I can only move about by crawling on all fours. Most people with my type of condition beg for alms on the roadside, but not me. Begging in the street cannot solve the difficulties facing disabled people. What we need is human dignity.
Ndifreke Johnson, Nigeria

There are over **50 million** disabled people in Africa

Only **2%** of disabled adults and children get any form of **rehabilitation**

Only **2%** of disabled children get any **education** at all

90% of disabled children **do not survive** into adulthood

70% of disabled adults are unemployed and live **in complete poverty** or by begging

LOOK OUT FOR THE SPECIAL SUPPLEMENT IN APRIL'S EDITION OF FOCUS ON AFRICA MAGAZINE

BBC World Service Education and **Index on Censorship** turn the spotlight on Disability in sub-Saharan Africa

- BBC World Service Education and the African Region produce **6 radio series** in **Hausa, Somali, Swahili, French, Portugues & English** - to be broadcast from April 1998
- Each radio series will be accompanied by a **free information booklet** which will be printed and distributed by partner disability organisations in Africa
- A **free educational supplement** on disability will be included in the April 1998 edition of Focus on Africa magazine
- Index on Censorship follow up Adewale Maja Pearce's article **(see page 177)** with a **media workshop** on disability in Autumn 1998

For further details about this or other education projects please contact:
BBC World Service Education
Bush House, Strand
London WC2B 4PH
Tel: +44 171 557 2295 • Fax: +44 171 240 3141
email: wsedu@bbc.co.uk

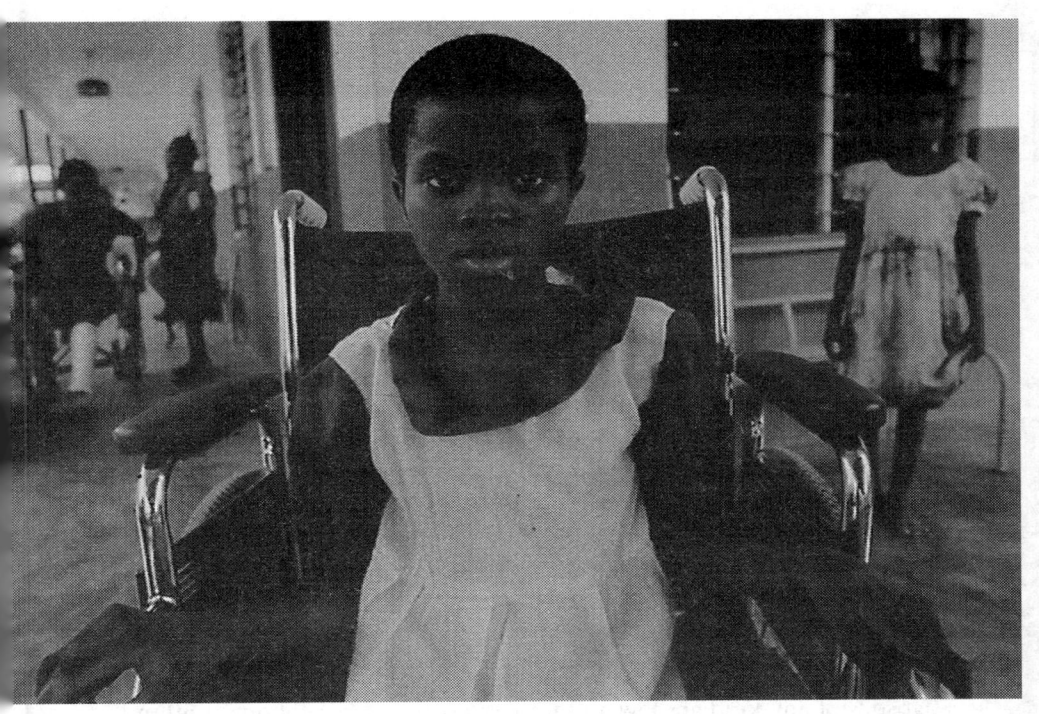

Disabled Africa: rights not welfare

BY ADEWALE MAJA-PEARCE

Compiled with the support of DANIDA and the European Commission

Above: Nigerian child with polio – Credit: Bruce Paton/Panos

❝There must be great power in disability and in being a human being. I do not know how disabled people have survived and are surviving up to now under very hostile situations of ignorance, marginalisation, poverty, neglect, powerlessness and lack of influence. All the same, the greatest thing to have happened to disabled people is the formation of **Disabled People's International**. Disabled people all over the world are organising themselves and setting the terms of their participation into society and so much energy has been released by the disabled people and the world will not rest until disabled people are liberated.❞

Joshua Malinga in 'Decade of Disabled People' published in *Proceedings of the Seventeenth World Congress of Rehabilitation International*, Nairobi, Kenya, 1992.

According to the World Health Organisation (WHO), roughly 10 per cent of the population in any country suffers one of the five broad categories of disablility: physical disability, blindness, deafness, intellectual impairment and mental illness. The figure for sub-Saharan Africa, where statistics of any kind are few and untrustworthy, is usually put at 50 million, but this seems low: the total population of the continent is nearer 600 million; moreover, the familiar problems of Africa – war, ignorance, superstition, poverty and politics – push the figures higher in most countries.

Take armed conflict, for example. In Mozambique, where a 20-year civil war followed the departure of the Portuguese, an estimated 10,000 soldiers on both sides of the fighting were disabled. They even have their own organisation, **Ademimo**, founded in 1982, to look after their interests, mostly by petitioning the government for free medication and prosthetics and running a rehabilitation centre to teach the usual skills given to disabled people in the continent: carpentry, shoe-repairing, sewing, pottery and metal-working.

In Angola, another former Portuguese colony and currently one of the most heavily mined countries in the world, there are upwards of 32,000 amputees in the civilian population as a result of unexploded mines in unmarked fields. In the words of Princess Diana, who visited the country in January 1997: 'These mines inflict most of their casualties on people who are trying to meet the elementary needs of life. They strike the wife or the grandmother gathering firewood for cooking. They ambush the child collecting water for the family.' The then British government was careful to distance itself from Diana's mission; and the USA and Egypt were unable to bring themselves to sign the recent Oslo Accord to ban all landmines by 2005. Both governments cited 'security reasons'.

You can see many of the victims of these landmines on the streets of Luanda, the capital, where they must beg for a living because the rehabilitation centre, which opened in 1992, can only cope with a few at a time. When I visited Adedimo's headquarters last April, I was told that the centre had only been able to train 500 people so far because of the lack of resources. This is a familiar problem all over Africa, which is why most disabled people in African cities are beggars. In this sense, they could almost be a metaphor for the continent itself: we, the non-disabled (or 'normal'), relate only to their disabilities (or 'deformities'), which they in turn use to solicit alms. In fact, the majority of the continent's disabled – up to 70 per cent – live in the rural areas without access to running water, electricity, health clinics, good roads, functioning telephones and all the rest of it. The poverty of the continent, in other words, is reflected in the plight of those least able to fend for themselves. Less spending on arms – and landmines – would go some way to help.

The problem is circular: poverty means few resources; few resources perpetuate poverty at the same time as they causes disability. So, for instance, lack of Vitamin A, which affects up to 40 million children worldwide, is a major cause of blindness; additionally, Vitamin A deficiency 'substantially increases the death rate as well as the severity and risk of the three main health risks facing children in the developing world, diarrhoeal disease, measles and pneumonia'. Again, a woman who contracts the rubella virus for the first time during pregnancy is likely to pass the virus to the foetus, with catastrophic results, including 'deafness, blindness, mental retardation and heart defects', all of which could be prevented by a simple innoculation. Deafness itself can also be caused by measles, mumps and meningitis, especially when exacerbated by malnutrition. It has been calculated that 40 per cent of all disabilities in Africa occur within the first four years of life; in Zimbabwe, for instance, up to half of all blindness is caused by measles.

Having been rendered disabled, the child must now acquire an education, the *sine qua non* for becoming 'a productive member of society';

and although the trend in recent years is for community-based rehabilitation whereby disabled children are encouraged as much as possible to learn alongside their 'normal' peers, some forms of disability obviously require extra facilities and specialist teachers. A blind child, for instance, should ideally be supplied with a Perkins brailler, a typewriter, a tape recorder and talking books. The brailler alone costs almost US$1,000; a ream (500 sheets) of the special paper to use with it costs over US$100. This is a tall order in a continent where school enrolment is falling because parents can't afford the fees, and where most of the available education is sub-standard because few governments are interested in raising a literate population that will be apprised of its rights.

Quite apart from the extra funds needed by disabled students, gestures can mean a great deal and needn't always cost anything. Deaf children can only be properly taught through Sign language, which is a seperate language with its own syntax, grammar and structure. Only Uganda, uniquely in the continent and only the second country in the world after Finland, has entrenched Sign language in its Constitution, which strongly discriminates in favour of that country's disabled. By contrast, in South Africa, where 11 languages were officially recognised in 1994 in the interests of democracy, Sign language, with more than 1.5 million users, is bigger than some of the smaller languages; yet there isn't a single tertiary institution in the entire country willing to present a course in Sign language interpreters' training. According to the **Deaf Federation of South Africa** (f 1929), this is because 'very few hearing people accept the existence of Deaf culture'. As a result, over 70 per cent of deaf people in the country are 'untrained and unemployed'.

The story is the same in most places. According to the **Tanzania Association of the Deaf** (f 1983), the Swahili word for deaf, 'bubu', means 'dumb' – in Uganda it is 'Kasiru', 'stupid' – which is why the deaf are usually kept at home to do household chores instead of going to school. Such a child is automatically assumed to be fitted only for a life of begging. But that is only the half of it: unable to read and write, most deaf people are deprived of access to even the most elementary information needed in order to function properly in society. This is why associations of the deaf lay great stress on television news in Sign. In Tanzania, where an independent station runs a twice weekly, half-hour news programme in kiSwahili and Sign, the percentage of deaf people who are better informed has increased significantly: 'Investigations done by *Voice* *of the Deaf* have shown that a good number of deaf people in Dar es Salaam are now sensitive to current issues in political, social and economic areas'. This can literally save lives. There is a higher incidence of AIDS among deaf women, for example, simply because they can't get the information they need to make informed choices – though the idea of informed choices for most women in Africa, disabled or otherwise, is something of a fantasy.

The fact of being a woman in Africa is enough in itself to create disability, almost always under the guise of 'traditional culture'. The most obvious and most tragic example is, of course, the widespread practice of female genital mutilation (FGM). This involves the removal of all or part of the clitoris and other external genitalia; in its most severe form, known as infibulation, the clitoris and both labia are excised and the two sides of the vulva sewn together, with only a small opening to allow for the passage of urine and menstrual blood. It is believed that up to 6,000 girls are forced to undergo this operation every day in Africa, usually under conditions that guarantee a high death rate. **Disability Awareness in Action** reported in 1997 that:

> A powerful women's secret society practised genital mutilation on about 600 girls in a camp for displaced people and many have developed complications, according to aid workers. The Bondo Society promotes female genital mutilation or "circumcision". It carried out the operations on 9 January [1997] in Grafton Camp in the eastern suburbs of Freetown [Sierra Leone]. Health workers say about 100 of the girls, aged between eight and 15, were suffering severe complications. The practice involves the removal of the clitoris and is usually performed with unsterilised knives and no anaesthesia.

In one study in Kenya, it was calculated that FGM, along with 'other harmful traditional practices', accounts for roughly half the maternal mortality rate. One of these 'other harmful traditional practices' is child marriage, itself an adjunct to FGM in its perverted need to control female sexuality; which is why little girls have bits and pieces of their anatomy sliced off. So, for instance, the case of the 13-year-old girl in northern Nigeria, married off to a 56-year-old businessman who complained to a midwife that there was something wrong with her because he had difficulty penetrating her:

> On reaching Amina's room, the midwife found that the little girl was bewildered, terrified, writhing in pain and bleeding from what looked like third degree vaginal tear...With tears in her eyes she pleaded with the nurse to take her away from that "wicked man" who, in her own words, "always pushed a hard stick into my private part".

Many of the girls who manage to become pregnant suffer permanent internal damage known as recto-vaginal fistula in which the wall between the vagina and the bladder and/or rectum is torn due to prolonged labour and lack of access to health care. Unable to bear children any longer and suffering from permanent leakage of urine and faeces through their vagina, these unfortunate girls become a social embarrassment to the people who have done this to them and are turned into the streets to fend for themselves.

'How many of our African women are handicapped by preventable problems of child bearing?' asked Salim Ahmed Salim, secretary general of the Organisation of African Unity, at an important international conference on the rehabilitation of the disabled in Nairobi, Kenya, in 1992. The possessive pronoun in this case was almost as insulting as his diplomatic refusal or inability to spell out the biggest single medical problem faced by women in the continent.

Shying away from 'sensitive' subjects is the best way to guarantee what you're trying to hide, what shames you, what makes you feel less: the plight of the disabled themselves. Superstition is another subject. According to the **Tanzanian Albinos Society** (f 1978), 'It is a common superstition in Africa that albino children have been substituted by the devil'; in pre-colonial days, they were usually killed at birth.

Albinism, from the Latin for 'white', is caused by lack of a pigment called melanin which provides protection against the ultra-violet rays of the sun. For this reason, albinos are prone to skin cancer, which is why they should stay out of the sun and keep their bodies covered. Most Tanzanians, including parents of albinos, are ignorant of this, and there is a high incidence of skin cancer, even in young children. According to Professor Henschke, a German cancer specialist who worked in the country in the 1970s and who was instrumental in setting up the society:

'We have seen frank skin cancer in albino children as young as four years.' He adds that despite these precautions, almost all albinos will develop 'multiple skin cancers, which present a horrifying appearance in later stages. Their final fate is still shrouded in mystery. We have not yet found a physician or layman who admits to having seen a dead albino'. The society, which has a membership of 4,000 out of an estimated 170,000 albinos in the country, wants to educate fellow albinos in particular, and society in general, that albinism is not a curse but a medical condition that can be managed; they want, as one of them told me when I visited their office at the Ocean Road Hospital in Dar es Salaam, 'to be counted as part of the community'.

Superstition affects the lives of disabled people in Africa in all sorts of ways. The **Namibian National Association for the Deaf**, for instance, complains that traditional laws forbid deaf people from getting married. In Lesotho, this stricture applies to disabled people across the board; additionally, disabled first-born sons are barred from succeeding to their father's chieftaincy title.

Superstition can also worsen an existing disability:

> Today a child is born with no disability. Two years later the child is paralysed by poliomyelitis. The mother and father are completely shocked, dazed and frustrated at the realisation that their child can no longer stand up on its own. Witchdoctors or traditional healers are next consulted on why the child has suddenly lost control of its daily living processes. The traditional leader advises that the deceased parental grandmother's spirit needs to be appeased if the child is to survive at all! The vicious circle has begun.

The appeasement is as bad as – if not worse than – the disease. Fred Koga of the **Kisumu Disabled Theatre** in Kenya contracted polio as a child. He was forced to undergo traditional treatment and describes how it left him mentally scarred:

> I contracted a disease when I was 4-years-old. My father took me to a witch-doctor. First, I was made to lie on a cowhide skin. Second, my legs were rubbed with cow fat and some greenish herbs. Third, a hot iron was passed all over my body. Later, I was

half-buried behind our hut for two hours on a daily basis. I became a target for stone-throwing kids and a laughing stock for the villagers. Very much later, polio was diagnosed and I was sent to stay with my maternal grandmother, humiliated, degraded and very bitter.'

Polio, which is 'easily preventable', used to account for over half of all disabilities in Africa, about 500,000 every year until 1988, when WHO announced the 'realistic hope' of eradicating the disease by 2000. The largest series of immunisations were carried out in 1996, when 80 per cent of the target population of 74 million children was reached. Currently, there are 12,000 new cases in Africa every year out of a worldwide total of 100,000, mostly in Asia.

Unfortunately, many of the children who do receive proper medical care suffer unnecessary complications when they leave hospital because of the lack of any follow-up, especially in the rural areas. 'We are all too familiar with the child who is admitted to hospital at two years with polio and then after discharge disappears into some distant communal land only to reappear at the age of six or seven years with severe contractures,' was the way that one Zimbabwean doctor put it. As one might imagine, paraplegics are in an even worse condition; according to a Zimbabwean social worker: 'Research undertaken a few years ago showed that the average discharged paraplegic patients did not live more than two years after leaving hospital.' He also pointed out that Zimbabwe was better off than most of the other countries in the region, especially since the enactment of the 1992 Disabled Persons Act.

The act, which aims to 'make provision for the welfare and rehabilitation of disabled persons', established a national disability board with the following aims:
- to bring about equal opportunities for disabled persons by ensuring...that they obtain education and employment, participate fully in sporting, recreation and cultural activities and are afforded full access to community and social services;
- to enable disabled persons, as far as possible, to lead independent lives;
- to give effect to any international treaty or agreement relating to the welfare or rehabilitation of disabled person to which Zimbabwe is a party;

SPECIAL REPORT: DISABLED AFRICA

- to prevent discrimination against disabled persons resulting from or arising out of their disability;
- to encourage income-generating projects for disabled persons unable to secure employment elsewhere;
- to encourage community-beased rehabilitation;
- to establish vocational centres; to co-ordinate services between different organisations helping disabled persons;
- to provide orthopaedic appliances and other equipment.

Kenya and South Africa are currently planning to 'review laws relating to disabled people', to quote the attorney-general of Kenya, a promise he made in 1993. In the meantime, the chairman of Kenya's electoral commission has proposed that five additional parliamentary seats be created and reserved for representatives of disabled people. President Bakili Muluzi recently spoke about the need for the same in Malawi so that 'they can represent themslves and be a part of the planning and formulation policy in Government'.

The fact that it has taken so long to get even this far, and that many countries in the continent remain indifferent or hostile to even the notion of rights for the disabled, is proof, according to the **Disability Rights Movement**, that disabled people remain the most marginalised group within any country, the result of society's 'negative attitudes' towards them, which is their main problem, more even in some ways than the disability itself:

> ❛Many non-disabled persons have a low opinion of physically disabled persons, especially those who use wheelchairs. A lot of non-disabled persons think that wheelchair users are sick; they think they are patients. They sometimes think that disabled persons have low intelligence and that they are not able to do anything useful.❜

> (From the *Development Activists Handbook*, published by the **Southern African Federation of the Disabled** (SAFOD), the Zimbabwe-based umbrella group of organisations of the disabled in the 10 countries in the region: Angola, Botswana, Lesotho, Malawi, Mozambique, Namibia, South Africa, Swaziland, Zambia and Zimbabwe.)

The distinction between organisations of the disabled and organisations for the disabled is everything. Organisations of the disabled, which have only emerged over the last 20 years, are run by disabled people themselves; organisations for the disabled, which have been around much longer, are run by experts known as 'service providers'. There is little love lost between them. Indeed, organisations of the disabled emerged precisely because disabled people themselves had finally tired of being treated as victims whose own views were resisted and even ignored by those who claimed to be helping them. Alexander Phiri, a disabled Zimbabwean activist, recounts how he and his colleagues were 'yelled at' by the minister of social welfare when they had the temerity to reject the first draft of the Disability Act. They refused to be intimidated, he said, because 'disabled people must control the issues that directly affect us. Our principles are self-representation, emancipation, self-determination and independence.'

Joshua Malinga, another disabled Zimbabwean activist and former mayor of Bulawayo, was particularly scathing about the attitudes of the entire rehabilitation industry vis-à-vis disabled people:

> ❛My quarrel with you is that you have presented a wrong image of disabled people and their needs, interests and problems. You have presented disabled people as people who are sick and stupid and as people whose needs and interests are different from other people's, and as people who are weak, who need care and protection. And as people who cannot do anything for themselves and who need other people to do things to them and for them. You have presented yourselves as experts in the field of disability and you pretend that you know all the solutions to their problems and that you have all the answers.❜

Malinga was speaking in his capacity as chairperson of **Disabled People's International** (DPI), the worldwide umbrella body of the **Disability Rights Movement**; the occasion was the 1992 World Congress of **Rehabilitation International** (RI, formerly the International Society of Rehabilitation) held in Nairobi, Kenya, to mark the end of the United Nations Decade of Disabled Persons (1983-92). The theme of the Congress, 'Accelerating Efforts to Equalisation of Opportunities: Strategies for the 1990s', was in keeping with both the spirit of the decade and the aims of DPI. The problem centred on areas

SPECIAL REPORT: DISABLED AFRICA

of activity. For Malinga, organisations for the disabled should confine themselves to 'prevention of disability (and not disabled people) and rehabilitation' and leave the third plank, the equalisation of opportunities, to organisations of the disabled.

A glance at the proceedings of the RI Congress proves his point. The note is struck early, in the opening speech from A A Moody, Kenya's minister of tourism and development:

> ‘Assembled here are men and women totally dedicated to serving a just cause. There are medical doctors, scientists, service providers, manufacturers, employers, Donors etc. In addition there are government ministers from seven countries whose portfolios cover rehabilitation. Their presence here is a testimony to [the] great importance attached to the absolute necessity of advancing the services to the people with disabilities.’

Assembled guests included the Kenyan President, Daniel arap Moi, who was pleased for the opportunity to be seen doing good work at a tricky moment in his long dictatorship. The President seemed confused as to whether his government had done a lot or a little on behalf of his country's estimated three million disabled people. On the one hand, he expressed 'deep satisfaction' that Kenya had done 'a great deal' for them, and then, overwhelmed by the 'honour' that Kenya should have been chosen as the first 'developing country' to host RI, he sought to play down 'our modest rehabilitation efforts'. And what did these efforts amount to? That the Danes had given money to the Kenya Institute of Special Education to train teachers, and that an ILO/UNDP project was helping unemployed disabled persons. In conclusion, the President announced himself 'happy' to support an application to the EU for funds to establish a rehabilitation centre.

It's difficult to know which is worse, the dependency occasioned by the over-reliance on donor money, or the fact that few African governments seem to care at all. Nearly every organisation I visited in East and Southern Africa – Kenya, Tanzania, Zimbabwe, Mozambique, South Africa, Namibia and Angola – was funded from abroad, mostly Scandinavia. Take Tanzania, a country with a long history of dependence on donor money. The **Tanzanian Association of the Deaf** is funded by the **Finnish Association of the Deaf**, which pays for office accomodation and equipment, a thrice-yearly newsletter, *Voice of the Deaf*, a Landcruiser and salaries for three full-time staff. The **Tanzanian League of the Blind** is 90 per cent funded by the **Swedish Association of the Visually Impaired**. The balance of their money comes from hiring out a mini-bus. Finally, a youth project for the mentally handicapped at Morogoro called **MEHAYO**, which provides vocational training in gardening, poultry-keeping and fish farming for nine students at a time, is supported by a private Swiss trust fund. The pity of it is that even the annual US$5,000 promised in 1982 by the then president, Mwalimu Julius Nyerere, to support organisations of the disabled under a 'Special Fund for the Disabled' hasn't been paid since 1994 because the government says it's broke.

One of the problems with donor money is that it's too far divorced from the culture it's trying to assist. Writing in the *Disability Rag and Resource* in 1994, Alexander Phiri recounts an experience he had in the 1980s:

> During the early-1980s there were a lot of development opportunities because there was a lot of international interest in Zimbabwe. While we had to take advantage of these opportunities, it also had the effect of underdeveloping our organisation. This was because the funding agencies had their own ideas about what projects should be started and many of these did not bear fruit. They did not correspond with our reality...Of course, these agencies wanted something tangible, something they could take pictures of so they could raise more money. For example, they wanted us to do poultry projects by keeping chickens to generate income. But what would happen is that the disabled members would become hungry and eat the chickens, which would diminish the project's viability. Another were vegetable gardens that were set up in areas where water was scarce; so the projects failed. This was demoralising as well. So when we analysed this, we recognised our main efforts had to be disability rights, not vegetables and chickens.

If you were a disabled Kenyan child you might have cause to be pleased that somebody at least was doing something. But donor funding serves to absolve African governments from carrying out their responsibilities to their own citizens. Yet it would be misleading to lump all governments together. The disability groups I spoke to in francophone Africa, principally in Benin and Togo, complained how far behind they had fallen compared with their English- and Portuguese-speaking counterparts. In the words of one delegate at the RI Congress:

> ‘Countries of francophone Africa remain the least endowed in terms of structures, programmes, projects or services in favour of handicapped persons. They also remain the countries where policies and strategies of integrating handicapped persons have the least impact or concrete results.’

Of the anglophone and lusophone countries, it's noticeable that those with more active organisations of the disabled and better legislation are those which fought most fiercely for their liberation.

The reasons are obvious: a Zimbabwean minister, for instance, spoke about the need for a disability act 'in view of our heritage and socialist philosophy' and because so many men and women were disabled in the course of the guerrilla war. In Zimbabwe, where an eight-year guerrilla war was waged against the white minority regime, there are five different organisations of the disabled: **National Council of Disabled Persons of Zimbabwe**, **Zimbabwe National League of the Blind**, **Zimbabwe Downs Syndrome Association**, **Association of the Deaf**, and **Zimbabwe Association of Disabled Sports.** They have come together to form a national assembly, the **Zimbabwe Federation of the Disabled**. Part of its task is to act as a pressure group, and they can, at least, count on a sympathetic hearing.

Again, in Mozambique, where most people earn under US$100 a year, the government has at least shown itself willing to help where it can. In 1992, the ministry of social action employed a Sign language user from Finland to teach a group of deaf school leavers in the capital, Maputo. Two of them were later employed by the ministry 'to work on the development of a formal sign language for Mozambique'. And in South Africa, where the bitterest of all the liberation wars was waged, the ANC government has consistently committed itself to full equality for all its citizens. In 1995, to mark the International Day of Disabled Persons (3 December), Jay Naidoo, then minister in the Office of the President, announced that a national strategy to promote equal opportunities for disabled people was to be included in the forthcoming Reconstruction and Development White Paper because, he said: 'Since April 1994, a fundamental priciple of our society has been that each individual is of equal importance and should have equal opportunity to participate fully in society, with equal obligations and responsibilities towards society'.

South Africa, of course, already possesses a well-developed rehabilitation industry, going back in some cases to the early part of the century. Some of the organisations for the disabled control vast resources, at least when compared with those in the rest of the continent, although the industry itself still continues to reflect the imbalance of the apartheid years that will take many years to erode. For instance, the **South African National Council for the Blind** (f 1929) has assets worth US$2.7 million compared with the paltry US$500,000 controlled by the **Kenya Society for the Blind** (f 1956). But while the former can only manage four mobile eye units for the rural areas, and performs only 3,000 surgical procedures a year, the latter manages 19 mobile eye units and 11,000 surgical procedures a year. Clearly, Kenya, for all its political problems, is still a more 'democratic' country than South Africa.

South Africa, on the other hand, has a range of facilities that others can only envy, the result of a well-developed industrial base which makes the country self-sufficient in the manufacture of appliances. The country is also internationally respected for its centres of excellence, for instance the Muscular Dystrophy Laboratory at the University of the Witwatersrand. To take another example: South Africa is the only country in the continent with an association to train guide dogs, the **South African Guide-dog Association** (SAGA f 1953). SAGA provides guide-dogs to blind people all over Southern Africa.

But the main problem, from the point of view of the **Disability Rights Movement** – the **Movement** – is not so much which country has done what, but the fact that disabled people are still largely ignored when it comes to decisions that directly affect them: that, 'many government officials and other decision makers prefer to listen to professional service providers than the spokespersons of the Movement'. For instance, when Phiri and his colleagues founded the National Council of Disabled Persons of Zimbabwe in the late 1970s: 'The rehabilitation industry tried to destroy us. They told the government we were part of the guerrilla movement at that time. This could have created very difficult problems for us; the white government could have crushed us.' At the RI Congress in Nairobi, Joshua Malinga accused the rehabilitation industry of doing 'very little to promote the World Programme of Action Concerning Disabled People (WPA)', and the United Nations Policy Document which accompanied the Decade of Disabled Persons – the policy document supersedes an earlier, discredited document which RI itself drafted in the late 1970s – of 'still speaking of training more professionals, the building of bigger and better institutions', without addressing 'the question of human rights, social and political changes and equalisation of opportunities'.

WPA asserts the rights of disabled people to be full members of society with an equal share in the distribution of resources, and enjoins member states to work toward 'making the physical environment accessible to all' by, for instance, incorporating ramps and lifts in public buildings (for only an additional 0.4 per cent of the cost) and making provision for public transport. In Africa, especially, where even the fittest must scramble for buses and trains, wheelchair users are effectively housebound and therefore unemployable, no matter how well educated. The WPA has since been beefed up by the UN Standard Rules on the Equalisation of Opportunities for Persons with Disabilities, adopted by the UN General Assembly in December 1993. The most important addition was the establishment of a monitoring mechanism to ensure that member states complied with the provision of the WPA. Unfortunately, the WPA is only a policy document and therefore voluntary, which means that no resources were allocated for governments to implement it. As an afterthought, perhaps, a voluntary fund was set up in Vienna to which governments and individuals could contribute, but why pay when you don't have to?

That African governments – and African people – should be more responsive to their disabled citizens is not a matter of welfare or charity but of rights, and with it a country's commitment to democracy in the fullest sense: the inclusion of all its citizens as equal members of society. Do we want to live in a society where everyone is able to partake to the fullest or don't we? And if not, why not?

This, after all, is what the great civil rights movements of our time, including the African struggle for full sovereignty, were about. And this is why the Movement questions even the notion of disability as anything more than a social construct, 'a complex system of social restrictions imposed on people with impairments by a highly discriminatory society'; and why it deliberately sets out to challenge the knee-jerk authoritarianism and power mania that is the bane of the continent.

The Movement is democratic, libertarian, inclusive, right down to the individual in the remote village who may not even exist as far as most governments are concerned: 'The grass-roots membership *is* the Movement. Without it there would be no Movement', says SAFOD's *Development Activists' Handbook*. The Movement also underlines the need for transparency and accountability within the leadership: 'As the leader of the Movement is a public figure, his or her private life should be clean and uncontroversial. Corrupt dealings and loose behaviour gets the Movement a bad name', says the same *Handbook*.

The Movement recognises the special problems of women, and why they are badly under-represented within it:

> 'Women are caregivers and mothers. They have more responsibilities than men and less free time. The traditional status of women as subservient to men means that many of them are still dependent upon 'permission' from their husbands, brothers, fathers or uncles before they can take part in out-of-home activities. Sometimes this 'permission' is not forthcoming. Because of the centuries-old tradition that oppressed women, many of them have [an] inferiority complex which constrains them from integrating in the widest sense. Until the time comes when there is equality, integration in the widest sense is not possible. Because of this, many women feel more comfortable working together, in situations they can control themselves, without domination by men.'

Even the way that people sit at meetings is 'important and has a direct bearing on the success of a workshop'. And in a continent where foreign adventurers and native officials chop down forests and poison rivers in pursuit of the profit motive, sometimes even hanging activists who raise their voice in protest, the Movement cautions against 'any project that has an adverse effect on the environment'. Such projects should be 'discouraged'.

The Movement has two primary functions: to 'change public negative attitudes towards disabled persons'; to increase membership at the grass-roots level. The first involves organising campaigns aimed at forcing change. These include street demonstrations, letters to eminent persons – not excepting heads of state – meetings with government officers, 'loud' public speaking using drama groups, radio and TV and 'silent' public speaking using wall posters, pamphlets, magazines, newspapers and T-shirts with slogans.

The second means keeping a register of members, providing information, training in awareness-raising, promoting self-reliance, identifying the needs of members and telling them where to go for services. The SAFOD *Handbook* gives advice on how to form groups at the local level, including the use of sympathetic contact persons – chiefs, village headmen, shopkeepers, teachers, church and youth leaders, etc – who are not themselves disabled but 'who are prepared to devote some time to the Cause of the Movement'. Ideally, of course, there should be a local activist in this role.

The Movement also monitors 'the functions and performance of the service providers', one reason at least why it is seen as 'threatening and interfering', and why, according to the *Handbook*: 'The service providers are suspicious of the motives of the Movement. They fear that the Movement's powers of advocacy will threaten their jobs and salaries.' The *Handbook* gives two examples of such monitoring. The first looks at vocational training at the **Jairos Jiri Association for Rehabilitation of the Disabled and Blind** in Bulawayo, Zimbabwe, the largest service provider in Zimbabwe. For Joshua Malinga, one of the centre's 'inmates' in the late 1970s, it was not a happy experience: 'Even from day one, I had an in-born attitude not to accept the attitudes at Jairos Jiri. These ideas were very bad; for example, disabled people were told when to eat, when to sleep, that we coudn't make love – it was banned!'

SAFOD's verdict is equally unequivocal:

> The training services do not seem to meet the needs of the clients. The services were sub-standard. The felt needs of the clients were not recognised, or were being ignored. The staff seem to be the main beneficiaries of the services. They do not seem to make any effort to identify the needs of their clients. Some clients seem to be content with the services they are receiving. Clients do not have any say about how the services are provided or about which services they receive. The JJA should adopt a consultative approach towards clients and associations of disabled persons.

Workshops are too small and not fully accessible. The toilets are not clean and not fully accessible. The services available to clients contribute to the under-development of disabled persons; but they help to contribute to the development and conscientisation of activists of the Disability Rights Movement. The services provided falsely raise the hopes and expectations of clients about their future job prospects in the open labour market.'

Its investigation into the Sheltered Employment Scheme at the **Association for the Handicapped**'s Ehafo Centre in Windhoek, Namibia, which caters for about 150 disabled people, found much the same, with the added insult that 'very few (if any) severely disabled persons' were employed at the centre.

Only disabled people – and women – are treated this way by societies that have usurped the definition of who is 'normal' and who isn't, and who in consequence deserves the lion's share of the resources. This is why the Disabled Rights Movement came into existence, and why it is among the most important liberation movements of our time. ❑

Adewale Maja Pearce is a writer and journalist based in Lagos, Nigeria. Copies of this report are available as offprints from Index on Censorship

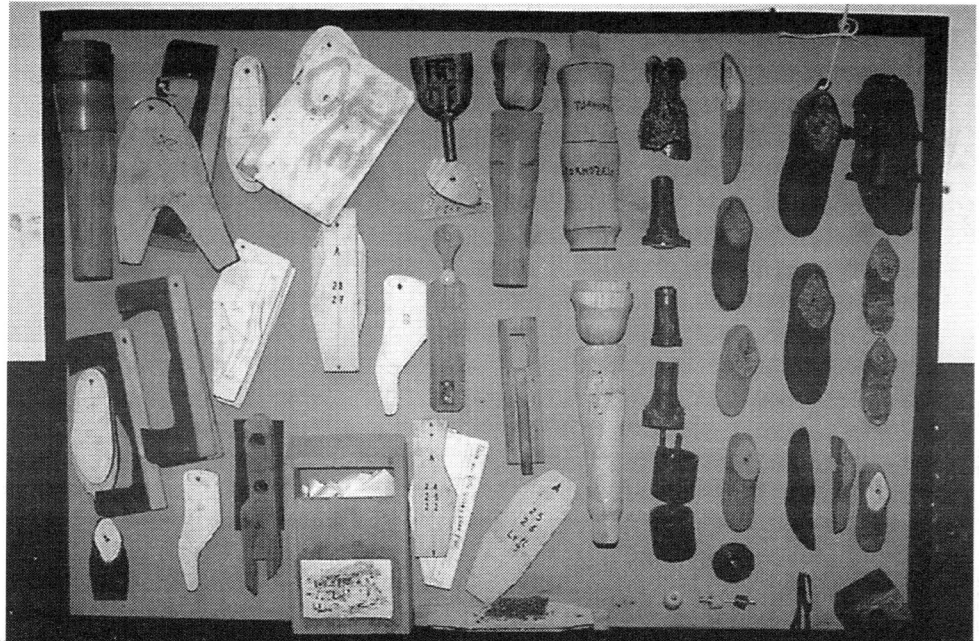

Prosthesis production facility, Maputo